The Vichy Past
in France Today

The Vichy Past in France Today

Corruptions of Memory

Richard J. Golsan

LEXINGTON BOOKS
Lanham • Boulder • New York • London

Published by Lexington Books
An imprint of The Rowman & Littlefield Publishing Group, Inc.
4501 Forbes Boulevard, Suite 200, Lanham, Maryland 20706
www.rowman.com

Unit A, Whitacre Mews, 26-34 Stannary Street, London SE11 4AB

Copyright © 2017 by Lexington Books

All rights reserved. No part of this book may be reproduced in any form or by any electronic or mechanical means, including information storage and retrieval systems, without written permission from the publisher, except by a reviewer who may quote passages in a review.

British Library Cataloguing in Publication Information Available

Library of Congress Control Number: 2016959290

ISBN: 978-1-4985-5032-1 (cloth : alk. paper)
ISBN: 978-1-4985-5033-8 (electronic)

∞™ The paper used in this publication meets the minimum requirements of American National Standard for Information Sciences—Permanence of Paper for Printed Library Materials, ANSI/NISO Z39.48-1992.

Printed in the United States of America

*In Memory of my Mother, Lucy Anne Broyles Golsan,
and my Friend, Wayne Merrill Ahr*

For my Sisters Maryanne and Katie

Contents

Introduction		ix
1	France's Fractured Legal Vector of Memory	1
2	The Le Pen Moment	21
3	Alain Badiou's *The Meaning of Sarkozy*: "Transcendental Pétainism" and the Ossification of History	43
4	Remaking the *Mode Rétro*: Perversion and the "Pulping" of History in Jonathan Litell's *The Kindly Ones*	65
5	Revising History, Betraying Memory: Yannick Haenel's *Jan Karski* and the *Jan Karski* Affair	89
Conclusion		111
Acknowledgements		121
Bibliography		123
Index		133
About the Author		139

Introduction

This book examines the memory of Vichy in the new millennium. Its central premise is that seventy years after the conclusion of World War II, the Vichy past, and all that that past has come to represent and signify, still resonates powerfully in contemporary France. Moreover, the forms that memory has assumed, and the issues raised, have evolved considerably since the 1990s. The proof can be found in political and intellectual exchanges, debates, and controversies; in movies and on television; in novels and histories; and in public ceremonies and commemorations. In a society and culture wracked by pressing and apparently unsolvable problems—chronic high unemployment, the social integration of an ever-increasing immigrant population, a political system (and parties) in flux and arguably moribund, and, in the wake of the *Charlie hebdo* and *hyper cacher* grocery store murders of January 2015 and the massacre of 130 people in Parisian streets in November that same year, fears of widespread terrorism—the memory of *les années noires*, the so-called "Dark Years," still maintains an abiding fascination and presence. All too often, it holds up a distorting mirror to the past as well as the present, and in political and social terms, encourages discord rather than reconciliation.

In politics, controversy erupts regularly over the use and abuse of the history and memory of Vichy, the person of Philippe Pétain, the Holocaust, and the legacies of the Resistance. In Spring 2015, the far-right leader and honorary president of the *Front National* Jean-Marie Le Pen shocked and angered many in France by reiterating a statement originally made in the 1980s that the Holocaust was only an "historical detail" of World War II. Le Pen also expressed his belief that Philippe Pétain was not a traitor. Even the current party leader, Marine Le Pen, was angered by her father's revisionist statements because they undermined her efforts to tone down the National Front's extremist image. This softening of the FN's image, she believed, was crucial to forwarding her presidential aspirations. But for many in France, the fact than Marine Le Pen *has* presidential aspirations, and legitimate ones at that, and that her party scored twenty-eight percent of the votes (6.82 million votes) in the second round of regional elections in Spring 2015, offers sufficient evidence of Vichy's long shadow in contemporary France.

Extreme right-wing and xenophobic politicians like Jean-Marie le Pen are not the only political leaders to invoke, problematically and controversially, memories of the Dark Years. Shortly after his election as president in Spring 2012, François Hollande angered many on the left and the right by appearing to assert in a speech to commemorate the *rafle du Vel d'Hiv*—the infamous roundup of some 13,000 Jews in Paris in July 1942—that the roundup was an exclusively French crime. Hollande stated: "The truth is that this was a crime committed in France, by France."[1] The only mention of Nazi Germany's role was to underscore the fact that not one German soldier or policeman participated in the roundups. Hollande concluded, also controversially, with a comparison of anti-Semitic acts in France today to the anti-Semitic crimes in Europe of the 1930s and 1940s—a problematic comparison, to say the least.

Earlier, Hollande's predecessor Nicholas Sarkozy had sought to "recycle the Resistance myth" to his own political advantage by repeatedly invoking the Resistance in awkward and self-serving ways. In 2007 he instructed the Ministry of Education to have a letter written by the young Resistance martyr Guy Môquet to his parents shortly before Môquet's 1941 execution by the Nazis read to all school children in France at the start of the academic year. Intended as an example of love for, and extreme sacrifice to one's country, the simple reading of the letter ignored the actual motives of Môquet—he was a militant Communist—as well as the historical circumstance of his *engagement*. Earlier, as a presidential candidate, Sarkozy had made "a pilgrimage" to the plateau of Glières where Resistance fighters had fought the Nazis and Vichy forces in 1944. He repeated this pilgrimage annually for the rest of his presidency. Where the Holocaust was concerned, Sarkozy demonstrated a similar penchant to recall the Dark Years in equally if not more dubious ways. In 2008, Sarkozy asked that each eleven-year-old school child in France "adopt" the memory of one of 11,000 French Jewish children killed in the Holocaust. As critics pointed out, this exercise was morbid, not to say frightening to the school children in question. And while Sarkozy's 2008 gesture, misguided as it was, served to express his sympathy for the victims of the Holocaust and their descendants, other gestures did not. In his declaration during his initial presidential campaign that France had never committed "crimes against humanity or genocide" Sarkozy made a mockery of the trials and prosecutions of the 1990s that convicted former Vichy officials on precisely such charges for their complicity in the implementation of the Nazi Final Solution in France. In characterizing Sarkozy's clumsy forays into the memory and history of the Dark Years, the historian Nicholas Offenstadt concluded that Sarkozy was the inventor and principle practitioner of a new kind of history, *l'histoire bling-bling*.[2] The reference, many will recall, was to Sarkozy's penchant for showy jewelry, Rolex watches, and rock star girlfriends (and later wives).

Finally, on a lighter note, during the primary season leading up to the 2012 presidential election, the memory of Vichy and World War II provided a moment of national hilarity when, in January 2012, the presidential candidate of the *Nouveau Centre* Party, Hervé Morin, declared that he had witnessed the Allied Landings in June 1944. Morin was born in 1961. As the internet site *Voilà.fr* quipped of the time-traveling candidate: "For a man born in 1961, to take part in the Allied landings of 1944 is a great achievement."

In literature and in the novel in particular, evocations of the Dark Years in historical as well as metaphorical terms are extraordinarily numerous in the new millennium, and are often met with critical and/or commercial success. Even when poorly received by the critics, these works occasionally enjoy a *succès de scandale* which also garners media attention and boosts sales. Some of the works in question have become global successes. For example, Irène Némirovsky's posthumous and incomplete 2004 novel *Suite française*, which deals with the disastrous French defeat in May–June 1940 and the first few years of German occupation (Némirovsky was deported to her death before she could complete the book) has been an international bestseller, as has Laurent Binet's 2009 novel *HHhH* focusing on the assassination of the Nazi leader Reinhard Heydrich in Prague in Summer 1942 by Czech and Slovak partisans. Jonathan Litell's controversial *Les Bienveillantes* (2006) (*The Kindly Ones*), whose protagonist is an intellectual and sadomasochistic SS officer named Maximilien Aue, was a commercial and critical success in France, Germany, and Israel, although it did not fare as well in other countries, including the United States.[3] Yannick Haenel's 2009 novel *Jan Karski* (*The Messenger*) a fictionalized account of the life of the real-life Polish resistance hero Jan Karski, provoked a storm of controversy after its publication, primarily for its hostile and historically inaccurate portrait of Franklin D. Roosevelt and its revisionist account of World War II. Haenel was also accused of plagiarism by Claude Lanzmann, who claimed that portions of his interview with the real Jan Karski in his classic 1985 film *Shoah* had been lifted without permission by the novelist.[4]

If these novels—and many others—reflect a fascination with the complicated historical realities of World War II and the Vichy past, (and in important instances to be discussed, willfully distort them), other works refer to the war and the Occupation more obliquely, often as part of a moral and ethical condemnation of present-day French society and culture. In her 1997 novel *The Company of Ghosts*, Lydie Salvayre links Vichy's soulless bureaucracy and murderousness to the horrors of the contemporary world through the deranged imaginings of an old woman about to be evicted from her apartment for failing to pay the rent. In her chilling and ironic 2005 novel, *Acidie Sulfurique,* Amélie Nothomb imagines a French television reality show, *Concentration,* whose participants live in a real concentration camp. Like Jews during the Occupation, the participants are first rounded up in the streets of Paris by French police. Having witnessed these roundups live, television viewers are then treated to the horrors of camp life and place bets on who will die next.

In film and on television, the Vichy past and the horrors of the Holocaust and French participation in it continue to inspire popular, if not always historically accurate representations of the Dark Years. These works include the enormously successful television "docu-drama" *Un Village français* about a French village and the lives of its inhabitants, from the defeat of May–June 1940 and the arrival of the Germans to the Liberation of France four years later. They also include a seemingly endless stream of documentaries about the war, as well as the television screening on the channel *Arte* of the proceedings of the landmark 1987 trial of the Nazi Klaus Barbie in Lyon. In the cinema, films dealing with the Dark Years include the 2010 docu-drama *La Rafle*, a largely (if not entirely) accurate and highly sentimentalized account of the *Vél d'Hiv* roundups of Jews in Paris, and their tragic aftermath. In an era in which the memory of other historical crimes and hecatombs also attract considerable public attention and debate (for example, the 2013 winner of the *Prix Goncourt* literary prize went to Pierre Lemaître for his novel *Au revoir là-haut,* about World War I and its tragic impact on postwar France, and the 2014 prize went to Lydie Salvayre for her novel about the Spanish Civil War and the crimes committed by Franco's Nationalists) the memory of the Dark Years and World War II is increasingly linked to the abuses of other eras. In the 2006 film *Indigènes* (*Days of Glory*) the experiences of four Algerian soldiers fighting with the free French in Italy and later in France are depicted. A blockbuster whose conclusion echoes the ending of *Saving Private Ryan* (The Algerian soldiers defend a French village from numerically superior German troops until French reinforcements arrive. Three of the four die heroically), *Indigènes* also focuses on the injustices of colonialism and decolonization. At the time of its release it called attention to racist attitudes of French officers toward their North African troops during the war, and also highlighted inequalities in postwar pensions of white versus North African Arab veterans. But in the process, liberties with historical fact were also taken. For example, the film shows white French officers standing by and watching while North African troops carry out attacks on German positions in Italy. In reality, white French officers were also involved in these assaults, along with their North African troops.

Historical distortions of this sort, if not outright revisionism, also characterize many recent public ceremonies and exhibitions commemorating crucial events of the Dark Years, suggesting that the French are not yet fully reconciled to the realities of the war or entirely comfortable with its legacies in France today. Marking the seventieth anniversary of both the D-Day landings of June 1944 and the liberation of Paris two months later, Summer 2014 provided two striking examples of such distortions and, indeed, manipulations. In June, the official French commemoration of D-Day and the battle of Normandy at Ouistreham was attended by many, including heads of state Barack Obama, Angela Merkel, Vladimir Putin, and of course François Hollande. It featured events that deliberately exaggerated the French role in the landings and, in an effort to forward European unity, emphasized expressions of Franco-German reconciliation that essentially whitewashed the animosities and hatreds of the combatants and the brutal realities of the Nazi war machine. In the first instance, the site of Ouistreham itself was chosen because this is where a small contingent of French soldiers, the Kieffer Commando, came ashore. The larger and more significant battles, involving vastly superior numbers of other Allied combatants—Americans, British, Canadians, and Poles—occurred elsewhere. On the second score, a high point of the ceremony featured a veteran of the Kieffer Commando being joined by, and shaking hands with a Wehrmacht veteran. For anyone familiar with the ferocity of the fighting, this seemed strained and artificial. On the German side an SS veteran might have been more appropriate, but of course the inclusion of such a disturbing presence in an exercise at least partially devoted to European reconciliation would have been impossible. At the conclusion of the ceremony, French military jets flew in from the sea over the assembled crowd, streaming red white and blue smoke behind them. If one did not know the history of the Normandy landings, one would have been left with the impression that the French were the principal liberators. While reassuring to (patriotic) French spectators, the ceremony smacked more of belated wish fulfillment than of an effort to pay tribute to the memory of those who fought and died to liberate France, and Europe, from the Nazi yoke.

If celebrations of D-Day were the order of the day in Normandy, in Paris Summer 2014 was devoted to commemorating the Liberation of August 1944, along with the centennial of the start of *La Grande Guerre*. Where the liberation of Paris was concerned, the Carnavalet Museum in the Marais mounted a photo exhibition original assembled shortly after the Liberation, in Fall and Winter 1944–1945. Consisting primarily of photos of resistance men and women fighting Germans in the streets of the capital and the arrival of French troops shortly thereafter, the paucity of images of Allied liberators in the exhibit seemed to detach the Liberation from historical realities that immediately preceded it. These included the Allied invasion earlier in the summer which made the liberation of Paris possible, and also the fact that, a few short weeks before the Liberation, most Parisians were going about business as usual with the German occupier. Huge crowds in the capital had also showed up earlier that summer to applaud Philippe Pétain on his final visit to German-occupied Paris. As if to confirm the Carnavalet exhibit in its historical myopia, a lengthy essay published in August in the newspaper *Libération* also emphasized France's "self-liberation," stressing De Gaulle's outwitting of the Americans, who are cast as rivals, in reaching Paris first. The essay concludes; "De Gaulle won. It was the [French] people who started the Liberation of Paris, not the Americans with their plans for a military administration. It was a French division that entered Paris, it was the Gaullists who took possession of the city's buildings, without firing a shot." The German occupiers are not mentioned here, and are hardly discussed in the essay as a whole.[5]

The commemorative activities of Summer 2014, and especially those surrounding the Liberation of Paris, seem to point—troublingly—to the return of the Gaullist or "Resistentialist" Myth, according to which the vast majority of the French resisted and only a few nefarious sorts collaborated and served Vichy and the Nazis. Historically, of course, this is completely false. Of greater concern is the fact that other developments point to a rehabilitation of Vichy itself, along with the denial, or deliberate attenuation of, French anti-Semitism during the Dark Years. In his provocative and inflammatory 2014 bestseller, *Le Suicide Français,* the right-wing journalist and polemicist Eric Zemmour revives the old saw that Vichy acted as a *bouclier*, or shield, during the war, protecting not only French non-Jews but French Jews as well. Deliberately ignoring the realities of Vichy's home grown anti-Semitism—the anti-Jewish statutes of 1940 and 1941, the willing participation in the Nazi Final Solution—Zemmour writes that the "strategy adopted by Pétain and Laval when faced with German demands" was "to sacrifice foreign Jews to save French Jews."[6] And Zemmour adds, the man who perverted France's self-understanding of its wartime years and the Vichy regime itself was the "austere American prosecutor," Robert Paxton. In his landmark 1973 book *La France de Vichy* (*Vichy France: Old Guard and New Order*), Paxton, according to Zemmour, paints an entirely Manichean portrait of wartime France, of Vichy, and of the French people themselves: "The Paxton equation: Vichy is absolute evil: Vichy is France; therefore France is absolute evil."[7] And Zemmour adds, Paxton's "victory," his successful imposition of a poisonous and culpable wartime self-image on the French nation, has been complete. The proof, Zemmour writes, is that the "Paxtonian doxa" has become the "official truth," voiced, for example, by Jacques Chirac in 1995 and by François Hollande in 2012 in their respective speeches commemorating the Vel d'Hiv roundups.

Given Zemmour's reputation for scandal-mongering and historically revisionist claims like those made in *le Suicide Français,* one is tempted—despite the book's status as a bestseller—to dismiss it as not representative of French opinion, and certainly not of an historically informed French opinion. Nevertheless, other evidence suggests that the revisionist impulse *Le Suicide Français* betrays regarding the realities of the Dark Years has indeed found its way into more legitimate historical and academic discourse. When the respected political scientist, historian of genocide, and professor at *Sciences Po* Jacques Sémelin published his massive, 800-page study *Persecutions et entreaides dans la France occupée: Comment 75 percent des juifs en France ont* échappé *a la mort* in 2013, he set off considerable controversy among historians and others by taking up and seeking to validate another strand of revisionist thought. Despite much evidence to the contrary, Sémelin argues that the fact that 75 percent of Jews in France during World War II survived the war was due to the fact that the French people were anything but anti-Semitic, and that they had actively rescued Jews during the war. While this was certainly true in some, indeed many instances, it is not valid as a rule. Even Sémelin's methodology—reading numerous memoirs of Jews who survived and interviewing others—is by definition anecdotal, and his logic can be highly dubious as well. For example, Sémelin argues that the very existence of the Vichy regime as an intermediary state between Nazi Germany and the French people, including Jews, meant that it served "structurally" to protect them.[8] This assumption ignores the core of Vichy's initiatives, many of which were designed to aid and support Nazi policies and initiatives.

To the extent that in their revision of history Zemmour's and Sémelin's books reflect both a kind of leveling of the moral playing field by arguing in effect that, as Sémelin put it in a subsequent defense of his book in *Le débat*, "the history of Vichy is not all black, it is all gray,"[9] they are not alone in this kind of endeavor. In a work that garnered little critical attention in 2013, the conservative philosopher Alain Minc chose to compare the "intersecting itineraries" of France's greatest martyr of the Resistance Jean Moulin, and Vichy's secretary general of police, René Bousquet. It was Bousquet who negotiated the Vél d'Hiv roundups with the Nazis in Spring 1942 and who would have been tried for crimes against humanity in the 1990s for his actions against the Jews during the war had he not been gunned down in his home by a crazed publicity seeker in Summer 1993. The linking of the two men and their careers and destinies in a single book is provocative enough, but the back cover reminds the reader that Moulin was a "diligent prefect" serving Vichy for the first six months of the war, and that Bouquet was a man "caught up in the machinery of bureaucratic ambition,"[10] an exculpating phrase worthy of Adolph Eichmann in the glass box in Jerusalem in 1961. And in blurring historical and moral distinctions in this fashion, Minc's work recalls Michel Foucault's famous critique of the 1970s *mode rétro* that had also, according to

Foucault, betrayed in its nostalgia for the Dark Years a similar urge to attenuate, if not erase, these kinds of distinctions.[11]

Finally, if the memory of Vichy lives on in historical debates and dubious revisionist claims about the Dark Years, it also lives on in a fascination and indeed reverence for the individuals associated with the great, or conversely, the terrible deeds of those years. The person of Charles de Gaulle, of course, towers above all others and serves, among other things, as a constant reminder of France's past glories. And those individuals whose remains were placed in the *Panthéon* in May 2015 alongside those of other national heroes like Voltaire and Emile Zola include Germaine Tillion, Geneviève de Gaulle-Anthonioz, and Pierre Brossolette, all Resistance fighters, and Jean Zay, the Popular Front minister and Jewish martyr, murdered by Vichy's paramilitary police, the *milice,* in 1944. On the other side of the coin, Pétain himself continues to enjoy a dubious notoriety as well, and his legacy is revisited (and revised) not exclusively by reactionary figures like Jean Marie le Pen and Eric Zemmour. In his 2013 book *Pétain en vérité*—a title which in itself suggests that the image and legacy of the head of Vichy'*s Etat Français* has been distorted—the historian Marc Ferro reexamines Pétain's career during World Wars I and II and, according to the book's back cover, addresses question's like "Did he play a double game during the collaboration (with the Nazis)? Did he save Jews? Was he the lesser evil? Was everyone behind him?"[12] By even raising these questions, the back cover of *Pétain en verité* suggests that the most fundamental and troubling realities of the Dark Years are once again up for discussion and debate, and that the many efforts, especially in the 1990s, to put the Vichy past to rest, to fulfill a "duty" to the memory of the victims of Vichy's and Nazi Germany's crimes, have been of little or no avail.

Why Vichy? Why now? And if, as Henry Rousso first argued, France has been dealing with the ebbs and flows of the "Vichy Syndrome" since the end of the World War II, what are the most salient and persistent attributes of the memory of Vichy and the Dark Years today? What evidence can be offered in support of specific claims made along these lines?

There are of course many reasons one could present to explain Vichy's presence as a "Haunting Past" in postwar France, and some of these reasons have evolved over time. First, there is the shock of the terrible and crushing defeat of French forces in May–June 1940 at the hands of the Nazis, and the resulting panic-stricken and chaotic *exode* of soldiers and civilians alike from the north to the south of France. The sheer number of historical, literary, and cinematic accounts of this disaster including, recently, Irène Némirovsky's moving and powerful narrative of it in *Suite française,* hardly do justice to the extent of the military, social, and political collapse, and resulting trauma. Following that collapse, there was also the betrayal of the French Republic and the republican tradition when French legislators voted dictatorial rights to Pétain and established the *Etat Français* in July 1940. And in *The Vichy Syndrome* Rousso argues that what France experienced especially during the latter stages of World War II was a veritable "Franco-French Civil War" a time when, as the then president Georges Pompidou put it euphemistically in the 1970s, "the French did not like each other." In the postwar years, the animosities and divisiveness generated by the conflict had to be put aside—indeed, obfuscated, according to many—in order for the nation to move forward. In Rousso's chronology in *The Vichy Syndrome,* the period of postwar "Mourning" was followed by a period of "Repressions" when the realities of the Dark Years were more or less swept under the rug. As novelists like Marcel Aymé in *Uranus* and Michel Tournier in *The Paraclete Wind* wrote, many French became overnight amnesiacs, forgetting their pro-Vichy pasts to become part of a "Nation of Resisters." For Rousso in *The Vichy Syndrome,* this comfortable illusion persisted until the late 1960s and early 1970s, when films like Marcel Ophuls' *The Sorrow and the Pity,* and Louis Malle's controversial *Lacombe Lucien* blew the lid off of postwar mythology, exposing the sordid realities of French collaboration, cowardice, and anti-Semitism to new generations of French people. Following this "Broken Mirror" phase that ended in 1974, France, according to Rousso, plunged into a period of "Obsessions" where the Vichy past was concerned. Up through the 1990s, political scandals, trials, historical debates, and works of literature and films dealing with all aspects of the Vichy past and the Dark Years marked and arguably defined the cultural landscape. This had reached such a point that in a 1994 work coauthored with Eric Conan, *Vichy. Un passé qui ne passe pas* (*Vichy: An Everpresent Past*), Rousso called for an end to the national fascination/obsession with the Dark Years and its crimes and abuses, all the while describing the latest installments in the ongoing saga of the Vichy Syndrome.

Increasingly in the late 1980s and 1990s, as numerous events and controversies confirm, the memory of Vichy became markedly "judeocentric," focusing primarily on Vichy and French anti-Semitism and especially the Pétainist regime's willing complicity in the Nazi "Final Solution." The 1987 trial on charges of crimes against humanity, primarily for the deportation of Jewish children, of the infamous "Butcher of Lyon," the Nazi Klaus Barbie, set the stage for the trials of Vichy servants Paul Touvier in 1994 and Maurice Papon in 1997–1998 on similar charges and for anti-Semitic crimes. It also lent impetus to the short-circuited prosecution of René Bousquet, gunned down as noted in 1993 before he could stand trial. The 1994 scandal over François Mitterrand's right-wing and xenophobic past during the interwar period, as well as revelations of the extent of his service to Vichy along with his being awarded the regime's highest honor, the *Francisque*, further stirred the pot. So did the political rise in fortunes of the National Front under

Jean–Marie le Pen, who did not try to hide his anti-Semitism. Alongside a remarkable historical interest in Vichy's crimes and especially its anti-Semitic abuses reflected notably in the outpouring of works about the trials for crimes against humanity, the subject of French anti-Semitism *before* Vichy, and the possibility of an indigenous French fascism, sparked debate (the latter often centering on the work of the Israeli historian Zeev Sterhell.)

In important ways, the judeocentric "turn" of the memory of Vichy in the 1990s leads up to the present. Outbreaks of violent anti-Semitism have been on the rise in France over the past decade. Although recent anti-Semitic crimes are not linked primarily to right-wing extremism but rather to Islamic fundamentalist terror or anti-Israeli sentiment, the spectacle of racist attacks, and even the murder of Jews cannot help by stimulate feelings of déjà vu and dark memories of the past, especially among French Jews. Returning to Summer 2014, in July protests against the Israeli-Palestinian conflict degenerated into violent attacks on a synagogue in the Marais District. A few days later, several Jewish businesses were destroyed in the suburb of Sarcelles. Roger Cukierman, president of the Representative Council of French Jewish Institutions (CRIF) compared the Marais violence to the Nazis' *Kristallnacht*, a linkage contested by many, but which echoed the comparison between anti-Semitism in France today and that of the Nazi and Vichy era made by François Hollande in his 2012 Vél d'Hiv speech. On July 21 the newspaper *Le Figaro* ran the headline: "Anti-Semitism: France in a State of Shock." Of course things would become much worse several months later, following the *hyper cacher* murder of four Jews by Amédie Koulibaly, who claimed to have acted on behalf of the Islamic state. Winter and Spring 2015 were remarkable for the number of Jews fleeing France for Israel or for other destinations, feeling that they were no longer safe and secure in their homeland.

Obviously, present-day anti-Semitism in France, and the specter of past abuses are only part of the explanation of Vichy's presence and resonance in contemporary French life. In a provocative 2006 essay "La tyrannie de la penitence" ("The Tyranny of Guilt")[13] Pascal Bruckner argues that France and also Europe are experiencing an ongoing malaise based on an obsession with past abuses and crimes, the Holocaust and the crimes of communism, of colonialism and decolonization, among other horrors. This self-indulgent fixation on the past, Bruckner continues, not only paralyzes France and Europe in dealing with the present and future. It also betrays a masochistic superiority complex: even in their crimes, French and Europeans believe they have surpassed what all others have done, and they take a perverse pride in this.

One may not share Bruckner's diagnosis of French and European guilty pleasures over the crimes of the past, but he is certainly right that France in particular, at least since the 1990s, suffers from what Charles Maier has labeled a "surfeit of memory"[14] and especially the memory of past crimes and abuses. Spurred in part by public efforts to fulfill a "duty to memory" of Vichy's crimes and the victims of the Holocaust, the 1990s witnessed the renewal or reemergence of other troubled memories, of other massive crimes and hecatombs. These included the abuses of France's colonial past and the destructive horror of World War I, among other disasters. Important works by prominent historians brought all of these issues to the public eye, and in effect amplified the weight of the past on French public life and in intellectual discourse. Following the 1997 publication of the *Black Book of Communism* which riveted public attention on the horror and sheer enormity of communism's crimes worldwide, the journalist and historian Jacques Julliard wondered somewhat despairingly in an essay entitled appropriately *L'année des fantômes* ("The Year of the Ghosts"), if the past in France and for the French had not been reduced a "Jurassic Park of horrors." Other intellectuals, among them Jean-Michel Chaumont, worried that this ongoing "memory fest" of crimes, genocides, and other human disasters tended to blur the boundaries between them, as well as the identities of victims they created. The result he argued, was an unseemly "competition" for recognition among the latter, which distracted from historical as well as the memorial issues at stake.[15]

Concerns over a "memorial culture" that place memory over history and historical understanding are of course by no means specific to France and the French context. They are in fact in many ways "global concerns," as they affect other European countries, and also Turkey, Japan, Israel, Rwanda, Argentina, the United States . . . the list goes on. But, apart from Pascal Bruckner's diagnosis of a French (and European) sadomasochistic focus on the past, what other accounts of the current French situation might explain the tenacity of memory, and the memory of Vichy and the Dark Years more specifically? Two recent explanations are particularly enlightening, the first by the historian Robert Frank, and the second by Henry Rousso in his book *La dernière catastrophe*.

In an interview published in the July 2014 issue of *Libération*, Robert Frank acknowledges that the French today are afflicted with a malaise he and others label *le déclinisme*, that is, a widespread anxiety over French "decline," over France's place in the world, and over a presumed loss of prestige on the international stage. That malaise, he argues, is attributable to *le syndrome de quarante*—"the syndrome of 1940." For Frank, the French are simply unable to get beyond the catastrophic defeat of May–June 1940 and its aftermath. In his book on *La hantise du déclin* Frank also stresses that in his experience this is a specifically French reaction to the memory of the war. The son of a Polish father and Scottish mother who immigrated to Paris after 1945, Frank states that while Poles and other foreign friends of the family who spoke of the war remembered heroic exploits and exhilarating moments along with the tragedies, the parents of Frank's French friends spoke only of "the debacle of 1940." For the latter, that disaster was experienced "not as a military event, [. . .] but as an internal wound, a trauma, a feeling of vertigo, a blow that annihilates."[16] In the interview in *Libération* Frank goes on to state that the subsequent loss of France's colonies only increased the weight of the 1940 defeat on the national psyche while reinforcing *le déclinisme* that imposes itself on the French mindset today. And linking his analysis of *le déclinisme* and its origins to the commemorative summer of 2014 and the memory of the two world wars, Frank notes that, as opposed to the annual November 11 celebration of the World War I armistice which "poses no problems" the May 8 celebration of the Allied victory over Nazi Germany, for all that it recalls, "is always divisive."

Frank is not alone in founding French *declinisme* in the traumatic defeat of May–June 1940. In a more recent assessment of the "the situation of France" in the wake of the terrorist attacks of January 2015 Pierre Manent— perhaps somewhat surprisingly given the pretext for has book—announces that the current malaise afflicting France today dates back "three quarters of a century" to the catastrophic defeat of May–June 1940. Manent affirms bluntly: "we have never recovered (from that defeat)."[17] Moreover, everything France has become and accomplished since is the result of the heroic efforts of the Resistance and de Gaulle to counter that defeat. But even though the latter experience "touches that which is most profound and most sensitive in our souls," the world it represents is nevertheless "as far from us as the Greeks and the Romans."[18] And no amount of commemorations can restore what amounts to a sacred flame for Manent. Given this loss of contact with the "only significant political experience" of recent times, France's *syndrome de quarante* has proven doubly ruinous in Manent's view.

In *La dernière catastrophe* ("The Last Catastrophe") Henry Rousso takes a broader historical approach in accounting for the tenacity of Vichy's memory in France today. For Rousso, the key to understanding the power of Vichy's memory, and the power of memory itself in France today, lies in the highly traumatic impact of modern wars themselves, and not in a specific historical moment, such as 1940. For Rousso, the extreme destructiveness of World War I in Europe, its terrible cost in human lives, and the absolute and unprecedented horror of World War II, were such that each created a profound rupture with the past, with what had preceded these conflicts in social, political, and cultural terms. At the same time, the two wars destroyed any confidence in and sense of the future, along with the idea of progress that inspires faith in it. In the case of both conflagrations—but especially in the case of the World War II—this new experience of a kind of historical "no man's land" created a powerful need, and indeed an obligation to think and experience the past *differently*. This transformation involved not only a fundamental change in perception but a concomitant "moral and political obligation" to construct a *souvenir collectif*, a collective memory, from it. But accomplishing the latter was, and is, no easy task, given the way the former is now experienced. As Rousso observes:

> The relationship of modern societies to history, and certainly recent history, is one that is profoundly marked by conflict: individual or collective conflicts shaped by insurmountable traumas, "memory wars," public polemics and scholarly controversies, often jumbled together. History is no longer defined primarily in terms of traditions to be respected, heritages to be transmitted, knowledge to be elaborated, or the dead to be commemorated. Rather it is defined in terms of problems to be "dealt with," of the work of mourning to be carried out or of memory to be taken up, so much has the idea taken hold that the past has to be rescued from the purgatory of forgetfulness, and only public and private actions will permit its recovery.[19]

Hence Vichy's—and History's—enduring "presence." But as Rousso also explains in *La dernière catastrophe*, this new attitude toward history, toward the past in today's "presentist society" embraces not *only* the notion that the past must be constantly recalled and rescued from forgetfulness. Once it has been recalled, it must be acted upon and judged in the present as well. This impulse to anachronistic judgment certainly helps account for the successful efforts to try and convict former collaborators and Nazis for crimes against humanity of the 1980s and 1990s. More recently, it also helps explain the impetus for the passage of several of France's highly controversial "memorial laws." Among other historical determinations, these laws condemn the slave trade from the sixteen Century as a crime against humanity or conversely, they offer ex post facto justifications of colonialism by expressing the nation's "appreciation" for the "positive role" played by French men and women in France's former extra territorial possessions." Finally, this impulse accounts, arguably, for the implicit historical *and moral* judgments evident in the 2014 commemorations of the Liberation of 1944 described here. Following a lengthy period in which the moral vacuity, corruption, and criminality of the Dark Years was constantly scrutinized, the pendulum appears to have swung in some quarters in the opposite direction. Now, France's World War II past is reimagined—if the 2014 commemorations described above are any indication—in morally bracing and even heroic terms. But as already discussed, this image is at best historically partial as well, and therefore also offers no real possibility of a kind of national reconciliation with the past. In the end, like Frank's analysis of *le déclinisme* and its origins in the defeat of 1940, Rousso's discussion of the hegemony of memory of the Dark Years and of memory itself also unfortunately offers no apparent exit strategy from the impasse that the memory of Vichy and World War II has become.

Although this book cannot claim to offer a way out of the "impasse" of Vichy's memory or, for that matter, a "cure" to the Vichy Syndrome so long present in French culture and society, it does attempt to define and delineate the characteristic forms and distortions of that memory today. By definition, this undertaking must be interdisciplinary, and it must also be somewhat selective, given the breadth of the subject at hand. The chapters that follow therefore deal with the law, with politics and intellectual debates, and with important and controversial literary works. All the topics discussed, or "case studies" chosen, are highly representative of Vichy's memory, its complexities and contradictions, as they manifest themselves now.

By way of justifying both my choice of subtitle, *Corruptions of Memory*, and also of distinguishing the approach taken here from other approaches in important recent works on the topic, I offer five propositions as to the nature of Vichy's memory as it exists in France today:

1. Whereas the preeminence of, or "obsession" with the memory of Vichy in the 1990s inspired numerous efforts in a variety of disciplines and discourses to better understand the historical realities of the Dark Years themselves,[20] in recent years the memory of the Dark Years inspires no such impulse to historical accuracy and understanding. Revisionisms are the order of the day in politics, commemorative exercises, intellectual polemics, and in fictional works—novels in particular—which deliberately revise the past in accordance with today's ideological prejudices, anti-Americanism, for instance.

2. Largely as a consequence of the preeminence and predominance of the memory of Vichy's crimes in the 1990s, what began as a "duty" to remember the Jewish victims of the Holocaust has expanded to include the victims of other crimes and other historical traumas, most notably the victims of colonialism and the brutalities of the Algerian war. While this is a legitimate and necessary development in historical as well as human terms, it also means that the memory of the victims and the crimes of Vichy and Nazi Germany are increasingly compared and conflated with those of other victims and crimes in such a way as to obscure important differences in motivation and practice between them. To paraphrase Jean Baudrillard, history in this instance risks being reduced to "collage" of its own toxic residues.[21]

3. As a corollary to "2" above, the trend begun in the late 1980s and 1990s to come to terms legally and judicially with the memory of Vichy and French complicity in the Holocaust has continued and expanded in the new century with the passage of aforementioned and highly controversial "memorial laws." As noted, these laws now address and criminalize retroactively not only moments and events from France's past but those of other national traumas as well. In defining and labeling past crimes "genocides" and "crimes against humanity" in this fashion these laws arguably simplify and distort the past and foreclose critical and historical reflection on it in the present and future.

4. Rather than refer in critically responsible ways to a particularly traumatic moment in France's history and to the victims of crimes committed at the time, "Vichy" as word and memory has increasingly become a metaphor for generalized social and cultural evil, for political, moral and ethical decline, and even decadence in the present. As such, it is used as a polemical cudgel of sorts to denounce specific cultural and political trends and practices, individual politicians and intellectuals, and even perceived malaises in the national psyche. While this practice may arguably shed light on some present realities, it does not clarify the past.
5. There has been an "ossification" of the memory of Vichy, along with the forms and imperatives associated with it, such that representations, commemorations and evocations of the Vichy past have become sterile, ritualistic, repetitive, and often anachronistic. Memory is "repeating itself," it is becoming a "memory of memory," or of memories, a kind of simulacrum, in which the image often takes precedence over the original. Historical knowledge and understanding are none the better for this.

How do these five propositions concerning the memory of Vichy as it exists now justify the use of the word "corruption" in my subtitle? By definition, corruption implies a "state of decay" or degradation, a "loss of integrity" and a "departure from the original that was pure and correct." It can also imply, of course, moral malfeasance and even depravity. Clearly, historical revisionism in the name of celebrating a dubious or faulty expression of "memory" implies a loss of crucial distinctions, a form of degradation, and therefore a loss of integrity. (This is not to argue that history is a fixed, immutable object that cannot and must not be reinterpreted. Rather, it is to affirm that it must be re-interpreted *responsibly*, on the basis of solid historical evidence.) So can the comparison and conflation of different and divergent memories and traumas, no matter how well intentioned the comparison may be. The use of the memory of Vichy as a metaphor for evil also implies a form of degradation, in that memory and history are morally "over determined" or tainted in the process. And the recycling of memory also implies a form of degradation of what was once more spontaneous and genuine.

Where other historians of the memory of Vichy are concerned, I want to stress that in articulating these five propositions I am not proposing the creation or addition of a new "phase of memory" along the lines of the four phases of the memory Henry Rousso outlined in *The Vichy Syndrome* and has revised in more recent works. As Rousso acknowledges in the Introduction to that book, the four phases, "Unfinished Mourning," "Repressions," "the Broken Mirror," and "Obsessions," discussed briefly above, follow something of a Freudian model of the repression and return of a traumatic memory. The prolonged "Obsessions" phase clearly encapsulates the outcomes of that "return of the repressed." Also, in more recent writings on the memory of

Vichy, Rousso emphasizes both the more broadly European and indeed global context for the memory of World War II, and also especially the "reparative" dimension of public and governmental practices related to the memory of Vichy. These would include in the first instance the 1997–1998 trial of Maurice Papon, and also the government's acknowledgement of important continuities between the Third Republic, Vichy, and the Fourth and Fifth Republics, in agreeing to pay important indemnities to Papon's victims following his conviction.[22] They would also include reparations paid to Jews whose possessions were "aryanized," i.e. stolen, as a result of investigations and recommendations made by the so-called Matteoli Commission created by then-Prime minister Alain Juppé in 1997. Both in the critical approach taken and in the choice of objects of study in the chapters the follow, this book will move in a different direction from Rousso.

By definition my approach to memory in France in this book also does not coincide with the approach taken in recent works by Michael Rothberg and Max Silverman, among others. Using somewhat different terminology— 'multidirectional' memory in Rothberg's case, and 'palimpsestic' memory in Silverman's—both argue, in effect, for the potential and reality of positive interactions between divergent memories of different historical traumas and events, of what Rothberg describes as "the dynamic transfers that take place between diverse places and times during the act of remembrance."[23] In accordance with this perspective, Rothberg is highly critical of the "competition" of memories, which "sometimes overrides other possibilities for thinking about the relation between different histories."[24] As much as I find Rothberg's and Silverman's approach to memory compelling, as my propositions here concerning Vichy's memory suggest, I remain convinced that the memory, or memories in question here remain fundamentally competitive, and even conflictive. In many ways they constitute what Susan Suleiman has labeled "crises of memory," in that they often embrace a "predicament or conflict about the remembrance of the past, either by individuals or by groups" and that they deal fundamentally with "questions of self-representation."[25] And as I hope to show in the chapters that follow, the examination of one traumatic past viewed through the prism of another can on occasion lead to significant distortions of one or both.

Of the five chapters that follow, Chapter 1, "France's Fractured Legal Vector of Memory" deals with the vexed legal efforts of the 1980s and 1990s to come to term with the crimes of Vichy and the Dark Years, and the consequences and "sequels" of these efforts in the new century. It reexamines the trials for crimes against humanity of the 1990s, along with their shortcomings and failings, especially in historical terms, in order to demonstrate the extent to which this century's "memorial laws" repeat these failings, and add a few of their own. Quite different in historical focus and legal articulation, the "memorial laws" nevertheless reveal the same anachronistic impulse to define, simplify, and/or proscribe the crimes of the past, and a similar problematic tendency to conflate the imperatives of history and memory to the detriment of the former.

Chapters 2 and 3 focus on French politics, and the ways in which political practice and commentary, as well as public perceptions of the former in the new millennium are inflected by, and in turn distort the shadow of Vichy and World War II more broadly. Chapter 2, "The Le Pen Moment," focuses on Jean-Marie Le Pen's shocking first round victory in the 2002 presidential election. It also addresses the related intellectual controversy that followed shortly thereafter, centering on the publication of Daniel Lindenberg's incendiary pamphlet *Le Rappel à l'ordre*. Jacques Chirac's extraordinary (80 percent) majority and victory in the second round were facilitated by massive public demonstrations and media campaign characterizing a potential Le Pen victory in terms of a "return of Vichy" and of fascism more broadly. In *Le Rappel à l'ordre* Lindenberg blamed Le Pen's initial success on a group of "new" reactionary intellectuals, who like 1930s right-wing and fascist intellectuals, Charles Maurras, and Drieu la Rochelle among others, prepared the advent of Vichy by poisoning French culture with anti-democratic and anti-Semitic pronouncements and broader claims of French decadence and decline. Both in the rhetoric of the presidential campaign and in Lindenberg's denunciations of his fellows, recycled historical and political myths, distortions, and clichés largely defamed the intellectuals in question, polarized political and intellectual exchange and in the process obscured the real political, cultural, and social threat a Le Pen victory would have posed.

Chapter 3, "Alain Badiou's *The Meaning of Sarkozy*: 'Transcendental Pétainism' and the Ossification of History" examines the controversy that followed the 2007 publication of Alain Badiou's *De Quoi Sarkozy est-il le nom?* in which Badiou likened Sarkozy's presidential victory to the advent of Vichy and the French nation that elected him to the supposedly abject and cowardly France that succumbed happily and readily to Hitler. It also examines in detail Sarkozy's own efforts to exploit the memory of the Dark Years, as well as the meaning and implications of "Bling Bling history." It concludes with a discussion of the fact that, despite profound political differences, Sarkozy and Badiou deploy similarly schematic and frankly clichéd versions of the Vichy past in grounding both their historical visions as well as their prognostications for political action in the present and future.

The final two chapters of *The Vichy Past in France Today* focus on two novels, their respective critical receptions, and the controversies that followed their respective publications. Chapter 4: "Remaking the *mode rétro*: Perversion and the Pulping of History in Jonathan Littell's *The Kindly Ones*" examines Littell's blockbuster and its critical reception in a global context. It focuses on the ways in which, despite claims for its originality and brilliance by its admirers, in its historical pretensions Littell's novel recycled clichés of the Vichy past and of fascism that in fact defined the *zeitgeist* of the 1970s *mode rétro* alluded to above. These include the link of fascism to sexual perversion, the leveling of historical and moral differences between ideologies, and a fascination with the figure of the *bourreau*, the torturer. Finally, in deploying, and in many instances distorting literary references from Greek tragedy to the pulp fiction of the American writer Edgar Rice Burroughs, Littell's narrator Max Aue effaces cultural boundaries and distinctions in linking other cultures to Nazi perversions and crimes. In this, Aue troublingly resembles Pascal Bruckner's contemporary European alluded to above, whose crimes are a license to accuse others as a means of affirming his or her own superiority.

The final chapter, "Revising History, Betraying Memory: Yannick Haenel's *Jan Karski* and the Jan Karski Affair" focuses on a novel that gained little notoriety in this country but raised significant issues in France concerning the novelist's right to rewrite history, and especially the history of World War II, as she or he wishes. The mix of fact and fiction, which the British historian Anthony Beevor labels "faction" is dangerous because, as Beevor writes, in an increasingly historically illiterate world, historical reality can be distorted and manipulated, often to political ends. Haenel's novel takes the privilege of the writer to revise history to extremes. In Haenel's version, Roosevelt is a lascivious old man indifferent to the Holocaust. What is more, Haenel's Karski claims that, in exterminating Europe's Jews, the Nazis were fulfilling the secret desire of the Allies, who also wished to be rid of them, albeit by different means. In its extreme revision of history *Jan Karski* not only betrays an anti-Americanism often linked to the memory of Vichy as it manifests itself today, but also serves as a reminder that the hegemony of memory has made historical accuracy, authenticity and integrity a matter of indifference, at least in some quarters.

In his account of the republican origins of Vichy, the historian Gérard Noiriel argues that Vichy and the Dark Years are second only to the French Revolution in terms of their impact on French history and in their status as a turning point in national memory whose impact is continuously felt. This is why Vichy emerges and reemerges—often spectacularly—in the public domain and in the national imagination, in one fascinating and often unsettling form or another. Hopefully, some of those recent moments are captured in the pages that follow in their complexity, their interconnections, and in their significance. Undoubtedly, there will be more such moments in France's future.

NOTES

1. François Hollande's speech was printed in its entirety in the 18 August 2012 issue of the *New York Review of Books*.

2. See Nicolas Offenstadt, *L'Histoire Bling-Bling. Le Retour du roman national* (Paris: Stock, 2009).
3. See my "The American Reception of Max Aue," *SubStance* 121 n. 39:1 (2010): 174–83.
4. Claude Lanzmann, *Le lièvre de Patagonie* (Paris: Galllimard, 2009), 510.
5. See Christophe Forcari and Laurent Joffrin "Août 1944: La liberté guidait Paris," *Libération,* 22 August, 2014. For a lengthier discussion of the commemorations of Summer 2014 in France (and Europe) see my "Where the Past is Always in the Present Tense," *Los Angeles Review of Books*, 15 February 2015.
6. Eric Zemmour, *Le Suicide Français* (Paris: Albin Michel, 2014), 89–90.
7. Ibid., 94
8. Jacques Semelin, *Persécutions et Entraides dans la France occupée: Comment 75% des juifs en France ont échappé à la mort* (Paris: Seuil—Les Arènes, 2013), 835.
9. Jacques Semelin, "Le Paradoxe français," *Le débat* 183 (2015): 191.
10. Alain Minc, *L'homme aux deux visages. Jean Moulin, René Bousquet, itinéraires croisés* (Paris: Grasset, 2013).
11. Michel Foucault, "Film and Popular Memory," in *Foucault Live: Interviews 1961–1984.* Sylvère Lottringer (Semiotext(e), 1996), 122–32. Foucault's analysis of the *mode rétro* will be taken up in greater detail in Chapter 4.
12. Marc Ferro, *Pétain en vérité* (Paris: Tallandier, 2013).
13. Pascal Bruckner, *The Tyranny of Guilt: An Essay on European Masochism* (Princeton: Princeton UP, 2012).
14. Charles S. Maier, "A Surfeit of Memory? Reflections on History, Melancholy, and Denial" *History and Memory* 5:2 (Fall-Winter 1993), 136–52.
15. Jean-Michel Chaumont, *La concurrence des victimes: génocide, identité, reconnaissance* (Paris: Editions la découverte, 1997).
16. Robert Frank, *La Hantise du décilin. La France de 1914 à 2014.* (Paris: Belin, 2014), 15.
17. Pierre Manent, *Situation de la France* (Paris: Desclée de Brouwer, 2015), 8.
18. Ibid., 9.
19. Henry Rousso, *La dernière catastrophe. L'histoire, le présent, le contemporain.* (Paris: Gallimard, 2012), 25.
20. Authoritative general histories such as Philippe Burrin's *La France à l'heure allemande,* and Gisèle Sapiro's massive study of writers during the Occupation and through the postwar Purge, *La guerre des écrivains*, are just two examples among many of excellent and exhaustive accounts of the realities of the Dark Years.
21. Jean Baudrillard, *Paroxysm: interviews with Philippe Petit* (London: Verso, 1998), 8.
22. See Rousso's discussion of this in the 2013 revised edition of *Vichy. Un passé qui ne passe pas* (Paris: Pluriel, 2013), 329–30.
23. Michael Rothberg, *Multidirectional Memory: Remembering the Holocaust in the Age of Decolonization* (Stanford: Stanford UP, 2009), 11.
24. Ibid., p. 10.
25. Susan Rubin Suleiman, *Crises of Memory and the Second World War* (Cambridge, MA: Harvard UP, 2006), 1.

Chapter 1

France's Fractured Legal Vector of Memory

Of the various ways in which the French have sought to come to terms over the past three decades with the troubled memory and legacies of the Dark Years, and primarily French complicity in the Holocaust, none have been more visible—and more problematic—than those involving French courts and French law. Certainly, events like the 1994 scandal over revelations concerning President François Mitterrand's service to Pétain's *Etat Français* and his prewar right-wing and xenophobic past generated considerable media attention and public outrage. But it was the 1987 trial for crimes against humanity of the Nazi Klaus Barbie, followed in 1994 and 1997–1998 by the trials on similar charges of two servants of Vichy, the paramilitary *milicien* Paul Touvier and the sub-prefect in Bordeaux, Maurice Papon respectively, that garnered the most national and international attention over the long term. Before Barbie's trial got underway the eminent historian Emmanuel Le Roy Ladurie predicted melodramatically that it would become an "enormous national psychodrama, psychotherapy on a nation-wide scale."[1] At least in terms of the riveting testimony it produced, it did not disappoint. Later, the trial of Maurice Papon, which took place in Bordeaux and lasted for six months from October 1997 to April 1998, often resembled a three ring circus[2] and produced a seemingly endless stream of controversies, revelations, and courtroom shenanigans. By the time the verdict was handed down and the accused sentenced, the Papon trial had exhausted nearly everyone involved, including the French public. Sales of the many books published about the trial following its conclusion were anemic, and public attention had already turned to another commemorative moment, the thirtieth anniversary of May 1968.

The fact that the French trials for crimes against humanity garnered the national and international attention that they did should come as no surprise, given the abiding importance and interest of the postwar trials of former

Nazis and their foreign accomplices. From the outset these trials raised numerous difficult legal, moral, and historical issues that still resonate today. The retroactive application of new legal categories like crimes against humanity at Nuremberg troubled many and raised the specter of "victor's justice." At the trial of Adolph Eichmann occurring in Jerusalem in spring and summer 1961, the nature of the political evil that motivated perpetrators like Eichmann, the role and responsibility of Jewish leaders in the destruction of their own people, and the testimony of witnesses who had never encountered the accused, among other issues, stirred considerable controversy globally. In a letter to Karl Jaspers written before she attended the Eichmann trial and published her landmark 1963 book, *Eichmann in Jerusalem,* Hannah Arendt had in fact wondered if the law and legal systems themselves were capable of dealing with the unprecedented nature of Nazi crimes and, by extension, those of their accomplices. Arendt wrote: "The Nazi crimes, it seems to me, explode the limits of the law; and that is precisely what constitutes their monstrousness. For these crimes, no punishment is severe enough. It may well be essential to hang Göring, but it is totally inadequate."[3]

To be sure, the French trials of the 1980s and 1990s did not achieve the historical status of the Nuremberg or Eichmann trials. They left behind no legal legacies on a global scale like Nuremberg, nor like the Eichmann trial did they help shape an emerging national identity and launch philosophical, historical and legal debates that continue today.[4] Nevertheless, occurring a half century after the commission of the crimes being tried, not to mention the demise of the Vichy regime and Hitler's Reich, the French trials did established their own distinctive and problematic legacies. First, at least arguably they more fully exposed the dangers of anachronism than the Nuremberg and Eichmann trials. The half-century interval separating the French trials from the crimes committed and the historical contexts in which they occurred encouraged multiple misunderstandings and allowed the intervention in the courtroom of other pasts and other crimes and traumas—not only crimes associated with Vichy and Nazism. These "interventions" in turn clouded legal and historical specificities in ways that did not occur (or not to the same extent) in earlier trials. The passage of time also posed a moral dilemma at the outset of each trial that many found troubling: how does one try a very old man for crimes committed forty to fifty years earlier, given that the individual in question may have changed entirely, and even become a different person? Also, at least arguably, the fact that the trials of Barbie, Touvier and Papon occurred decades after the postwar French Purge trials of collaborators that took place before the amnesty laws of the early 1950s means that the 1990s trials of Paul Touvier and Maurice Papon could ultimately appear to be just pale imitations, *simulacra* of these earlier, historically more *authentic* and urgently necessary trials, given the political context of the postwar era. Indeed, the phrase "the second Purge" was not uncommon in media references to the trials of Touvier and Papon at the time they took place, and continued afterward.

In the new century these trials also inspired another controversial legacy; the so-called "memorial laws." Most of these laws have been passed (and in one instance, repealed), since 2001. In expanding the reach of ex post facto legal condemnation and criminalization over space and time, that is, well beyond Metropolitan France during the Dark Years, these laws have highlighted problems already revealed during the trials, such as the confusion and conflation of different pasts and different traumas, and the consequent "dilution" or corruption of legal categories and the historical and moral specificity of the crimes committed. They have raised other concerns as well, especially where the role of the historian is concerned.

In order to better understand the troubled legal and historical legacies of the trials for crimes against humanity and the "memorial laws," and therefore the law's ultimate failure as a vector of memory reconciling the nation to its past, a closer look at both the trials and the memorial laws is in order.

THE TRIALS

Klaus Barbie, Paul Touvier, and Maurice Papon, the accused in the three trials, all led eventful postwar lives.[5] Barbie worked for American intelligence in Germany under assumed identities after fleeing France at the end of the war. It was also the American intelligence services, along with groups in the Catholic Church that eventually helped him to flee to South America. There he worked as a businessman and also trained extreme right-wing paramilitary groups in several South American countries. Barbie was arrested and extradited to France in 1983, and remained imprisoned in Lyons, the same prison where Resistance fighters had earlier been detained, and often tortured, until his trial some four years later. Following his conviction in Summer 1987, Barbie spent the remainder of his life in prison. He died there in September 1991.

Following the war Paul Touvier, who like Barbie had served in wartime Lyon and survived afterwards under aliases, made a living as a petty criminal and con man, selling his stories of woe to those who would listen. Among those who were willing to help him were powerful figures in the Catholic Church.[6] In 1971, Touvier's allies in the Church succeeded in securing a presidential pardon from President Georges Pompidou so that Touvier could inherit property from his father in his native Chambéry. The pardon, however, did not cover crimes against humanity, charges of which in any event would only be filed against Touvier later. When scandal erupted following the revelation of the presidential pardon to the public, Pompidou tried to calm passions at a press conference in September 1972, during which he suggested that it was time to draw a "veil" over the past of the Dark Years. Pompidou's left-footed effort to justify his pardon only succeeded in further stirring public outrage. Touvier was forced to go into hiding once again, this time in a series of right-wing, *intégriste* monasteries throughout France. He was finally arrested at the priory of Saint-François in Nice in May 1989. He was tried in spring 1994 in Yvelines near Paris, and died in prison in July 1996.

Maurice Papon's itinerary after the war was quite different from those of Touvier and Barbie. Following his service to Vichy in the prefecture in Bordeaux during the Nazi Occupation, he stayed on, with a promotion, under the Gaullists. In retaining him, the latter sighted his "acts of Resistance."[7] Following his tenure in Bordeaux, Papon went on to become a powerful figure in the Fourth and Fifth Republics, both in Metropolitan France and in Algeria. He was Prefect of Paris Police in the late 1950s and early 1960s, and later Minister of Finance under President Valerie Giscard-d'Estaing. Papon's role in the deportation of Jews from Bordeaux during the Holocaust first came to light in May 1981, when the satirical newspaper *Le Canard enchaîné* revealed previously undisclosed documents concerning his activities along these lines. Papon was finally brought to trial on charges of crimes against humanity in October 1997. As noted, he was convicted and sentenced six months later, in April 1998. After multiple efforts to avoid imprisonment, including flight to Switzerland under a false name, Papon was briefly imprisoned before his release in 2002 under a new law that amnestied elderly prisoners unable to withstand the rigors of prison life. Papon died in 2007.

Given its legal consequences and implications, at least from the Touvier trial on, it is ironic that the incorporation of crimes against humanity statutes into French law did not begin as a "French affair," that is, it was not intended to make possible the prosecution of *French* criminals against humanity. Rather, the intent of the original 1964 legislation passed by the National Assembly making these crimes imprescriptible under French law was to make possible the prosecution of Nazi criminals still at large after the statute of limitations of war crimes had run out in 1965. One Deputy in the National Assembly went so far as to speculate during deliberations over the law that Hitler himself might well still be alive. The deputy in question added that it would be a supreme injustice if Hitler could not be prosecuted for his crimes, were he to turn up in France! And, as Marc Olivier Baruch observes, in promulgating the law from his home in Colombey-les-Deux-Eglises a short while after its passage, President Charles de Gaulle would never have imagined that the law would one day be applied to Maurice Papon, then serving as de Gaulle's Prefect of Paris Police.[8]

Both in legal decisions leading up to the trial of Klaus Barbie in 1987 and also during the trial itself, the inherent limitations and unforeseen difficulties of the 1964 law began to emerge. First, because the text of the 1964 law did not explicitly define crimes against humanity under *French law*, but merely referred to the statutes used at Nuremberg, the French statute was in some ways a "fill-in-the-blank" law that could be written and re-written as needed. In Lyons, this problem arose because French resistance fighters—and among them Jean Moulin, France's national martyr and symbol of Resistance against Nazi oppression—were also among Barbie's victims, along with his Jewish victims. Indeed, the last deportation train that left Lyon on 11 August 1944 contained three hundred Jews and three hundred resistance fighters.[9] This being the case, French Resistance associations lobbied to have Barbie's Resistance victims included in the charges leveled against him by the prosecution, in homage to their memory. As a result, in 1985 the French court of appeals ruled that Barbie's crimes against the Resistance could be prosecuted as crimes against humanity as well. In effect, this merged the categories of war crimes and crimes against humanity, thus breaking with precedents set at Nuremberg, where the two were distinct charges.[10] It also, paradoxically, cast the resisters in the role of *victims* of the Nazis, thus depriving them of their status as enemy combatants, a status they had long fought for and claimed.[11] And in human terms, it suggested an equivalency that even lawyers involved in Barbie's prosecution found dubious. Looking back on the trial more than thirty years after its conclusion, Michel Zaoui wondered: "Is there really anything in common between a resister arrested because he is a resister, and a child arrested because he is a Jew?"[12] Finally, the decision set a dangerous precedent according to which the law could be revised to meet the circumstances of the moment, in this case the demands of civil party pressure groups and of the prosecution.

When the Barbie trial finally got underway in spring 1987 other difficulties arose. Taking advantage of the time elapsed between Barbie's and Nazism's crimes and the late 1980s, Barbie's attorney Jacques Vergès pointedly emphasized what he viewed as the hypocrisy of the proceedings by drawing parallels between the Nazi extermination of Europe's Jews and what he considered to be comparable French crimes during the colonial period and decolonization. One strategy for emphasizing this comparison, and thereby implicitly challenging the very historical and legal foundations of the trial as a whole, was to include on his defense team individuals from former French colonies whose presence was intended to recall France's past colonial abuses and crimes. Reflecting on this tactic and its implications, Alain Finkielkraut observed that "the presence on the bench of Jacques Vergès, Nabil Bouaïta, and Jean Martin M'Bemba for the defense said in itself that the extermination of the Jews was a crime of local interest, a drop of European blood in the ocean of human suffering, and thus offended the conscience of only white people."[13] Henceforth, Finkielkraut added, the word "Nazi" was "a word without a referent, anchored in nothing, a word that is no longer a fact but simply a label, a floating word—available, completely adaptable"[14] ready to hand for all self-proclaimed victims not of Nazism but of white European hegemonic practices. Earlier, Vergès had supported the demands of Resistance organizations that Barbie be tried for his crimes against the Resistance, also to muddy the legal and historical waters and thereby diminish the specificity of Nazism's crimes against the Jews. And during the proceedings themselves, Vergès sought as well to cast Jewish aid organizations during the Occupation obliged to work with Vichy and the Nazis in the role of "collaborators," despite the fact that these "collaborators" also, among other things, prepared false identity papers for Jews fleeing to Italy and Switzerland.[15] All of these distractions or diversions were of course set in relief by the notable absence in the courtroom of the accused himself, who refused to appear after the first few days, only returning for his sentencing. According to Claude Lanzmann, Barbie himself was not even really the man on trial. It was Vergès who had dismissed him in order to cast *himself* in the martyred, if in his case untouchable, role of the accused! The "perversity of the story," Lanzmann continued, was that Vergès had realized his dream of being "judged" while at the same time running no risk himself, and all the while parading without restriction or restraint in front of the press. In the end, Lanzmann concluded lugubriously, the trial was a "false" one, a "simulacrum:" the only thing that was real were the "six million [Jewish] dead."[16]

Despite Vergès' tactics and shenanigans, in the end the Barbie trial remained largely focused on the crimes of the accused, and of Nazism itself. But as Tzvetan Todorov has observed, this itself was problematic. For Todorov, historical trials such as the Barbie trial are flawed by definition, in that by their very nature they focus all the blame on the accused in the dock (and what he or she represents), while those not accused, at least implicitly, are considered entirely innocent. By extension—and referring directly to the Barbie trial—Todorov writes that "regardless of the intention of the public authorities who organized the trial, its lesson was: the persecutors were the Germans, the victims were the French."[17] If Todorov's assessment is accurate, then in the end, the Barbie trial offered only a skewed and partial justice based on a Manichean vision of history.

It is to the credit of the French legal system and also to French public opinion that the prosecution of Klaus Barbie, despite its failings, accelerated efforts to bring French criminals to justice on charges of crimes against humanity. But by the time Paul Touvier was tried in Spring 1994, French law had once again been egregiously manipulated, apparently in an effort to forestall coming to terms with precisely the inequity Todorov detected in the outcome of the Barbie trial. This time, in April 1992, the Paris Court of Appeals stunningly dropped all charges against Touvier, arguing that his crimes for which he was being charged—the murder of seven Jewish hostages at the Cemetery of Rillieux-la-Pape in June 1944—were not crimes against humanity under French law. Referring to the 1985 court decision prior to the Barbie trial which stipulated that crimes against humanity can only be committed on behalf of a regime practicing a "politics of ideological hegemony," the Appeals court argued that since Vichy's *Etat Français* was *not* such a regime, and since Touvier was an agent of that regime, his crimes could not be considered crimes against humanity. Therefore, Touvier could walk.

To make this argument the court, in effect, rewrote history and, as the French jurist Jean-Denis Bredin lamented, all 213 pages of the decision, "well-constructed, often well written," seemed "slanted toward an acquittal."[18] Where history was concerned, the appeals court argued that Vichy was not inherently racist and anti-Semitic, and thus not like Nazi Germany. This argument ignored the most fundamental proofs of Vichy's culpability along these lines, the anti-Jewish statutes of 1940 and 1941, for example.[19]

Although the Appeals court decision was partially overturned by the Supreme Court in November 1992, the higher court did not reverse the lower court's revision of history where the realities of Pétainist anti-Semitism were concerned. Rather, it argued, ironically—following some of the accused's own claims—that the murder of the Jews at the Rilleux-la-Pape cemetery had been ordered by the Germans, and therefore, as a "German crime" *could* be tried as a crime against humanity.

The deliberations of the trial itself two years later revealed the fallacy of this claim. Touvier had in fact *not* acted on German orders at Rillieux. So as a means of overcoming this new obstacle, another twist, again involving the manipulation of history and the law, was introduced by one of the civil parties lawyers.[20] Because Touvier's superior and the head of the *Milice*, Joseph Darnand, had sworn an oath of loyalty to Hitler, the *Milice* itself, *ipso facto*, could be considered a Nazi organization and therefore one practicing a politics of ideological hegemony. Having found a means, dubious as it was, of confirming Touvier's guilt, the court convicted him of crimes against humanity. In the process however, legal responsibility for the Rilleux crimes in institutional and even national terms had in effect migrated back across the borders of time and space, back to Nazi Germany.

Shortly after the conclusion of the Touvier trial, and as a result of the revisions and manipulations of crimes against humanity statutes up until then, the legal expert Christian Guéry questioned in an essay in the review *Le genre humain* if crimes against humanity had any substance and coherence, if they *existed at all*, in French law. After having been "corrected," "adapted," and "made to satisfy" numerous external exigencies of the moment, the law as it stood, had become "narrow, volatile, out of date, and invalid."[21] But rather than serve as a warning to courts where future prosecutions were concerned, Guéry's admonition fell on deaf ears. Between the end of the Touvier trial and the beginning of the trial of Maurice Papon some three years later, crimes against humanity statutes continued to be revised to facilitate an eventual prosecution of Papon. For example, after initially requiring that the accused have *full knowledge* of Nazi intentions in collaborating with them in the deportations of multiple trainloads of Jews between 1942 and 1944—a claim that would be hard to prove, and that the accused would surely deny—the court backtracked under pressure. It declared that the accused did not have to "adhere to the politics of ideological hegemony" of the Nazis—code for knowing their ultimate aims—in order to be charged and convicted of crimes against humanity. On this fragile basis, the trial of Maurice Papon could proceed.

From the outset what Marc Olivier Baruch has described as the "temptation to confuse myth and history, symbol and reality," and the procedural necessity of "leafing through the past" willy-nilly marred the proceedings of the Papon trial.[22] Unlike Barbie and Touvier who for all intents and purposes had become historical and political non-entities after the war, Maurice Papon, as noted, went on to have a distinguished political career in the postwar years, primarily as a servant and representative of Gaullism. As such, according to the curious, not to say ludicrous testimony of some former Gaullists reading backwards in time at his trial, Papon was not a criminal against humanity under Vichy but an important servant of the Fifth Republic and even an admirable representative of *la France Libre*. For these witnesses, the trial itself was not about Papon's crimes under Vichy. It was rather an attempt to put Gaullism and France itself on trial.

Before the trial in Bordeaux was a week old, perhaps the most memorable moment in the entire proceedings occurred, and one which also underscored the dangers of anachronism, of reading backwards in time. Moreover, the legacy of this moment still resonates today, although not in relation to French complicity with Nazism, but rather in relation to French Fourth and Fifth Republican crimes during decolonization. The moment in question was the discussion, during the required review of the accused's CV, of the brutal and murderous repression of Algerian protesters by Parisian police under Papon's command on the night of 17 October 1961.

In many ways the deliberations inside the courtroom and the controversy that swirled outside concerning Papon and 17 October 1961 serve as a perfect microcosm of the complications and paradoxes inherent in France's crimes against humanity trials. More so than the trials of Barbie and Touvier, the Papon trial as it was trumpeted in the media (and by other interested parties) was the quintessential trial of "History" and "Memory." But, one should ask, whose memory? The victims of official French complicity in the Nazi Final Solution deported by Papon during the Occupation, or his Algerian victims in the streets of Paris almost two decades later, and by extension, all those who had experienced the brutal realities of French colonialism? And what History? During his testimony Papon claimed that all the protestors killed were not killed by the police but rather died as a result of violent clashes between rival factions of the Algerian liberation movement. He testified, first, that not one Algerian was killed by police fire, but rather all those shot died at the hands of assault groups of the FLN. Papon went on to claim, all the while diminishing their number, that the bodies recuperated from the Seine in the days following 17 October all belonged to the PPA, the *Parti du peuple algérien* [The Party of the Algerian people], the FLN's fierce rival.[23] Then Papon's lawyer Jean-Marc Varaut introduced into the record a letter written at the time from then Prime Minister Michel Debré congratulating Papon and his men for their courage in protecting the security of the capital. Following all of this, the historian Jean-Luc Einaudi testified, on the basis of years of research, that the Algerians killed *were* in fact the victims of the police rather than of rival Algerian factions. Moreover, Einaudi testified, Papon had already given ample proof of his brutality while serving as Prefect in Algeria before its independence. As the journalist Eric Conan, who was present throughout the trial, wrote following these testimonies: "A beautiful demonstration of the fate of History before the tribunal: one day it goes in one direction, the following day in another direction."[24] And since, as Michel Zaoui observes, in a French criminal trial such as this only the judges, and *not the jury* get to see the dossiers containing evidence, the latter are at the mercy of, and indeed can be more influenced, by the oratorical skills of the witnesses and the attorneys than by the facts of the case themselves. And unlike the American system, where the accused and witnesses swear an oath to tell the truth, the French justice system has no such requirement. As a result, the accused can say anything he or she wants with relative impunity, as Papon amply displayed[25] Meanwhile, outside the walls of the courtroom, the distinguished historian Pierre Vidal-Naquet took the debate beyond the realm of history and to the heart of the legal issue at hand. In an article in *le Nouvel Observateur* Vidal-Nacquet argued that Papon's crimes against the Algerians in 1961 were *also* crimes against humanity, and that Papon should be tried in Bordeaux for these crimes as well.[26] Would this mean that, after all, the French Fifth Republic itself had practiced a politics of "ideological hegemony," like Nazi Germany?[27]

In the end, Papon was sentenced to ten years in prison, a "bastard decision" according to his lawyer, and one that seemed to underscore the paradoxes and ambiguities of the trial itself. How does one receive a sentence of only ten years' imprisonment for the worst crimes imaginable, when lesser crimes receive lengthier sentences? The answer lies in the verdict handed down by the court. Papon was found guilty of complicity in the "illegal arrest" and "arbitrary sequestration" of Jews during the deportations from Bordeaux between 1942 and 1944. But he was acquitted on all counts of "complicity to murder" or "attempt to murder" in his involvement in implementing the Final Solution. While this verdict satisfied some, including the lawyers and activists Serge and Arno Klarsfeld, who from the outset sought to make the trial a "pedagogical" exercise for the French people[28] others saw it as yet another failure of crimes against humanity law in France. In an essay published in *Le débat* shortly after the conclusion of the trial entitled: "What is the purpose of the Papon trial?" Jean de Maillard argued that the verdict was "rational" in its acknowledgment of the facts presented. But it was also "contradictory" in that without Papon's *knowledge* of the fate of those Jews rounded up and deported, that is, their *extermination*, the other crimes he committed and for which he was convicted hardly seemed to amount to crimes against humanity. As the defendant himself testified in his closing remarks, a crime against humanity cannot be "sliced up," and one cannot be a "criminal against humanity at fifteen, or thirty, or sixty percent."[29] In the end, the verdict was one of "compromise" in legal terms, a "mixed one" at best, according to the legal expert Leila Sadat-Wexler.[30]

What of the justice of the verdict? Although no one knew what Maurice Papon actually knew during the Occupation except, obviously, the accused himself, Michel Zaoui for his part remains reluctant to accept the idea of Papon's ignorance of the Nazis' intentions and therefore unconvinced by his acquittal on charges of complicity in murder. Zaoui notes that in Bordeaux during the Occupation Papon voluntarily served as the individual in charge in the *prefecture* of the "service for Jewish questions." And, Zaoui writes, "To direct such a service in itself implies assuming responsibility for a program which, if its objective was evidently not the physical elimination of Jews, still had as its final aim the implementation of a shared Franco-Geman will, made concrete through signed agreements, whose end was to get rid of all Jews, seize their belongings, and deport them to a "cruel fate."[31]

If the law and justice were ill-served by the Papon verdict, at least for some history and historical understanding were served worst of all. According to Eric Conan, the fact that the trial of Papon was cast as the "symbolic trial of Vichy" meant that the verdict constituted a "trap": the judgment of Papon would also constitute an historical judgment of Vichy. In acquitting Papon on the charges of complicity to murder, the court in Bordeaux thereby in effect diminished the crimes of Vichy, suggesting that Pétain and the *Etat Français* were less knowingly responsible for their complicity with the Nazi Final Solution than they were. As Conan argues, "this constituted a *formidable regression* [my italics] where recent developments in the historiography of the Occupation are concerned."[32]

For Jean de Maillard, the historical "regressions" implicit in the verdict in the Papon trial were symptomatic of even grosser historical distortions suggested by the proceedings themselves. According to Maillard, what the latter accomplished was to offer a perverse, global/historical pedagogical lesson whose purpose was to "make future generations believe that [during World War II] there existed only, on one side, the Nazis and their accomplices, whose energies were totally given over to the elimination of the Jews and their friends [which constituted the other side], and that everyone was obliged to pick sides, *in full knowledge of the meaning and implications of his or her choice.*"[33] For Maillard, this "strange and disquieting vision of History," this "Manichaeism imposed *a posteriori* for expiatory purposes" occulted specific historical issues at stake at the very heart of the trial, not the least of which was French anti-Semitism, and the anti-Semitism of the accused himself. While the trial made it seem that Papon's willingness to load the trains in Bordeaux with Jews sprang from a racial hatred akin to that of the Nazis, in reality it sprang from a "French anti-Semitism, with different origins and significations but about which one never speaks."[34]

For Maillard, the ultimate meaning of the Papon trial, and the other "trials of Collaboration" as he refers to them, lies elsewhere than in specific legal and historical failures and shortcomings. All of these "remakes" of the trials of the postwar Purge, as Maillard labels them, aspire to something much larger, and that is the "de-scientification" [Maillard's term] of History and its "re-enchantment" to the benefit of "a hermeneutics of Good and Evil whose consequences are most dangerous in the public arena."[35] In the era of human rights this kind of moral manichaeism, in Maillard's view, allows for the demonization of the modern nation-state itself, since Nazi Germany and Vichy, are finally, only representatives of, or stand-ins for the latter.[36]

Henry Rousso, for one, would disagree with Maillard's claim that the Papon trial constituted nothing more than a "remake" of the earlier purge trials of Vichy's leading political and cultural figures. In the Afterword to the new edition of *Vichy, un passé qui ne passe pas*, Rousso states in fact, that unlike the Purge trials "whose debates and deliberations focused on the anti-Semitic fury of a partisan of Nazism," the Papon trial focused instead of "the role of the French government and the French administration in the internment and deportation of the Jews, a subject hardly discussed at the moment of the Liberation."[37] Still, as Rousso had acknowledged earlier in discussing the Touvier trial, over the proceedings hung the shadow of the *real trial* of Vichy and French complicity in the Holocaust that never took place, and that was the trial of René Bousquet, Secretary General of French Police under Vichy. It was Bousquet who negotiated Vichy's accords with the Nazis to implement the Final Solution in France in spring 1942. That agreement led to the *Vél d'Hiv* roundups of July 1942, which as noted resulted in some 13,000 Jewish deaths, and many other roundups of Jews as well. Bousquet was gunned down in his Paris apartment in July 1993 by a deranged publicity seeker shortly after the final legal obstacles to trying him on charges of crimes against humanity had been removed.[38] As Maurice Papon stated in a self-serving interview in March 1996, he was only a "scapegoat" for bigger fish that got away, implicitly pointing the finger at Bousquet.[39] While Papon's attempt to whitewash his own crimes in this Girardian strategy is transparent, the fact remains that as a *comprehensive* exposition and judgment of Vichy's crime in the Holocaust, Papon's trial, and Touvier's before his, were only "stand-ins," simulacra of sorts, of what the trial of Bousquet would in all likelihood have been.

If Rousso's and Maillard's views diverge over the question of the Papon trial's status as a "remake" of the earlier purge trials, their views concerning contemporary relations to the past—for Maillard revealed directly in the Papon trial and for Rousso, strongly influenced by the Papon and other trials of the 1980s and 1990s—bear striking resemblances. What Maillard describes as the "de-scientification" and re-enchantment of the past in order to impose a hermeneutics of Good and Evil on it recalls the way History is experienced in today's presentist culture as described by Rousso in *La dernière catastrophe*. Remembered in terms of unresolved conflicts to be judged and (hopefully) repaired in the present, the recent past, recent History, is nevertheless cast, anachronistically, in specifically moral terms. In the process it is simplified, degraded and distorted.

THE MEMORIAL LAWS

In the new millennium, both the legal means as well as the chronological and geographical scope of French efforts to come to terms with the crimes of the past changed significantly, not to say radically, with the passage of three "memorial laws." Of these laws, two were passed in 2001. The first law officially recognized the Turkish genocide of Armenians in 1915. The second law, the so-called Taubira Law, recognized the slave trade and slavery itself since the Fifteenth Century as a crime against humanity. The third law, often referred to as the Meckachera Law, was passed in 2005, and expressed the nation's gratitude to French men and women who served in France's former colonial possessions. It also mandated the teaching in secondary schools of France's "positive role" in these former possessions, especially in North Africa. The Meckachera law was partially annulled one year later in 2006, after the Constitutional Council ruled that it was not in the purview of the legislature to pass laws determining the content of school textbooks.[40] A fourth "memorial law," or more accurately a precursor of and inspiration for the other "memorial laws"—the "mother-law" of the "memorial laws," according to Pierre Nora[41]—was the Gayssot law of 1990. The Gayssot Law made the denial of the Holocaust, or "negationism," to use the French term, a crime punishable with significant fines and up to a year in prison. Of these four "memorial laws," only the Gayssot law includes penalties involving fines and imprisonment, although recent efforts have been made to attach similar penalties to the other laws, especially the law which labels the Armenian genocide a crime against humanity.[42]

Taken as a whole, the origins, evolution, and controversies that have surrounded the Memorial laws from the Gayssot law of 1990 to the Meckachera law of 2005 seem to mirror those of the French trials of the 1980s and 1990s in interesting ways. Indeed, both the trials and the Gayssot law itself grew out of a common political and cultural matrix of the late 1980s and early 1990s. At the time, the memory of and controversies surrounding the Holocaust were acute in France. The profound shock that accompanied the release of Claude Lanzmann's 1985 film *Shoah,* coupled with the Historians Debate raging in Germany were instrumental in launching or fueling both initiatives.[43] Also, Paul Touvier's belated 1989 arrest in an *intégriste* monastery in Nice once again brought French crimes of the Holocaust to the fore, and aroused as well public suspicions about both governmental and religious institutions that had allowed Touvier to remain free for so long—hence the need for the passage of a law to recognize and penalize the denial of those crimes in the present.[44]

Like the trials before them, the memorial laws also exposed the danger of anachronism, which opened the door to the revision of history, or at least to partial and highly partisan interpretations of it. If the Meckachera Law retroactively downplayed or even erased French crimes and abuses in its former colonies and possessions by insisting on the "positive role" of the colonizers, the Taubira law labeling the slave trade and slavery itself a crime against humanity was also partial in its representation of the past. Even those generally favorable to the law like Gilles Maceron, observed:

> The law is limited, in reality, to facts that form a part of our national history, or of European history in which the former is inscribed—and admittedly with a certain looseness—because the Taubira law designates slavery from the Fifteenth Century on, which corresponds to the beginnings of the slave trade on the Iberian Peninsula but not to the French slave trade. The latter only began at the beginning of the Seventeenth Century.[45]

For harsher critics of the law, this was only a small part of the problem: What of the African slave trade, or the slave trade in the Muslim world? Were these crimes against humanity under French law as well? If not, why not? What of slavery in the United States in the antebellum south, whose brutal practices covered not just the capture and transport of black Africans, but the harshest of oppressions throughout the lives of the victims in question? And as for the

2001 Law dealing with the Armenian genocide, although few outside Turkey deny the crime, Bernard Lewis's defense of his views on the genocide and the circumstances of its occurrence following his 1995 conviction in France for statements "susceptible to unjustly reawakening painful sentiments in the Armenian community" point to important historical nuances that the French law leaves out or effectively passes over. For his part, Tzvetan Todorov noted that the passage of a French law covering the Turkish genocide of the Armenians underscored a hypocritical willingness to condemn the recent crimes of other nations while ignoring France's own recent crimes. As an example of the latter, Todorov pointed to the French abandonment of the *harki* population following the liberation of Algeria. Tens of thousands of *harkis*, who fought with the French during the Algerian war, were massacred as traitors by the new Algerian government shortly after the conflict ended.[46]

Other critics of the Memorial Laws, and especially the historians and authors of the *Liberté pour l'histoire* petition published in *Le monde* in December 2005[47] raised additional concerns, also related to the danger of anachronism. But these concerns dealt less with questions of historical accuracy and thoroughness than with the practice of history itself in the present. If it is possible to legally and retroactively declare past crimes or abuses "crimes against humanity" in the name of memory of victims and the latter's descendants, and make any historical challenge to this determination punishable with prison time and fines, this creates an obvious bind for present and future historians. Most will logically decide to work in a less dangerous area, and important historical events that *need* further exploration will become taboo. And what of those historians who persevere in working in these prescribed areas despite the risks? A cautionary tale along these lines already exists. In 2005 the historian Olivier Pétré-Grenouilleau in an interview in the newspaper the *Journal du Dimanche* did not challenge the Taubira law's affirmation that the slave trade was a "crime against humanity." But he *did* claim that the slave-trade was not genocide, since the goal of slavery was to have slaves available for labor and not to kill them. Angered by these comments, an association of individuals from France's former colonies brought suit against Petré-Grenouilleau for "negationism," citing both the Taubira and Gayssot laws. Although the suit was eventually dropped, the fear of a future legal muzzling of historians seemed justified to many.

Another anxiety raised by the passage of the Memorial Laws concerned their status as precedents that called for further legal actions criminalizing the past. If the Barbie trial and conviction provided momentum and justification for trying French criminals against humanity like Touvier and Papon, the passage of the Memorial Laws produced a similar impetus, but without the restraints of actual criminals to indict. The memorial laws passed to date thus risked opening a veritable Pandora's Box of additional laws indiscriminately incriminating *any number* of historical events and traumas. This danger had in fact first been voiced in 1990 by Madeleine Rebérioux after the passage of the Gayssot law. Rebérioux also worried that, although this was not the law's intent, prosecuting violators of the memorial laws could and would make martyrs of them.[48] By way of validating Rebérioux's first concern subsequently shared by many others, in 2008 Françoise Chandernagor noted that more than twenty new proposals for laws labeling as genocides or crimes against humanity had been submitted since the passage of the Taubira and Meckachera laws. These included crimes from France's past like the repression of the Vendée in 1793–1794. But they also crossed national borders and traveled backward and forward in time to propose the retroactive criminalization of the massacres in Palestine during the Crusades and the Ukrainian famine of 1932–1933. Chandernagor added that often proposals for new Memorial laws were based on divergent national and ethnic memories in competition with each other. For example, proposals for laws made subsequent to Papon's 1997–1998 trial and conviction sought to label as a crime against humanity the suppression of Algerian protesters in Paris in October 1961, and also the FLN's assassinations of *pieds noirs* and *harkis* during and after the Algerian war.[49] In the end, if the passage of these laws were to go unchecked, René Rémond argued that this would mean "the death of objective historical research."[50]

A final concern with the Memorial laws, implicit if not explicit in their temporal and geographical expansionism, has to do with the legal definitions of genocide and crimes against humanity themselves. If the trials stretched, revised, and modified the statutes dealing with crimes against humanity to the breaking point within the "narrow" context of the Nazi Final Solution and French complicity in it, by their very range and reach the Memorial Laws signaled a similar or perhaps even greater danger. Although, with the exception of the Gayssot law not intended for prosecutorial purposes when originally passed, the Memorial Laws nevertheless stretched and arguably diluted the definition and meaning of "crimes against humanity" to the point that—as the proposed laws mentioned above by Chandernagor suggest—the term could be applied, or misapplied to virtually any historical trauma. And as René Rémond had warned, such dilution and loss of specificity through multiplicity could only aid these crimes' deniers.[51]

In tracing France's fractured legal vector of memory over the last twenty-five to thirty years, the dangers the application of the law poses to history and historical understanding, both in the courtroom and in governmental attempts to legislate the past become clear. It is not surprising, therefore, that in March 2008 a government commission presided over by the president of the National Assembly Bernard Accoyer concluded that no more Memorial Laws should be drafted or passed into law. The commission also affirmed that it is not the role of the National Assembly "to adopt laws that characterize or carry an appreciation of historical facts, especially if these laws carry criminal sanctions."[52] Timely as it was, the recommendation of the Accoyer Commission only served to validate observations made earlier in discussions of the shortcomings of the memorial laws as well as the trials for crimes against humanity. Summing up, Tzvetan Todorov had already observed that, "Justice does not aspire to historical equity."[53] And Madeleine Rebérioux had written: "the very concept of historical truth rejects the authority of the state."[54]

Still, for all its failings, the law's forays into French history have produced—at least arguably—some positive outcomes. For example, where the trials are concerned, it should not be overlooked that it was the heated discussions and exchanges early in Maurice Papon's trial that reintroduced the events of 17 October 1961 to public scrutiny. As a result, in addition to powerful novels and films being written and made about these events and the brutality of Papon's police, the events themselves have now been carefully studied and debated by historians, and have claimed a rightful and central place in the history and memory of decolonization. If the revelations of these events were viewed as an impediment to justice and the law at the time as I have described here, that is certainly not their exclusive legacy today.

Similarly, if the passage of the Taubira law and its declaration that slavery and the slave trade were crimes against humanity appeared to open the door, as many argued, to an unlimited criminalization of French (and European) history, others have underscored its value in different, but arguably equal "historical" terms. Françoise Vergès writes, for example, that the Taubira law serves as an eloquent counterargument to those "advocates of the republican myth who continue to conceive of slavery as something that happened 'over there.'"[55] Opposition to the slave law, she continues, is symptomatic of "a blind spot in French thought where the role played by race in the construction of national identity is concerned."[56]

Still, both positive and negative assessments of the law's impact on French *history* and our understanding of it leave off what is perhaps the most important and least quantifiable of its long-term consequences, and that is its impact on the French nation's self-image, its collective psyche. Already in the late 1990s Henry Rousso worried that the relentless focus at the time on the Vichy past and French complicity in Holocaust, encouraged by the trials of Touvier and Papon, and the short-circuited prosecution of René Bousquet had the effect of criminalizing the nation's past in the eyes of the French. And, he continued, that process could only have a negative impact on the nation's ability and will to focus on the present and on the future.[57] If anything, the passage of the Memorial Laws only encouraged this tendency. As Albert Camus wrote in the *Algerian Chronicles,* while it is necessary for a strong nation to confront its past "errors," it is also essential not to lose sight of the "reasons for it self-esteem," what Pascal Bruckner has more recently referred to as the "duty to our national glories." If this latter capacity is lost in present-day France through the criminalization of the past, it can only contribute to what Robert Franck among others refer to as the nation's sense of decline, its *déclinisme*. At the same time, however, as the ceremonies celebrating the Liberation in summer 2014 described in the Introduction confirm, appropriate and historically responsible celebrations of the "nation's glories" are not easy to come by, for a variety of reasons.

On a different, and more ominous concluding note: following the *Charlie Hebdo* and *Hyper Kacher* attacks in January 2015 the *le Monde* journalist Alain Frachon pointed to a sinister and frankly murderous by-product of French efforts to legislate the past. In a televised interview Frachon suggested that the real impetus behind the tragic murders of the *Charlie Hebdo* staff and the Hyper Kacher near the Porte de Vincennes in January 2015 was *la concurrences des victimes,* the "competition of victims." This perverse competition, he argued, haunts present-day France and was triggered by the Memorial Laws, and the Gayssot Law in particular.

Franchon's reasoning, or better, perhaps, his leap of logic is disturbing, not to say shocking. It does suggest however, that the law's intervention in history in an effort to fulfill a duty to memory, to the victims and descendants of past crimes and traumas, can be dangerous and indeed lethal in ways no one could have foreseen.

NOTES

1. Quoted in Rousso, *The Vichy Syndrome*, 210.

2. The "inner circle" of the Papon trial was the courtroom itself. Just outside the courtroom, in the "second ring" or entry hall to the building, the lawyers for the various parties met with the media and camera crews during recesses to give their account of what had happened. Outside the building, "memory militants" staged regular demonstrations in the "third ring" of the circus.

3 Hannah Arendt and Karl Jaspers, *Correspondence: 1926–1969* (New York: Harcourt, Brace, Jovanovich, 1992), 54.

4. The ongoing interest, indeed fascination with the Eichmann trial is at least partially attributable to the brilliant and controversial book it inspired, Hannah Arendt's *Eichmann in Jerusalem*. The most recent iteration of the debate surrounding the trial and Arendt's book followed the publication of Bettina Stagneth's *Eichmann before Jerusalem*, (2014 for the English translation) which once again challenged the validity of Arendt's take on Eichmann and especially the banality of evil he supposedly represented.

5. Barbie's life and career have been the subject of numerous books as well as the classic 1988 documentary by Marcel Ophuls: *Hotel Terminus: The Life and Times of Klaus Barbie.*

6. For Touvier's postwar Itinerary, see the Introduction to my *Vichy, the Holocaust, and French Justice: The Bousquet and Touvier Affairs* (Dartmouth/UPNE, 1996). For an excellent fictional portrait of Touvier, see Brian Moore's *The Statement*, later made into a film starring Michael Caine.

7. See Van Kelly's essay, "Papon's Transition after World War II" in my *The Papon Affair: Memory and Justice on Trial* New York: Routledge, 2000) for a detailed account of Papon's postwar career.

8. See Marc-Olivier Baruch, 44–45.

9. In Marcel Colin, *Le Crime contre l'Humanité*, 94.

10. As Michel Zaoui, Noëlle Herrenschmidt, and Antoine Garapon point out, this was in fact ironically expedient in historical and legal terms, since France had earlier refused to ratify international conventions making war crimes imprescriptible as well. If France had ratified these conventions, it would have been obliged to try *French* soldiers who had fought in Indochina and North Africa for war crimes, something it very much wished to avoid. See *Mémoire de justice. Les procès Barbie, Touvier, et Papon* (Paris: Seuil, 2009), 51.

11. See Henry Rousso, *The Vichy Syndrome* (Cambridge: Harvard UP, 1991), 210.

12. Michel Zaoui, Noelle Herrenschmidt, and Antoine Garapon, 79.

13. Alain Finkielkraut, *Remembering in Vain: The Klaus Barbie Trial and Crimes against Humanity* (New York: Columbia University Press, 1992), 25.

14. Ibid., 37.

15. Zaoui et al., 83.

16. "Le masochisme de Vergès: Entretien avec Claude Lanzmann," in *Archives d'un procès: Klaus Barbie*, Bernard-Henri Lévy, ed. (Paris: Le Livre de Poche, 1986).

17. Tzvetan Todorov, *La Signature humaine. Essais 1983–2008.* (Paris: Seuil, 2009), 236. (Paris: Livre de Poche, 1986), 190–91.

18. Jean-Denis Bredin, "The Touvier Affair: History and Justice Abused," in Richard Golsan, ed., *Memory, The Holocaust, and French Justice: The Bousquet and Touvier Affairs.* (Hanover: Dartmouth/UPNE, 1996), 110.

19. For an exhaustive and up-to-date account of Vichy's anti-Semitic policies and practices, see the new edition of Robert Paxton and Michael R. Marrus's *Vichy et les Juifs* (Paris: Calmann-Lévy, 2015).

20. Arno Klarsfeld, who later published his statement before the court, *Touvier. Un crime français* (Paris: Fayard, 1994).

21. Christian Guéry, "Une interrogation après le procès Touvier: le crime contre l'humanité existe-t-il?" in *Le genre humain 28: Juger sous Vichy* (Paris: Seuil, 1994), 119.

22. See Baruch, 85–88.

23. *Le Procès de Maurice Papon, Volume I* (Paris: Albin Michel, 1998), 198.

24. Eric Conan, *Le Procès Papon. Un journal d'audience* (Paris, Gallimard, 1998), 29.

25. See Zaoui, 79–80. Zaoui also notes that the Act of Accusation containing the facts is read out in the court room at the beginning of each court session, but that this reading is often long, tedious, and convoluted, and is therefore often of little help to the jurors wishing to establish the facts for themselves.

26. Pierre Vidal-Naquet, "Ce qui accable Papon," *Le Nouvel Observateur* 23–29 October, 1997): 56–57.

27. One of the glaring ironies of the Papon trial is that, afterward, Papon sued Einaudi for defamation of a public official, although by any measure it was not Einaudi who was lying and making false accusations during the trial. For the ensuing "second Papon trial" which occurred in 1998, see my *The Papon Affair: Memory and Justice on Trial* (New York: Routledge, 2000), 224–44.

28. Arno Klarsfeld served as a lawyer for one of the civil parties during the trial. In his recently published memoir with his wife Beate Klarsfeld, Serge Klarsfeld explains that from the outset he and his son considered Papon's crimes to be lesser than those of Barbie, Touvier, and René Bousquet, to be discussed shortly, and therefore deserved a lesser sentence. As a "pedagogical lesson" for the French public, the punishment should fit the crime. See Beate and Serge Klarsfeld, *Mémoires* (Paris; Fayard/Flammarion, 2015), 576.

29. Quoted in Conan, 311.

30. Leila-Sadat Wexler, "The Legal Legacy of Maurice Papon" in Golsan, *The Papon Affair*, 148.

31. Zaoui, 114.

32. Conan, 315.

33. Maillard, 36–37.

34. Ibid., 37.

35. Ibid., 40.

36. Ibid.

37. Eric Conan and Henry Rousso, *Vichy, un passé qui ne passe pas* (Paris: Fayard/Pluriel, 2013), 323.

38. For a detailed discussion of Bousquet, the convoluted legal efforts to bring him to trial, and his murder, see the Introduction to my *Memory, the Holocaust, and French Justice: The Bousquet and Touvier Affairs* (Hanover: Dartmouth/UPNE, 1996).

39. In Golsan, *The Papon Affair*, 166.

40. Accoyer, 33.

41. Quoted in Accoyer, 71.

42. A law passed in late 2011 penalizing the Armenian law was later declared unconstitutional by the *Conseil constitutional*. See Marc-Olivier Baruch, *Des Lois indignes? Les historiens, la politique, et le droit* (Paris: Tallandier, 2013), 55.

43. Baruch, 34.

44. René Rémond, *Quand l'Etat se mêle à l'histoire* (Paris: Stock, 2006).

45. See Gilles Manceron, "La loi: régulateur ou acteur des guerres de mémoires?" in Pascal Blanchard et Isabelle Veyrat-Masson, *Les Guerres de mémoires. La France et son histoire.* (Paris:La Découverte, 2008), 247.

46. Tzvetan Todorov, "Letter from Paris," *Salmagundi* 177 (Winter 2013): 33–34.

47. The text of the petition can be found in Baruch, p. 318. The petition was signed by many of France's most esteemed historians and public intellectuals including Pierre Nora, Jacques Julliard, René Rémond, and Pierre Vidal-Naquet.

48. Rebérioux's article "Le génocide, le juge, et l'historien" originally appeared in *L'Histoire* 138 (November 1990). It is available on the *Liberté pour l'histoire* website.

49. Françoise Chandernagor, "L'histoire sous le coup de la loi," in F. Chandernagor and Pierre Nora, *Liberté pour l'histoire* (Paris:CNRS Editions, 2008), 35.

50. René Rémond, *Quand l'état se mêle à l'histoire* (Paris: Stock, 2006), 41.

51. Ibid., 31.

52. Baruch, 173.

53. Todorov, *La signature humaine*, 234.

54. Quoted in Baruch, 62.

55. Françoise Vergès, "Wandering Souls and returning Ghosts: Writing the History of the Dispossessed," *Yale French Studies* 118 and 119 (2010): 143.

56. Françoise Vergès, *La mémoire enchaînée: Questions sur l'esclavage* (Paris: Albin Michel, 2006), 29.

57. Conversation with the author.

Chapter 2

The Le Pen Moment

On 14 July 2002, a twenty-five-year-old neo-Nazi named Maxime Brunerie drove a rented car from his family residence in suburban Courcouronnes to Paris to attend the annual parade along the Champs Élysées to celebrate France's national holiday.[1] Brunerie carried with him a guitar case, inside of which he had hidden a recently-purchased twenty-two caliber rifle. The day before his trip into Paris, on the British neo-Nazi website Combat 18 ("1" for the letter "A," as in "Adolph," and "8," for the eighth letter in the alphabet, "H," as in "Hitler"), Brunerie had posted this message: "Watch the television on Sunday, I'll be the star."

Once at the parade site, Brunerie blended in with the crowd. As President Jacques Chirac's vehicle approached the spot along the route where Brunerie stood, the young neo-Nazi extracted the rifle from the guitar case and took aim at Chirac. According to most accounts, he managed to get off two shots before a spectator standing in front of him grabbed the rifle barrel and wrested the gun from Brunerie. The would-be assassin was then wrestled to the ground by other spectators present at the scene, who held him until the police arrived to arrest him.

Following his arrest, Maxime Brunerie, was examined by doctors and determined to be mentally unstable and indeed suicidal. He was taken, at least temporarily, to a psychiatric hospital in Villejuif. Later, Brunerie was judged competent to stand trial and in 2004, he was tried and sentenced to ten years in prison. He was later released, in August 2010.

In some ways, Maxime Brunerie's failed, and indeed pathetic attempt to assassinate the president of the Republic on Bastille day can be seen as

---

Portions of this chapter were previously published as Richard J. Golsan, "The Le Pen Movement," *SubStance* 32:1 (2003): 125–143. © 2003 by the Board of Regents of the Unviersity of Wisconsin System. Reproduced courtesy of the University of Wisconsin Press.

a metaphor for—or a caricature of—France's 2002 presidential election. Between the National Front leader Jean-Marie Le Pen's stunning victory in the first round and equally crushing defeat in the second round two weeks later, many in France felt the nation itself was threatened. The extreme right, in the person of Le Pen, sought nothing less, they believed, than to assassinate the French Republic. Indeed, the National Front's program of a "national preference" for "true" French—*Français de souche*—in terms of employment, social security and health benefits, coupled with policies mandating the exclusion and indeed the deportation of some categories of immigrants, violated, as Robert Badinter argued, not only the French constitution and the principles on which it was based but European conventions involving the rights of individuals.[2] (On the last score, at least, Le Pen could not have cared less, as his hostility to "Europe" and his intention to promote "la France seule" were at the very core of his ideology and rhetoric.) And if the National Front's policies were viewed as a threat to French democracy, the political "tactics" of the National Front—a willing recourse to bullying, intimidation, and violence evident in the behavior of Le Pen himself, most recently in his infamous physical assault on the Socialist candidate Annette Peulvast-Bergeal—were considered to be nothing less than fascistic in their brutality. Finally, no one has ever operated under the illusion that the National Front itself is organized and run along democratic lines. At the time, Le Pen was the absolute master of his domain, and those who would challenge his authority within the movement or pose as his successor soon found themselves on the outside. This was already clear in 1998, when Le Pen and then second-in-command Bruno Mégret broke violently, and the latter was exiled from the fold.

If Le Pen's one percentage point (seventeen to sixteen percent) victory over the Socialist Prime Minister Lionel Jospin on 21 April, and his qualification to face Jacques Chirac in a runoff on 5 May, shocked the nation to the core—the press referred to Le Pen's victory as *le séisme Le Pen* [the Le Pen earthquake]—the surprise should perhaps really not have been so great. The campaign leading up to April had been singularly lackluster and uninspiring. The favorites, Jacques Chirac and Lionel Jospin, both absolutely confident of victory in the first round, failed to impress anyone in their rush to claim the political middle ground while seeking to prove their toughness in announcing that among their highest priorities as president would be to deal with "insecurity" and crime in the streets. Despite their many disagreements, Chirac and Jospin seemed content to embrace, at least for the moment, a kind of presidential *pensée unique,* a derogatory expression commonly used at the time for unimaginative, one-track political thinking. Theoretically at least, real differences would emerge in the second round when they faced each other in the run off.

The humorist Yves Lecoq, for one, expressed his dissatisfaction with the campaign by referring to the two front runners as "blanc bonnet" and "bonnet blanc," and the right-wing polemicist Jean Dutourd, who would throw in his lot with third party candidate Jean-Pierre Chevènement, lamented: "there is no more boring regime than a democracy." Even the corruption charges facing Chirac for the apparent gross misuse of public funds while mayor of Paris, as well as the earlier "scandal" over Jospin's Trotskyist past as a Lambertiste, seemed to stir little outrage, irritation, or even interest. Only the psychologist Boris Cyrulnik, apparently, found the situation encouraging. He described the presidential campaign as "mournful," but argued that this was a good sign because it proved that France was at peace. Only wars, he asserted, stimulated the kinds of strong ideological passions and hatreds that made elections interesting.

Despite the general lethargy, there were signs of the "earthquake" to come. First, Le Pen had been climbing in the polls. In an article in the 31 January 2002 issue of *L'Express* devoted to Le Pen's surprising come back in the wake of the split with Mégret, the Peulvast-Bergeal fiasco, and the French victory in the 1998 World Cup (during the competition, Le Pen had lamented the presence of "non-French" players on the team, that is, players of color), his strong standing in the polls at the time (eight to eleven percent) was noted. The article also stressed the fact that in the 1988 and 1995 elections, when Le Pen had similar scores in January, he had ended up with 14.3–15 percent of the vote. Given these figures, the author of the *Express* piece, Romain Rosso, speculated that it was conceivable that Le Pen might even finish as high as *third* by pushing past Jean-Pierre Chevènement. If he succeeded in this, Rosso concluded, he would be turning what would certainly be his electoral "swan song" into a formidable "last-ditch stand."[3]

In at least one significant way, Le Pen's rise in the polls and eventual first round victory were facilitated by the rhetoric of the frontrunners themselves. In taking tough stands against crime and urban insecurity and making this the central focus of their respective campaigns, Chirac and Jospin were, of course, aping Le Pen's line and thereby cutting the ground out from under the best position from which to attack him. For Jospin, the left's standard bearer, this was particularly costly, as it confirmed for many that the Prime Minister and the Socialists were out of touch with true leftist ideals and aspirations. In fact, it was the fragmentation of the left—which accounted for forty-three percent of the total vote in the first round but dispersed its strength over third party candidates including the National Republican Chevènement and especially the Trotskyist Arlette Laguiller—that was the principle reason for Le Pen's victory.

Once Le Pen's victory and Jospin's elimination were confirmed on the night of 21 April, attempts to assess the nature and extent of the "disaster," as well as efforts to mobilize the population to defend or, as *Le Monde* magazine later put it, to "re-elect the Republic" were rapidly forthcoming.[4] In the first wave of assessments, genuine expressions of pain (Jean-Marie Colombani entitled his editorial in *Le Monde* the next day "La blessure [The wound]") and outrage at France's self-inflicted "disgrace" were coupled with denunciations of the Left's costly self-indulgence in not making sure Jospin made it into the second round. Colombani blasted the Left for the "shopkeeper's mentality" of the leaders of its various factions for promoting their narrow interests and for, in effect, declaring open season on Jospin. When the dust settled, Colombani lamented, Jospin would be remembered for his accomplishments: the euro, the thirty-five hour work week, the reduction of unemployment.[5] But it was too late to crown these achievements with electoral success now.

In assessing the Left's failure, others took the opposite tack from Colombani. On 25 April Jean-Louis Andreani argued in *Libération* that the Socialists had forgotten their bedrock supporters: "the people who struggle," that is, workers and small wage earners.[6] The further one moved down the social ladder, the more people felt abandoned. Andréani believed that while Jospin sensed this disaffection and even wished to combat it, his will to do so was not evident enough in his campaign to be convincing.

In his criticism of the "shopkeeper's mentality" among leaders on the Left, Jean-Marie Colombani had singled out Jean-Pierre Chevènement in particular, especially for his anti-establishment rhetoric (he was not above trumpeting the Lepeniste slogan "Sortez les sortants" "Throw the bums out!") and for turning against Jospin, who had, as Colombani noted, rescued Chevènement from political oblivion in 1997. But the context in which Colombani presented his criticisms of Chevènement—a *chef de file* on the left—was misleading to the extent that Chenènement was not a traditional Leftist but preferred to present himself—as his anti-establishment rhetoric suggested—as a kind of "third way" candidate. Indeed his supporters ranged across the political spectrum and included such disparate figures as the aforementioned monarchist Jean Dutourd, Régis Debray, nominally on the left but recently most visible for his vehement opposition to NATO's bombing in Kosovo and his pro-Serb attitudes (something he shared with Dutourd and other Chevènement supporters like Patrick Besson), and former Mitterrand loyalist Max Gallo. They also included, perhaps to Chevènement's discomfort, figures like Michel Houllebecq, the *louche* novelist who was then becoming visible following the smashing success of the novels *Elementary Particles* and the more recent, even more highly provocative, *Platform*. The latter deals, not disapprovingly, with sexual tourism and is anti-immigrant, anti-Arab, and anti-Islamist in tone and action. At about the time Houellebecq announced his support for Chevènement (and contributed to a volume in support of his candidacy edited by Régis Debray), he expressed his personal distaste for

Islam as the "stupidest religion" in an interview published in France, and his disgust for Muslim women in an interview in the Austrian publication *Profil*. In the latter interview Houllebecq described Muslim women as "grotesque" in their chadors and as "fat whores needing a lay." Apparently Chevènement did not comment on these statements, but he did say that he liked *Elementary Particles* which he considered "tough" but "good." Clearly Houellebecq was enjoying a certain literary success among presidential candidates. Le Pen, in fact, had been seen reading *Platform* on the campaign trail.

For Michel Wieviorka, Jean-Pierre Chevènement was ultimately less a candidate of the Left than he was a latter-day *Maurassien* attempting to benefit from an archaic but anti-racist nationalism of the Left *and* Right.[7] No wonder then, given the hybrid nature of the political currents on which Chevènement wished to draw, the *Canard enchaîné* defined him as "the most confused (confusing) adverb in the French language." [the suffix "–ment" in French is the equivalent of "–ly" in English.] Under any circumstances, his candidacy, even given its limited success, could be said to embody what many commentators perceived to be displeasure and even disgust with the political status quo. Wieviorka described the overall presidential vote as "anti-system" in nature, and found it to be symptomatic of nothing less than the "decomposition of the French political system." The crisis was of course particularly acute for the left, certainly at its more extreme end, because it had been reduced to a purely oppositional role in the absence of any real faith in a future utopia, of *"les demains qui chantent,"* the "tomorrows that sing" to use the old Communist phrase. This, in turn, was symptomatic of another problem facing what François Ascher labeled "hypermodern" French society: with no great ideologies or socio-economic issues to bind citizens together, democracy itself worked less and less well. People voted for one candidate for one plank in his or her platform, and another candidate for another plank. No overarching political creed made people vote for "the big picture" and sacrifice their smaller interests and concerns. Under these circumstances, political candidates—with the exception of fanatical and simplistic extremists—were forced to navigate between many small and occasionally contradictory positions to attract voters.[8]

Despite these deeply pessimistic and indeed apocalyptic assessments of France's political present and future generated by the *séisme Le Pen*, there is no doubt that the "earthquake" also galvanized the nation and produced protests and demonstrations in the streets the likes of which had not be seen in years. The vast majority of these were of course vociferously anti-Le Pen (there were also poorly attended rallies in his support) and the overwhelming presence of angry youths carrying banners was reminiscent of the heady days of May 1968. Among the slogans on the banners, some expressed earnest, heartfelt disgust—"I'm ashamed of being French"—or militant, generationally-based hostility to the Le Pen candidacy: "Youth against the Extreme Right." But other slogans and banners were more colorful. One had a large photograph of Le Pen attached to the inside of a toilet seat with the slogan, "On May 5, let's pull the chain!" Others, referring to Le Pen's claim many years before of having been blinded in one eye in a street fight and his penchant for sporting an eye patch over the bad eye, either showed a picture of Le Pen with his patch accompanied by the slogan "in the kingdom of the blind, the one-eyed man is king" or stated simply "Let's cry with one eye, and open the other." While mocking Le Pen's apparent blindness in one eye might have struck some as cruel, in reality it was not, because, as the journalist Annette Lévy-Willard had shown years before, the eye patch and blindness were both fakes. Photographs assembled by Lévy-Willard showed that Le Pen's eye patch had in fact migrated from eye to eye over time.

If some expressed their revulsion at Le Pen's candidacy through humorous banners and slogans, other protestors preferred to link Le Pen and the National Front to fascisms past. One banner announced "The FN (spelled *F-Haine*, or "hatred") will not pass," a reference to the Republican slogan of resistance to Franco and his Italian Fascist and Nazi supporters during the Spanish Civil War. Another showed a photo of a hand giving the Nazi salute with the slogan: "Let's not wait for them to come back." Finally, referring to Le Pen's 1987 dismissal of the importance of the Holocaust, one poster stated simply "Six Million Dead = A Historical Detail."

Street protest and banners were, of course, only a few of the forms of activism intended not simply to defeat Le Pen at the polls but to bury him politically on 5 May. Innumerable petitions denouncing his candidacy and calling for a massive turnout for Chirac as a symbol of the Republic itself circulated over the internet and were signed by people from all walks of life. In the pages of *Le Monde* on 25 April, Daniel Cohn-Bendit, Bernard-Henri Lévy, André Glucksman and others called for a "ninety percent vote for Chirac" which would be "an immense plebiscite for democracy." To make clear just how ideologically repugnant Le Pen was, in its 26 April issue *Libération* offered a sampling of his most outrageous statements on a variety of topics. His comment on the Holocaust as a "historical detail" was quoted in full, as was his obscene play on words when he linked a Jewish politician Michel Durafour to the Holocaust in calling him "M. Durafour-Crématoire"—a *four* in French is an oven, and a *crématoire* is a crematorium. *Libération* also noted Le Pen's characterization of AIDS victims as "lepers," his assertion that women's claims to own their own bodies were "ludicrous," and his statements that races were not all "equal."

Politicians also joined in the groundswell against Le Pen's candidacy. Despite a noticeable but fairly brief delay, Lionel Jospin threw his support to Chirac, as did virtually all the other third party candidates. (A notable exception was Arlette Laguiller, for whom all insiders of the political system were corrupt and unworthy of support). Even Chirac, in his role as candidate, did his part to exclude Le Pen by refusing to debate him, thus denying him at least the appearance of participating fully in the normal democratic electoral process. According to Perry Anderson, however, Chirac had his own personal reasons for refusing to debate Le Pen on television which were less than admirable: he was afraid of being bested by Le Pen in the debate, and was also afraid the latter would "embarrass him by recounting past secret tractations between [the two men]."[9]

On the morning of 5 May, shortly after having voted, Le Pen stated "If I get less than thirty percent, it will be a great disappointment." That night, French television affirmed that Jacques Chirac had received 82.1 percent of the vote of the vote, and Le Pen only 17.9 percent—barely a percentage point higher than his first round score.[10] Chirac's victory, Anderson notes ironically, was "worthy of a Mexican president in the heyday of the PRI," and his vote tally on the Left Bank "reached virtually Albanian heights."[11] After the votes were in, true to form, Le Pen offered a sour, ideologically barbed concession: "This is a crushing defeat for French hope. The victory of Jacques Chirac is equivocal, and it has been won through the Soviet method." Chirac for his part, stated: "I have heard and understood your call for the Republic to live, for the nation to come together, for politics to change." Some self-congratulatory commentators observed that the national groundswell of support for Chirac (and against Le Pen) was "France's finest hour since 1914, when the nation closed ranks in a sacred union against another deadly enemy."[12] Others, however, including Perry Anderson offered, more cynical—and sinister—historical comparisons. Anderson writes that "if analogy were needed, the unanimity of 2002 was closer in spirit to that of Bordeaux in 1940, when the national Assembly voted overwhelmingly to hand power to Pétain, convinced that this was a patriotic necessity to avert catastrophe. On this occasion tragedy repeated itself as farce, since there was not even a trace of emergency to warrant the consecration of Chirac."[13] Setting aside historical comparisons like these, in his prescient editorial in *Le Monde* published two weeks before the final round, Jean-Marie Colombani underscored what would prove to be truly equivocal in Chirac's later landslide victory: "Jacques Chirac will succeed himself. Thus, the president who inspires the weakest support in all the history of the Fifth Republic [with his first round showing] and who, for seven years, has presided over a weakening of the presidential function will be elected by the greatest margin in our long political history."[14]

Given Le Pen's crushing defeat—percentage -wise, at least—on 5 May 2002, coupled with the convincing victory of Chirac's center-right coalition in the legislative elections several weeks later, it does not appear unreasonable to assert that Le Pen's frightening first-round victory on 21 April was in reality little more than a "historical detail," to turn the National Front leader's infamous phrase about the Holocaust against him. Or, to use a literary analogy, one could invoke Stendhal's classic metaphor of the irruption of politics in the novel in *The Red and the Black* to describe Le Pen's first round victory. That victory was like a gunshot in a concert: it was "earsplitting" but lacked point, it did not harmonize with any instrument, and it horrified some while boring others, who preferred to read about it in their papers the next day.

Still one could argue that Le Pen did, after all, receive six million votes on 5 May. And, as a poll conducted by *Sofres* after Chirac's election indicated, despite his final tally of eighteen percent in the second round some twenty eight percent of the French populace actually adhered to the ideas of the extreme right regardless of their vote (or lack thereof).[15]

But, as Perry Anderson has written, in the final analysis Le Pen and the National Front's support was always limited. There was never any viable path to power for them, and this was obvious to most if not all of the French, despite the hyperventilation of protesters and the media:

> The limits of the [National] Front as a political phenomenon were . . . always plain. Shunned by the right . . . over dependent on the personality of Le Pen, it lacked any professional cadre and never acquired administrative experience, vegetating between polls in a resentful subculture. Its brawling style at hustings alarmed as much as it attracted. Above all, its main calling card—the immigrant issue—was inherently restrictive. The appeal of Fascism between the wars had rested on massive social dislocation and the specter of a revolutionary labor movement, a far cry from the tidy landscape of the Fifth Republic.[16]

If Anderson is correct about Le Pen's ultimate lack of viability and credibility as a presidential candidate in May 2002, then there seems to be a substantial disparity between the nation's extreme reaction to it and the extent of the actual political threat posed. Therefore, are there other ways of looking at *le séisme Le Pen* that are less explicitly and overtly political and social, and more broadly historical and cultural? On a superficial level, protestors' signs (described above) portraying the struggle against Le Pen as a reprise or successor to the struggle against fascism, along with comparisons of the closing of the political ranks around Chirac with a similar cohesion around Pétain some sixty years earlier, point broadly to the specter of the past, and specifically the memory of Vichy and Nazism. As Henry Rousso demonstrated in *The Vichy Syndrome*, the rise of the extreme right, and scandalous "eruptions" of xenophobia and anti-Semitism have, at least since the 1980s been linked to, and proven to be an integral part of, the presence and tenacity of Vichy's memory.

In the remainder of this chapter, I want to examine two controversies related to *le séisme Le Pen*, one roughly concurrent with it and the other a direct consequence of it. These controversies strongly suggest that the real scandal of Le Pen's first round victory was in fact that it conjured up memories of the Dark Years as well as the turmoil and tragedy of what Eugen Weber has labeled France's "Hollow Years," the 1930s, which prepared the ground for the catastrophe that followed. These memories in turn, in some quarters at least, stirred fears and provoked widely publicized accusations of a frightening and widespread cultural and intellectual complicity in the reemergence of a new French fascism embodied in the person—and success—of Le Pen. As noted in the Introduction, one of the hallmarks of the memory of Vichy in the new century has not only been its tenacity, but also its encouragement, so to speak, of the need to "re-experience" the past vicariously, and pass judgment (again) on its excesses and crimes. Locating and condemning Le Pen's ostensible "collaborators," as we shall see, furnished precisely this kind of opportunity.

The first of the two controversies mentioned centered on the politics of the writer Renaud Camus, and the publication of his book *Du sens* in April 2002, precisely at the time of the first round of the elections. The second controversy occurred in Fall 2002, and followed the publication of Daniel Lindenberg's incendiary essay or pamphlet, *Le Rappel à l'ordre*. The work's subtitle, *Enquête sur les nouveaux réactionnaires*, "An Investigation of the New Reactionaries" gives a clear idea of its content—and purpose.

Renaud Camus's *Du sens* is a five-hundred-and-fifty-page journal, of sorts, published by the trendy and respected publisher P.O.L. It purports to deal objectively—in sweeping philosophical, historical, and linguistic terms—with the meaning of words like "French, France, European, English, Italian" in order to arrive, ultimately, at the meaning of the word "meaning" itself.

But Camus's investigation of "meaning" in *Du sens* is hardly *politically* innocent. In Spring 2000, the writer had already created a highly mediatized controversy by expressing his distaste, in his 1994 journal *La campagne de France* (published in 2000 by Fayard) at hearing so many "non-French"—read "Jewish"—names on a radio program and for stating, as he reiterates in *Du sens* that the "Jewish collaborators" of the *France Culture* radio program "Panorama" "exaggerated somewhat" in treating so many "Jewish subjects."[17]

After recalling the incident in *Du sens*, Camus hardly backs away from his earlier statement, along with its troubling implications. Instead, he reiterates it in unequivocal terms: "But it happens that we believe we can confirm that Jewish participants on "Panorama" of *France Culture* do in fact have a slight tendency to exaggerate [Camus uses the verb *abuser*] because of their numbers, and one can't ask us to act as if we have noticed absolutely nothing."[18] Moreover, taking the 2000 controversy and the issues it raises as his cue, Camus then ups the ante by offering a series of "reasoned" reflections on hot button issues including the Holocaust, "Frenchness," and racism. In the end, these reflections prove to be far more provocative and extreme than his original pronouncements about an excessive Jewish presence on "Panorama."

In a discussion of the meaning and appropriateness of the word "Shoah," Camus begins by stressing its essential *artificiality*. It first crops up, he notes, in Claude Lanzmann's classic film by that title, and it therefore refers to the *representation* of suffering and not to the actual suffering itself. When the term is used in memoirs of Holocaust survivors, Camus continues, "Something rings false: it's as if, fifty years after the French Revolution, one had decided to designate it differently and to give it a more theatrical and resounding name, such as the Great Upheaval, or Chaos, or the Dawn of Time."[19]

Having established the word's fundamental "artificiality," Camus then stresses its usage as a sign of contemporary *conformity*, of wishing to belong to the "right group" and of proving one's *chicness*. It is used by

> Young girls (*petites jeunes filles*) with cigarettes between their fingers, who say *Shoah* as if *they were there* [emphasis mine] with a natural, disarming conformity: one recognizes in the word the pure mark of appurtenance that it is just like that of the cigarette: I belong to the "in crowd" they both proclaim, I speak like one should speak, I smoke like one should smoke, with an arm gesture dictated by the prescribed code, *I belong*. And no doubt one should congratulate oneself that that the signs of appurtenance to "right thinking" are virtuous, that "right thinking" is virtuous as well, that [the young girl in question] pronounces the word *Shoah* with the right intonation at just the right time, the moment of flipping her hair back or of picking a tobacco flake off her lip.[20]

Concluding his reflection, Camus writes "In the word *Shoah* the real does not unfold, or rather a 'real' unfolds, but it is altogether temporary."[21]

Earlier in *Du sens* Camus treats "Frenchness" in an equally troubling, and perversely anecdotal fashion. He refers to a "Professor of French in the United States" who, he stresses, is "French, of Jewish and Egyptian abstraction" and who argues that one is "French" by birth *or* by naturalization, and for only as long as one has been born and living in France or has been naturalized. Obviously, for this unnamed (but not culturally anonymous) professor, *ancienneté* [Camus's term and italics] has nothing to do with being French.

To this, Camus responds:

> But it is not inconceivable that, to belong to a family residing in a country for a very long time gives one greater intimacy with its history, its language, its customs, its *folklore* . . . such that the latter would designate this history, this language, and these *folklorized* customs, shared through habit, by constant rumor and repetition, by the gaze of the tourist, by regional accents and pride—a greater intimacy, then, than is conferred by birth or education in an immigrant family of the preceding generation which itself is seeking to discover this language, this history and these customs, because they have not imbibed them. *Not inconceivable.*[22]

In discussing his ideas on racism, Camus once again returns to the context of World War II because, as he puts it, "it is the touchstone of all moral judgment."[23] He notes, first, that many things are classified as forms of racism, which in reality they are not. Moreover, while the term is readily applied to certain peoples and their prejudices, no one, Camus asserts, would think of applying it to the philosopher Vadimir Jankélévitch for refusing to read German philosophy in the wake of the Holocaust, or to Isaac Stern for refusing ever again to perform in Germany. While agreeing that these are not "racist" attitudes, Camus insists that they are nevertheless "unquestionably anti-German." And while they can be justified "psychologically," or as evidence of deep personal anguish or trauma, they cannot be legitimately characterized as "*pure* moral judgments," which Camus labels "intellectual abstractions." Why not? Because the "culpability of Germany and German people at a moment in the nation's history does not automatically entail the guilt of *all* individual Germans, and certainly those of another epoch, today, for example."[24]

Few would contest Camus's final claim here, and his other assertions on racism are arguably "reasonable." That being said, the context, the examples used and the string of propositions assembled points to a very different, much less "reasonable" and more insidious mode of argumentation. Why should "racism," even while denied as such, come up in the context of a *Jewish* philosopher's and a *Jewish* musician's respective refusals to have *contact* with Germany and German culture in the wake of the Holocaust? Apparently so that Camus can label this attitude "anti-German" and move to an *intellectual* rejection of it from the standpoint of a "*pure* moral judgment." Moreover, to legitimize it only in "psychological" terms denies it any *collective* identity or justification, while at the same time leaving open the possibility that it might be an *individual* aberration or pathology. In short, in this passage Camus seems more interested in exploring—and condemning, at least "intellectually"—the traumatized reaction of two Jews against German culture and Germany (not German *individuals*) than he is in exploring and denouncing the history of German racism, brutality and murderousness during World War II as well as the issue of collective and individual German guilt.

Camus's remarks concerning the word "Shoah" and "Frenchness" in *Du sens* are equally loaded politically, and are also clothed in a language that falsely purports to be imminently "reasonable," equally "measured." Moreover, in the themes and strategies they deploy, the thrust of these remarks is noticeably reminiscent of many postwar extreme right-wing French writers, from "literary" figures like Maurice Bardèche and Céline to Holocaust deniers from Robert Faurisson to Roger Garaudy, and beyond. To insist on the essential "artificiality" of the word "Shoah" is obviously to diminish it, along with the event it purports to represent. Moreover, to compare the word's anachronistic application to the event to those who would belatedly refer to the French Revolution as "Chaos," or the "Dawn of Time," or the "Great Upheaval" is to accomplish the same aim, this time by intimating a deliberate and dishonest *inflation* of the event in question through language. No matter how historic or monumental the French Revolution was, it did not and could not achieve the *cosmic* stature that phrases like "The Dawn of Time," or the "Great Upheaval" or "Chaos" would clearly confer upon it. Similarly, Camus implies, the same deliberate distortion and enhancement of the event is evident when one belatedly uses the word "Shoah" to describe Hitler's persecution of the Jews. Finally, in describing an imaginary, vulgarly superficial girl's (hardly depicted in "objective" language!) attachment to the term in order to be "in style" and in with the "in crowd" Camus diminishes and indeed denigrates the term "Shoah" and the event it connotes once again by linking the status and meaning of both to a kind of feminine, adolescent "fad." By definition "fashionable," they are also therefore transitory phenomena. And—to link Camus's reasoning on "Shoah" with his earlier reflections on "Frenchness" in *Du sens*—neither the word nor the event possesses *ancienneté* which alone in Camus's view confers real, legitimate "Frenchness." But this fact would of course be lost on the French Professor of Egyptian Jewish origin with whom Camus had earlier conferred.

As noted, Renaud Camus's pseudo-"reasonable" approach along with his deliberately convoluted language, and indeed his strategies of delegitimization and denunciation are hardly new to right-wing and negationist rhetoric of the postwar period. The emphasis on "Frenchness," the allergy to a superabundance of "foreigners," whether they be Jews on French radio or *métèques* in the streets of French cities, dates back to the Occupation, the 1930s, the Dreyfus Affair, and beyond. If there is any "originality" in Camus's approach, it is the fact that his diminution of the Holocaust through an insistence on the facticity of the word "Shoah" is essentially linguistic in nature, as opposed to earlier strategies involving "scientific" arguments against the gas chambers, or statistical arguments that the number of Jews supposedly killed is grossly exaggerated, or—as argued in the mid-1990s by Roger Garaudy—that the number of Jews killed by Hitler is negligible compared to the number of Palestinians killed by Israelis and black Africans killed by the European and American slave trade.[25]

On 29 May, a month after *Du sens* appeared in book stores, the "Society of the Readers of Renaud Camus" organized a public debate over the book at the *Amphithéâtre Boutmy* at the prestigious *Fondation Nationale des Sciences Politiques,* where Camus had once been a student. The two featured speakers were Alain Finkielkraut and Edwy Plenel, then the managing editor of *Le Monde*. Their exchange turned for the most part on Plenel's decision not to publish recent and, once again, politically disturbing writings by Camus in the pages of *Le Monde* during the period of the presidential elections. Taking what might be described as an "American perspective," Finkielkrait defended

Camus's right to publish in the name of freedom of the press. Plenel, obviously, disagreed.

But for our purposes here, the issue of the freedom of the press in "Round Two" of the "Camus Affair" is a secondary one. At the core of the controversy—as well as during "Round One," the 2000 controversy following the publication of *La Campagne de France*—is a different dynamic. In both rounds, Camus's nostalgia for a "true France" as well as what Maurice Bardèche would have called his "refined anti-Semitism" provoked widespread outrage, and also hyperbolic comparisons linking Camus to the worst horrors of Vichy and Nazism. Camus, Laure Adler had asserted, was "worse than Hitler," an excessive claim, to say the least. But in response to Camus's attackers, his defenders only muddied the waters worse by claiming that he was the victim of a "lynching." Or, as Alain Finkielkraut wrote in *L'Imparfait du présent*, he was condemned in a media trial before the trial ever took place. Warming to his subject, Finkielkraut added: "The sentence came down immediately. The court issued its symbolic death sentence without ever being in session."[26] Clearly, the media and France's intelligentsia that had condemned Camus was itself guilty of a rush to judgment. And, Finkielkraut added, this was precisely what an earlier generation of France's *intellectuels engagés*—committed intellectuals—had *not* done at the time of the Dreyfus Affair. Had these "virtuous condemners" of the "rancid France" Camus supposedly extolled bothered to actually read his work, they would have discovered, "with growing perplexity," their "prey" escaping the condemnation they had prepared for him. Camus's writings were neither "essentialist," nor "racist," nor for that matter "criminal" as his accusers made them out to be. Seconding Finkielkraut's defense of Camus, the novelist Emmanuel Carrère argued that even if one should peruse Camus's journals, one would not understand Camus's meaning without reading "the sentence within the paragraph, the paragraph within the page and the page within the book." Doing so, presumably, would prove their essential political and ideological innocuousness.[27]

What is one to make of Emmanuel Carrère's, and especially Alain Finkielkraut's defense of Renaud Camus? Apart from being caught up in a highly mediatized controversy, both were right in demanding that at the very least Camus deserved a reading of his works, and both were also right that accusations of him being "worse than Hitler," that is, the absolute personification of evil—were excessive to say the least.

But in their zeal to defend Renaud Camus, his writings and his supposed fundamental political innocence, both Finkielkraut and Carrère were themselves guilty of overlooking the very *real* racist, extremist, and quasi-negationist content of the passages from *Du sens* discussed above. Given the clear import of these assertions in Camus's journal, it is not surprising that before the most recent presidential election, Renaud Camus came out in favor of Le Pen's daughter and successor, Marine Le Pen.

So what are the actual dynamic of "Round Two" of the *Affaire Camus*? As stated in the Introduction of this volume, among the characteristics or attributes of the memory of Vichy in the new millennium are that the word and the memory itself have become synonymous with moral and political evil in intellectual discourse and in public debate. Moreover, their invocation in this guise generally breeds obfuscation rather than clarity where historical issues are concerned. So both the excessive accusations against Camus, but also, *especially* Alain Finkielkraut's and others' overzealous defense of the writer, actually ended up obscuring political *and historical* implications of the latter's arguments and claims made in *Du Sens* by essentially whitewashing them. These arguments and claims in Camus's work *are* in fact part and parcel of a disturbing historical revisionism where "the Dark Years" and their implications and consequences are concerned. Finally—and this is also symptomatic of the memory of Vichy today—if the rhetoric of the controversy itself had not become overheated, or veered off into other matters related to the circumstances of the moment (Le Pen's first round victory, and the question of freedom of the press) it would have been more clear that the *Affaire Camus* in most of its essential aspects had played out several times before in the postwar period, with different protagonists to be sure, but also with many of the same basic issues at stake. Whether deliberate or not, in *Du Sens* Camus was aping in tone and content, if not in strategy, some of the negationist and racist affirmations of earlier extreme right-wing provocateurs including the film-maker Claude Autant-Lara and the critic Maurice Bardèche. And Camus's nostalgic remarks on a kind of pure and eternal "Frenchness' in *Du sens* anticipate similar views and postures of the novelist and critic Richard Millet, who in 2012 provoked his own scandal and eventual disgrace with the publication of racist and inflammatory pamphlet's purporting to defend the purity of French culture and the French language in particular.[28] In the end, in Round Two of the *Affaire Camus*, neither the ends of history *nor* memory were well served.

THE LE PEN MOMENT: *SUITE ET FIN*

One of the more surprising aspects of the controversy that erupted in France in Fall 2002 following the publication of Daniel Lindenberg's *Le Rappel à l'ordre* is that the book—mediocre at best, according to virtually all of its critics—provoked a scandal at all. Lindenberg's book is a slim volume, and it is more of a thinly disguised polemical and political pamphlet than it is an analysis or investigation into what Lindenberg labels France's "new reactionaries." Rather than systematically examine the political thought or ideas of all of the "new reactionaries" it targets, it offers a pastiche of seemingly randomly chosen and often isolated assertions taken out of context and lifted from novels, interviews, or essays by one individual on the disparate list of the "accused." By insinuation or by direct reference, this assertion is then treated as entirely representative of the views of the group as a whole. Although the book does conclude with portraits of two of Lindenberg's targets, the novelist Michel Hoellebecq and the philosopher Maurice Dantec, it offers no such focused discussions of the most important—and influential—thinkers among the figures it characterizes as "new reactionaries." These include Alain Badiou, Alain Finkielkraut, Marcel Gauchet, (an editor of *Le Débat*), Alain Besançon, and Pierre-André Taguieff. As critics of *Le rappel à l'ordre* observed, this was certainly a "motley crew" in that despite Lindenberg's attempts at "amalgamation" the views of many of the figures discussed were and remain miles apart on any number of issues. Moreover, in "amalgamating" their views and lumping them all together in the category of "new reactionaries," *Le rappel à l'ordre* inadvertently or more likely deliberately (some critics believed) lent an air of conspiracy to the group as a whole.

I have used the word "accused" above to designate the "new reactionaries" Lindenberg discusses because the author does in effect accuse them of a "crime." Their collective ideas and attitudes, Lindenberg insists on the first page of the Introduction, have had a destructive effect on French democracy and are, moreover, directly responsible for paving the way to Jean-Marie le Pen's stunning first round victory in the presidential elections of 21 April. According to Lindenberg, discussions of the emergence of a new "populism" in Europe and France supposedly responsible for the success of figures like Le Pen and Jorg Haider in Austria are, in the French case at least, misleading. They are no more than a smokescreen to cover up for the renewal of something older and more sinister, that is, the reinvigoration of "corrosive ideas" and attitudes, the "aromas of which are somewhat forgotten," that Lindenberg links to the figure of Charles Maurras[29]

These ideas and attitudes include a taste for "order, authority, the restoration of values, and "true Frenchness" (*le peuple réel*). They also include an increasingly pronounced and articulated distrust and suspicion of democracy, the state of law," and the "foundations of an 'open society.'"[30] They manifest themselves in attacks by the "new reactionaries" on mass culture, liberal social and sexual mores, the memory and legacy of May 68, human rights, racially and ethnically mixed society, Islam, and equality. According to Lindenberg, each of the latter is part and parcel of a democratic society and has been "put on trial" by the "new reactionaries." And while their targets may be somewhat scattershot, at stake are ultimately nothing less than the foundations of the Republic as well as France's revolutionary tradition.

Moreover, rather than remain faithful to republican thinkers like Tocqueville, these "new reactionaries" have turned sharply rightward, reading and admiring thinkers like the Nazi Carl Schmitt or America arch-conservatives of the Bush years like Benjamin Barber (lumped together in *Le Rappel à l'ordre* despite their differences). Assessing the ultimate danger these "new reactionaries" pose to France, in a section entitled "From 1930s to the 'Rock Years'" Lindenberg asserts that the "inegalitarian, hierarchical, and counter-revolutionary ideas" that seduced so many prominent intellectuals in the 1930s are making a comeback in the France of 2002. He adds, "we also know that there comes a time when the critique of parliamentary democracy can attract impeccable logicians into the 'magnetic field' of totalitarianism."[31] It is therefore not surprising, he concludes, that "the 1930s and the Second World War that followed immediately on them continue to obsess us."[32] Explaining his motivation for writing *Le Rappel à l'ordre* Lindenberg asserts that it is not simply in the name of a "duty to memory" invoked "willy nilly." Rather, while cognizant of the dangers of historical comparison ("comparison does not confer reason") he argues that it is important to underscore "similitudes" that "can exist between periods of disorder."[33] And, he implies, the French ignore these similitudes at their peril.

As noted, the reaction to the publication of Lindenberg's essay was extreme, immediate and very largely negative. In an interview in *Le Monde* on 21 November, Pierre Nora characterized *Le Rappel à l'ordre* as simply absurd in its arguments, among these that "all criticisms of democracy are made exclusively by enemies of the latter," and that Le Pen's first round victory was proof that a "true fascist peril" existed in France in 2002.[34] If the latter had been the case, Nora observed derisively, there would have hundreds of thousands of "national populists" pounding the pavements in Paris just as the "SA in brown shirts" paraded in in Weimar. And, he added: "Marx was right: history repeats itself in burlesque form, with le Pen as stand-in for the blond beast and Lindenberg as impersonator of Malraux, as there are impersonators for Dalida or Elvis."[35] Elsewhere, Nora insisted, Lindenberg's book was nothing more than "gruel for cats, some very bad intellectual work." It reflected, moreover, "a return to the reflexes of the *belle époque* of Stalinism."[36]

The sociologist Catherine Pauchet's editorial in *Libération* on 29 November was equally acerbic, except that she charged Lindenberg with forgetting the old, true reactionaries in his zeal to attack the "new ones." She included among the latter Jean-Marc Varaut, Maurice Papon's lawyer and his 1997–1998 trial, but also cited the return to respectability of Charles Maurras as a political thinker, "the theoretician," she added, "of the 'rupture between the people and their leaders.'" She concluded that there was in fact a "Lepenization of the minds" underway, an "intelligent fascism" taking hold, but it was not where Lindenberg located it.

Later, on 20 December, Liliane Kandel attacked Lindenberg's book for another reason: it was, she argued, fundamentally anachronistic. Although it pretended to be timely in its attack on a dangerous cabal of 'new reactionaries" it ignored what was actually going on in the world of 2002: "coups, wars, terror, 11 September" were absent. Writing also in *Libération* on 3 December, Thomas Clerc criticized the book and its approach on different grounds: in casting the concept of "reaction" and "the reactionary" in exclusively *political* terms, Lindenberg had reduced the debate to a series of binary oppositions, and therefore any judgments made would be essentially Manichaen in nature. For Jacques Julliard, the entire controversy seemed ludicrous, in that French intellectuals were rushing to the barricades over loose and unsubstantiated allegations of reaction being made by the *sans culotte* Lindenberg. Moreover, when a real threat of a renewal of fascism had emerged in Europe in Serb aggression against, and "ethnic cleansing" of its neighbors in Croatia and Bosnia less than a decade before, most French intellectuals—and presumably Lindenberg himself—stood idly by.

In his dismissive remarks concerning the entire affair, Julliard also criticized at least some of those condemned by Lindenberg for jumping into the meaningless fray surrounding *Le Rappel à l'ordre*. Many, if not most, of the latter had been interviewed or had published written responses to Lindenberg. On 27 November in the pages of pages of *Le Figaro* Pierre-André Taguieff accused Lindenberg of fear mongering because the implicit message of the entire book was "reactionaries today, fascists tomorrow." He also accused Lindenberg of perverse intellectual gymnastics in the latter's insistence that any critique of anti-racist ideology paved the way to racism and xenophobia, and support for Israel in any guise automatically made one a Nazi (Lindenberg had also criticized the "new reactionaries" for their support of Israel in a chapter oddly entitled—in English in the original—*When Jews turn Right*). Turning the table on his attacker, Taguieff noted that in his own public pronouncements Lindenberg had shown a dangerous tendency to downplay recent acts of violent anti-Semitism in France by dismissing a recent "wave of Judeophobia" as an "intellectual construction." While not accusing Lindenberg of a contemporary "negationism" outright, Taguieff was clearly alluding to the tactics of French Holocaust deniers like Faurisson and Rassinier.

Earlier, in *le Figaro* of 14 November, Finkielkraut had also invoked the shadow of Nazism in asserting that according to Lindenberg in criticizing mass culture and *métissage,* among other things he, Finkielkraut, had "aligned myself with those intellectuals who at the time of the 'Brown Plague' had unleashed attacks on racial outsiders and the values of democracy." And while not one of those labeled "New Reactionaries" by Lindenberg, the journalist and historian Eric Conan brought the Nazi reference home to France, so to speak, and invoked the Holocaust in suggested that the "New Reactionnaries" had in effect been *raflés*-rounded up-and put in a police paddy wagon by their accuser to be taken away for good. And, Finkielkraut opined in his comments on Lindenberg's tactics, that if he, Finkielkraut, and his fellow "new reactionaries" could not be executed for real, they could at least be made to understand that they "should be dead."

To be sure, not all the reactions of those accused of being "New Reactionaries" couched their responses in terms of a return to the Dark Years: Vichy, Fascism, Nazism, and the Holocaust. In the 28 November issue of the magazine *L'Express* several of them—Finkielfraut, Gauchet, Manent, Muray, Yonnet, and Taguieff published a manifesto entitled, somewhat pompously: "A Manifesto for the Freedom of Thought," which responded to Lindenberg in relation to more contemporary issues. In the Manifesto they argued that what the entire controversy signaled was the end of the "anti-totalitarian parenthesis" in France, a time when most leftist and centrist intellectuals had shared an anti-totalitarian ideology in the wake of the publication of Solzhenitsyn's *Gulag Archipelago* in 1974 as well as other events underscoring the abuses of communism in the mid- to late 1970s, the *Khmer Rouge* catastrophe in Cambodia in particular. (This was certainly the view of many subsequent commentators on the entire controversy, Perry Anderson most notably.[37])They also insisted that the shock of the Socialist loss in the first round and the failure of the Left that it signaled were being deliberately manipulated to justify a neo-Stalinist politics of intimidation and denunciation, an "extremism of the center," Gauchet had asserted in another context.[38]

But even after having couched their initial response to Lindenberg in more contemporary and arguably more pertinent, and historically and politically accurate terms, the signees of the petition returned to the context of the 1930s and the Dark Years in their concluding remarks. In effect, they charged that they were being accused of being the new "non-conformists" of the years leading up to World War II, of being the new French fascists. They damned Lindenberg's efforts to tar them with that brush as an effort to "fascisticize" the malaise created by Le Pen's first round victory, and they considered this both "ludicrous and monstrous."

In September 2009, Daniel Lindenberg published a kind of sequel to *Le Rappel à l'ordre* entitled *Le Procès des Lumières*—"The Enlightenment on Trial." As its title suggests, Lindenberg's more recent work is also an attack on the "New Reactionaries," on those who would challenge, indeed "put on trial" the ideals and ideas of the enlightenment. Lindenberg also provides updates on new individuals placed in this category, and new publications in France that supposedly promote conservative and reactionary ideas.

More global and globalizing in its scope than *Le rappel à l'ordre, Le Procès des Lumières* also claims to discern not just a French but also, in fact, an "international" wave of reaction that includes the thinkers and ideologues of the Bush Administration, intellectuals in places like Japan, and, most provocatively, conservative and radical Islamists. According to Lindenberg, all these reactionaries share a powerful animosity toward human rights, a hatred of decadent modernity ("une modernité malade d'elle-même") and an exaltation of national dignity. Even though the New Reactionaries as defenders of the West are assumed to be radically opposed to Islamic fundamentalists, in their shared hatred of modernity, of the Enlightenment and of democratic ideas they are locked in a Girardan mimetic rivalry that ultimately makes them virtually indistinguishable from each other.

Perhaps because it only repeated the same charges against France's "New Reactionaries" uttered seven years previously ("Nothing has truly changed, except for the worse, among French intellectuals since 2002, and the publication of my *Le Rappel à l'ordre*") or perhaps because Lindenberg had "gone global" in his denunciations in *Le Procès des Lumières,* making them at once more (overly) generalized and further removed from the French context, the second book stirred little reaction, certainly not one on the scale of its predecessor. But another and I would argue more opposite way to understand the *succès de scandale* of *Le Rappel à l'ordre* as opposed to *Le Procès des Lumières*—admittedly a more substantial and ambitious, if equally unconvincing work—has to do with the moment of the former's publication and the principal charge initially leveled by Lindenberg against the so-called "New Reactionaries." However limited the real threat posed by Jean-Marie le Pen's first round victory in the presidential elections of 2002, the Front National leader's unsettling success produced both a widespread, if false sense of *déjà vu*, of a "return of fascism" and the Dark Years, and a rhetoric as well as an iconography of protest that emphasized precisely this mindset and its accompanying anxiety. Into this situation, only a few short months after the *séisme Le Pen*, Daniel Lindenberg introduced another dark element of that past, the specter of "collaboration," or worse, on the part of many of France's leading intellectuals. And many of the responses of the latter, rather than break with such anachronistic accusations, only closed and in fact expanded the circle. As noted, they alluded ominously to an implicit, if not explicit negationism on Lindenberg's part where recent acts of anti-Semitism in France were concerned, while also accusing him of attempting to "fascisticize" the malaise created by Le Pen's first round victory.

In the exchanges between Lindenberg and his adversaries that dominated intellectual debates in the media for several weeks, the memory of the World War II past, of "Vichy" and its legacies were clearly present and palpable. Moreover, implicit in the very violence of the accusations by both sides was a retrospective urge or impulse to judge that past by condemning its crimes and abuses, now apparently ominously emerging in the present. The very real historical incommensurability of France in the 1940s (and late 1930s) and the France of 2002 was never raised, and was in fact obfuscated by the debate itself. While Le Pen's first round victory along with its aftershocks never in fact produced a real "return of fascism," it certainly reaffirmed the haunting power of an historical moment when fascism in all of its forms and manifestations was a crushing and brutal reality in France and Europe as a whole.

NOTES

1. Portions of this chapter was previously published as Richard J. Golsan, "The Le Pen Movement," *SubStance* 32:1 (2003): 125–43. © 2003 by the Board of Regents of the Unviersity of Wisconsin System. Reproduced courtesy of the University of Wisconsin Press.

2. Rober Badinter, "Une autre idée de la France," *Le monde* 4 May, 2002.

3. Romain Rosso, "Au secours, Le Pen!," *L'Express*, 31janvier 2002, 14–15.

4. As Vaérie Igounet reports in her recent book, *Le Front National: De 1972 à nos jours: le parti, les homes, les idées* (Paris: Seuil, 2014), le Pen was shocked by his victory, and to the alarm of his inner circle, even seemed lugubrious after the results were in. According to Igounet, many thought that his moroseness was due to the fact that he had never actually *thought* about being president and the responsibilities that would entail, 363–64.

5. Jean Marie Colombani "La blessure," *Le Monde* 22 April, 2002.

6. Jean-Louis Adréani, "La gauche a oublié les gens qui peinent,' *Libération* 25 April 2002.

7. Conversation with the author.

8. François Ascher, "l'Echo d'une société hypermoderne," *Libération* 25 April 2002.

9. Perry Anderson, *The New Old World* (London: Verso, 2009), 176.

10. Le Pen did however increase the number of votes he received by almost three fourths of a million (Igounet, 367).

11. Anderson, 176.

12. Anderson, 177.

13. Ibid.

14. Colombani, La blessure," op. cit.

15. Anderson notes that there were an extraordinary number of blank ballots cast, as well as abstentions.

16. Ibid., 174.

17. Renaud Camus, *Du sens* (Paris: P.O.L., 2002), 381.

18. Ibid., 398.

19. Ibid., 400.

20. Ibid., 401.

21. Ibid., 402.

22. Ibid., 84.

23. Ibid., 438.

24. Ibid., 439.

25. Roger Garaudy's specious "historical" comparisons of the Holocaust to other genocides in *Les mythes fondateurs de la politique israélienne* and other pamphlets are discussed in detail in my *Vichy's Afterlife* (Lincoln: University of Nebraska Press, 2000), 124–26.

26. Alain Finkielkraut, *L'Imparfait du present* (Paris: Gallimard, 2002) 51.

27. Carrère later renounced his support of Camus, as the latter's anti-immigrationist posture became increasingly apparent.

28. In 2012, Millet joined forces with Camus, contributing an essay to the first number of Camus's journal *Les Cahiers de l'Innocence*.

29. In addition to being a right-wing nationalist and founder of *Action Française* he was a mentor, of sorts, to fascists and collaborationists like Robert Brasillach and others.

30. Daniel, Lindenberg, *le Rappel à l'ordre* (Paris: Seuil, 2002), 7.

31. Ibid., 53–54.

32. Ibid., 54.

33. Ibid., 53–54.

34. Pierre Nora, "Trois questions pour Pierre Nora," (*Le monde*, 21 November, 2002).

35. Ibid.

36. Ibid.

37. Anderson, 169.

38. Quoted in "Marcel Gauchet, au chevet de la democratie," (*Le monde*, 21 November 2002).

Chapter 3

Alain Badiou's *The Meaning of Sarkozy*
"Transcendental Pétainism" and the Ossification of History

In February 2010 the weekly magazine *Marianne* published a profile/interview with the radical leftist philosopher Alain Badiou under the provocatively flippant title, "Badiou, le star de la philo est-il un salaud?"[1] ["Is the star of philosophy Alain Badiou a bastard?"] The occasion for the publication of the profile/interview was the recent commercial success of, and controversy surrounding, Badiou's essay on the presidential campaign—and person—of Nicolas Sarkozy, *De quoi Sarkozy est-il le nom?* [*The Meaning of Sarkozy*]. In *The Meaning of Sarkozy* the new president and the nation itself are compared to Pétain and Vichy France in their fear of change, their subservience to outside power, their self-interest and complacency, and their cowardice. For Badiou this state of affairs marked the return in France of an historical and for Badiou "metaphysical" phenomenon he labeled "transcendental pétainism."

Despite the occasion of the profile/interview with Badiou, it is striking that the author of the piece, Eric Conan—himself a specialist of the history and memory of Vichy and the Dark Years—spends little if any time analyzing Badiou's text and the plausibility of the historical comparisons Badiou seeks to establish. Rather, Conan summarizes Badiou's career as a radical leftist and Maoist and an unrepentant supporter of radical and murderous causes, from Mao's Cultural Revolution to the Khmer Rouge in Cambodia. For Conan, Badiou is a "fossil" of the 1960s and 1970s, an "old loser whose originality consists in his defense of lost causes that had died bloodily: Stalinism, Maoism, and the Cambodian genocide."[2] Conan also stresses Badiou's vociferous hostility to democracy and his championing of the idea of revolution. He touches briefly on Badiou's philosophical *oeuvre,* and especially what he describes as his "tragi-comic" radical works from the 1970s. In these works, Conan locates—and quotes—some chilling passages. He cites Badiou's condemnation of the 1979 Vietnamese invasion of Cambodia that ended the

Khmer Rouge's reign of terror as "an act of military barbarism" and a "violation of a people's right to exist and the right of nations to have their borders guaranteed."[3] In other philosophical texts like *The Theory of Contradiction*, Conan quotes Badiou as affirming that "the resolution of a contradiction requires that someone disappears." The implications of this assertion when applied to concrete political situations are, Conan implies, frighteningly clear.

In its highly partisan tone and take on its subject—Conan makes no bones about the fact that for him Badiou *is* a "bastard"—the *Marianne* profile is representative of many if not most of the critical reactions by journalists, scholars and others to Badiou and his work. For Badiou's critics, he is essentially "one of those writers, so numerous in the Twentieth Century, who lent their considerable talents to the service of a politics that one has the right to consider atrocious."[4] Rather than take his work seriously, these critics generally stop with a denunciation of Badiou's politics. On the other hand, Badiou's admirers consider him a philosophical deity, a thinker on the level of Kant or Hegel—an assessment with which Badiou tends to agree. For these admirers, the philosopher can do no wrong, no matter how extreme the political positions he takes or pronouncements he makes.

In assessing a work like *The Meaning of Sarkozy* it is especially important to avoid both extremes. If, as Conan writes in his profile, Badiou was a virtual unknown in France before the publication and *succès de scandale* of the book, what is it about Badiou's brief and polemical reflections on Sarkozy and the "meaning" of his victory in the presidential elections of 2007 that captured the public's attention and, in many instances, stirred such strong reactions? One could argue of course, that because the memory of the Dark Years remains more of a vexed issue in contemporary France (and sells more books) than does the memory of the 1960s and 1970s radicalism, in writing his polemical book about Sarkozy and Vichy, Badiou was simply "cashing in." But to dismiss *The Meaning of Sarkozy* in this fashion would be to ignore what Badiou's book actually has to say about the memory of the Dark Years and the ways in which they resonate in contemporary France. There is little question that *The Meaning of Sarkozy* hit a nerve with the French public. For the purposes of this study, it is important to understand why.

To explore the broader meaning and implications of *The Meaning of Sarkozy* and the controversy it stirred up, it is necessary, first, to consider the work in relation to Badiou's politics and political philosophy. And because the book is ultimately about Nicholas Sarkozy and his historical meaning and function in France in 2007, it also is instructive to compare Badiou's perspective with Sarkozy's own views, not only where his place in French history is concerned, but also how he understands its history in the first place. In the end, surprising similarities between the respective visions of the two men emerge. Together, they offer additional insights into how the memory of Vichy and the

Dark Years are remembered and instrumentalized politically, as well as how that memory, in their hands, has proven corrosive in historical terms.

Alain Badiou's intellectual forays into the Vichy past and the history, memory, and legacies of World War II and France's Dark Years did not begin with *The Meaning of Sarkozy*. First, among other reasons, Badiou has repeatedly demonstrated a strong fascination and admiration for those who fought Vichy and the Nazis because his father, who served as mayor of Toulouse for many years, was in the Resistance. Moreover, in Badiou's philosophy of the Event, the Resistance plays a crucial and indeed foundational role. A more provocative intervention on the philosopher's part concerns his statements about the meaning and "grammatical" function of the word "Jew" in works like *Circonstances 3* and elsewhere. Finally, in the wake of Jean-Marie Le Pen's first-round victory in the presidential elections of 2002, Badiou weighed in on the political and social implications of that victory and the supposed "return of fascism" the National Front leader's success heralded.

All three of these interventions have proven problematic in philosophical and historical terms and/or highly controversial in political terms. In an essay on Badiou's interpretation of Samuel Beckett's (and others') decision to join the resistance during World War II, Barbara Will dissects and exposes the weaknesses of Badiou's philosophy as a means to understand what are, for Badiou, crucial and positive world-changing moments or "Events." These include not only resistance to fascism during World War II, but also the French Revolution in 1789, the Paris Commune of 1871, the 1917 Bolshevik Revolution, the Cultural Revolution in China, and finally the student and worker uprising of May 1968 in France.[5]

For Badiou, an Event occurs when "the rational or conventional laws of this world are interrupted or put out of their normal effects by something which happens."[6] In politics, these events or upheavals are usually revolutionary moments, and they herald what Badiou describes as "a change of the degrees of existence of a lot of the multiplicities [read: humans] which appear in the world."[7] Put differently, they effect a change "of intensity in the existence of something the existence of which is minimal."[8] In layman's terms, to understand and to commit oneself to the Event—what Badiou calls "fidelity" to the Event—changes a person from a "multiplicity" into a "subject," and the result of the commitment is the creation of "truth." Those who recognize the Event and commit themselves together to it often form a revolutionary vanguard or elite. Finally, Badiou adds, there is no way to anticipate or cause an Event to happen. The crucial issue is to recognize its impact and meaning and remain faithful to it.

As Will points out with regard to the French Resistance during World War II, the problem with this notion of the Event when applied to a specific historical situation or occurrence is that it effectively eliminates individual human (or group) agency, and also the impact of the historical circumstances themselves leading up to the Event. On the first point Will writes: "The idea that a change can take place without recourse to any group renders the French Resistance into something radically individualistic and miraculous."[9] On the second, Will notes that in *Metapolitics* Badiou raises the Resistance to a transcendent, Platonic ideal, to be coupled with an opposing (negative) ideal, which Badiou in *The Meaning of Sarkozy* will label "transcendental Pétainism." The two then form the two poles of an ongoing dialectical struggle, of crucial importance to the French past as well as the French present, in Badiou's view. But as a hermeneutical frame for analyzing the complexities of the present, Badiou's recourse to such "eternal, transcendental forms" risks "diffusing or, at worst, banalizing the force" of his critique, according to Will.[10] In historical terms, it also abstracts and removes the event from its crucial historical backdrop or bedrock, while also erasing the complexities and ambiguities of individual political commitment, or *engagement*.

There are also other problems and limitations—as well as dangers—with Badiou's concept of the Event that emerge in politico-historical, and other contexts as well. Among them, "fidelity" can only follow a sudden, transformative (or traumatic) and unprecedented event. Speaking of Saint Paul's conversion on the road to Damascus which qualifies as perhaps the quintessential Event, Badiou writes: "It is of the essence of the Event that it can be preceded by no sign, and that it surprises us with its grace, no matter what our vigilance has been."[11] But, as Nick Hewlett asks, why can "fidelity" as defined by Badiou not *also* be fidelity to a state of affairs that itself proves transformative? To return to politics and history, In *Homage to Catalonia*, George Orwell writes that what inspired his commitment to the Spanish Republican cause was not a revolutionary upsurge or upheaval, but the "state of affairs" he experienced on arriving in Barcelona in 1937 and witnessing a truly egalitarian society: "Practically everyone wore rough, working-class clothes or blue overalls or some variant of the militia uniform. All this was queer and moving. There was much in it that I did not understand, in some ways I did not even like it, but I recognized it immediately as a *state of affairs* [*my italics*] worth fighting for."[12]

One could argue of course, that the anarchist Barcelona of 1937 did form part of a revolutionary "Event" according to Badiou's definition, but the crucial point is that Orwell himself recognizes *not* the revolutionary moment, but the society *transformed*, as the object of value. As Simon Critchley observes, Badiou's fascination with revolution is in the end a fascination with the revolutionary *moment*, and *only* the revolutionary moment: "it is [the] sudden transformation of febrile sterility of the nothing of the world into a fecund something, this moment of radical rupture that obsesses Badiou, a seizure by thought in the event that is a seizure of power."[13] And this absolute commitment to the revolutionary moment, to the moment of violent rupture, reveals something else about Badiou's politics. Critchley writes: "there is an affectionate and, to my mind, misguided nostalgia for revolutionary violence. Seductive as it is, Badiou's politics suffer from a heroism of the decision, a propaganda of the violent deed in all its deluded romance."[14] Here, Critchley makes reference to affinities between Badiou's revolutionary politics and the "decisionism" of the Nazi jurist Carl Schmitt, itself a controversial issue,[15] but beyond the scope of this chapter.

The reference to Schmitt and through him to Nazism itself does however call to mind a second intellectual foray on Badiou's part into World War II and its legacies in the present. This concerns the meaning and origins of the word "Jew," its connection to anti-Semitism, and the implications of both, especially with regard to Israel, today.

From the outset, Badiou's speculations along these lines, published in 2005 in *Circonstances, 3: Portées du nom juif* have provoked controversy, not to say outrage among his critics. In *Circonstances, 3*, Badiou suggests first, that "the "word" Jew now constitutes an "exceptional signifier . . . even a sacred signifier"[16] that confers a dubious privilege and even political immunity on its bearer. More concretely, Badiou writes:

> Today it is not uncommon to read that 'Jew' is indeed a name beyond ordinary names. And it seems to be presumed that, like an inverted original sin, the grace of having been an incomparable victim [of the Holocaust] can be passed down not only to descendants and the descendants of descendants but to all who come under the predicate in question, be they heads of state or armies engaging in the severe oppression of those whose lands they have confiscated.[17]

Moreover, for Badiou it was Hitler and the Nazis who in effect "created" the Jews as a category. They created the predicate "Jew" and "with a rare zeal for following through, drew all the consequences from making the signifier 'Jewish' into a radical exception—it was, after all, the only way that they could give some sort of consistency, in their industrial massacre, to the symmetrical predication 'Aryan' the particular vacuity of which obsessed them."[18]

For Badiou's critics, attributing the creation of the category or "predicate" "Jew" as it is now understood—and for Badiou, overvalued—to Hitler and the Nazis is provocative, not to say offensive enough. But among the perverse correlatives this entails is that, to claim for oneself (or one's people, or one's nation) the predicate "Jew" now, in the present, is to embrace the project Hitler launched, and thereby to stimulate the anti-Semitism from which it is inseparable. According to Eric Marty, this means, ultimately, the erasure of the distinction between claiming the predicate "Jew" in a positive "identitary" sense and using the word pejoratively, as an insult. Marty writes: "Badiou's entire thesis lies in the act of establishing . . . the virtual synonymy between the 'kike' that the Nazi enunciates and the 'I am a Jew' enunciated by one subject or another."[19]

But for Marty, this is not the only nefarious consequence of Badiou's speculations on the predicate "Jew," nor does it constitute his final aim. Marty notes that the Nazi revolution is not a real Event according to Badiou's philosophy because it has no universal import; it serves the interests of the German race, the "Aryans" alone. Therefore, in Badiou's terminology, it is a "simulacrum" of an Event, a false imitation of one. So, logically according to Marty, the Holocaust itself is *also* a "simulacrum" whose memory belongs *not* to the victims but to the *Nazis* themselves: "Thus, the memory of the extermination, fidelity to the dead, can only be absorbed into the simulacrum of Nazism, and passed on integrally by it."[20]

What is Badiou's goal in all this, what animates his thinking along these lines? For Marty, the answer is clear:

> The logical delirium that organizes these effects is a delirium of negation, of denial. It is a question of twice over negating or denying the signifier "Jew": in identifying it with the Hitlerian idea, in dismissing as a fable the founding word that brought it into the world, and in positing the imperative to forget that this signifier was in the Twentieth Century the object of a project and of a process of destruction never before seen in human societies.[21]

One may well disagree with Marty's analysis—Badiou himself certainly does.[22] But there is no doubt that one of Badiou's main goals is to remove the memory of the Holocaust from the equation of the Palestinian-Israeli conflict as a justification of Israeli actions and Israeli oppression of its neighbors. In an interview in Israeli daily *Haaretz* in May 2005 Badiou stated bluntly: "The question of the destruction of the European Jews is a German and European question. If we are to come to a resolution of the Middle East problem, we must manage—I know it's a difficult thing—to forget the Holocaust." And he adds

> There is always something monstrous about determining a state from a racial, mythical, or religious point of view, or more generally, by appealing to a particularity. That went as much for the German fascists as for the French fascists. It goes for the Serbs as much as for the terrorist conception of a "Muslim state" (with Sharia, etc.). It goes for the Jews too.[23]

If (as discussed in the last chapter) many in France including prominent intellectuals saw Jean-Marie Le Pen's victory in the first round of the French presidential elections in April 2002 as a return of French (and European) fascism as well as a threat to French republicanism and democracy itself,

Badiou, in his essay "On Parliamentary 'Democracy,'" strongly disagrees on each of these counts. To begin with, democracy in what Badiou describes as "this politically sick country"[24] is a sham. It is not about freedom but about conservatism, about maintaining the status quo. Political candidates, be they of the left or right, are ultimately "homogeneous" to the system, and ultimately represent no potential for real change, regardless of what they say, or what voters believe.

Le Pen, on the other hand, *appeared* to be "heterogeneous" to the system, and therefore theoretically posed a devastating threat to it, at least in the eyes of the public. This is why, according to Badiou, people, and especially young people, poured into the streets in the thousands and tens of thousands to protest Le Pen's presence on the second-round ballot. In the end, however, even though they *thought* they were fighting a potential fascist threat and protecting democracy, they were in reality only protecting what Badiou calls the "homogeneity principle."[25] The fact that Le Pen's first round victory was alarming was not because he received the *number* of votes that he did, but because his score made him an interloper of sorts in a "pre-coded" place ordinarily reserved for a "homogeneous" candidate of one of the traditionally more acceptable parties.

But for Badiou, Le Pen is not really an outsider to French republicanism and democracy at all. In fact, he represents the secret, dark conscience of every Frenchman. He is "like the hideous spectacle of what one is oneself but taken to the extreme, or proclaimed rather than hidden."[26] He is "the extreme, odious image of a secret and subservient public conscience."[27] And even if Le Pen *were* truly a threat to the French Republic, what is there actually worth defending in that Republic? Is it the Republic "of the terrifying massacre of 1914–1918? That which voted full powers to Pétain? That of the atrocious colonial wars? . . . of Mitterrand? Of the pair Chirac-Jospin? Or that of De Gaulle?"[28]

The institution of democracy fares no better in Badiou's essay. Because democracy is profoundly conservative, once one is elected to power the only way to stay there is to "do nothing." Democracy is increasingly, moreover, a "minority ritual," to the extent that true electoral majorities are going the way of the dinosaur. And, most importantly, what makes power through the accumulation of numbers sacrosanct to begin with? Badiou points out that Hitler, like Pétain, came to power through the vote. Finally, what is needed according to Badiou, is a distinction between "passive" and "active numbers," and a reliance on the latter. Today's French voters, and in fact all those of Western democracies, accumulate "passive numbers." These passive numbers should ultimately have no say in politics. Rather those who account for the "active numbers,"—"the *résistants* of the 1940s, those of the 1950s opposed to the 'sordid' colonial wars, the leftists of the 1960s and 1970s"[29]—even though they constitute absolute minorities should in Badiou's view lead the way. Otherwise France and the French will continue to succumb to the "siren song," the "blackmail of 'democracy.'"[30]

THE MEANING OF SARKOZY

The Meaning of Sarkozy is divided into nine chapters. The first two chapters, "Before the Election" and "After the Election" deal with the threat posed by Sarkozy, the political climate and circumstances that prepared his rise to prominence, and Badiou's thoughts on the meaning of Sarkozy's victory. The final chapters of the book examine the broader meaning and historical implications of Sarkozy's ascent to power. In Chapter Six, Badiou elaborates at length on his notion of "transcendental pétainism" and its implications not only for the present, but for the past two centuries of French history. This section deserves particular attention.

From the outset *The Meaning of Sarkozy* is a politically and ideologically charged book. It opens with a renewed condemnation of French democracy, and the electoral process upon which it depends. The latter is characterized here as an "irrational process," and "parliamentary fetishism" takes the place of true democratic practices. Not surprisingly, the occasion for these initial reflections is not the candidacy and potential election of Sarkozy but rather, once again, Jean-Marie Le Pen's first round victory in the 2002 presidential election. And here again, it is not Le Pen per se—an "old Pétainist," a "knackered old horse from a ruined stable"[31]—that interests Badiou but the role played by the "ideological state apparatuses"—political parties, the press, trade unions, and the civil service—in the 2002 election. Following the *Front National* leader's first round success, these entities set out to create what Badiou here calls the "Le Pen psychosis." This psychosis "threw masses of terrified young *lycéens* into the streets and right-minded intellectuals into the arms of Chirac."[32] The result was the latter's massive second round victory.

Five years later, with the candidacies of Ségolène Royal, whom Badiou dismisses as "a hazy *bourgeoise* whose thinking, if it exists, is somewhat concealed"[33] and especially Nicolas Sarkozy, whom Badiou characterizes as a "twitchy accountant, visibly uncultured," the "fatal consequences" of the "Le Pen psychosis" are being reaped. France is in the grips of a phenomenon resembling the "Great Fear" of French revolutionary times. Implicitly at least, the French will vote for any "homogeneous" candidate, to use the language of Badiou's earlier essay, to thwart the "heterogeneous" threat that Le Pen had supposedly posed.

As Badiou explains, the Great Fear of the present is actually composed of two different but related "fears." The first fear, which Badiou labels the "essential" or "primitive fear," derives from France's loss of standing in the contemporary world, and an accompanying anxiety over the nation's increasing insignificance. In real terms, this fear translates according to Badiou (although the process is not explained) into "a fear of foreigners, of workers, of the people, of youngsters from the *banlieues,* Muslims, black Africans. . ."[34] This "essential fear" is a "conservative and gloomy fear" Badiou writes, and one which "creates the desire for a master who will protect you, even if only while oppressing and impoverishing you all the more."[35] This is precisely the kind of fear, Badiou concludes, that can result in the victory of a figure like Sarkozy, a "jittery cop," a "miniature Napoleon," "a reinforced-concrete heterosexual" intended by his supporters to deal with "foreigners and foreign ways."

The second fear, which Badiou labels a "derivative fear," occurs among those who are frightened by those subject to the first fear, along with the protective master the latter seek to install in power. (Badiou likens this "master" to a police chief and in particular to Jean Genet's police chief in *Le Balcon* who, as Badiou reminds the reader, dreams of incarnating a giant phallus.) This second fear is typical of "Socialist petty bourgeois" who, for all their opposition to the "jumpy cop" Sarkozy, are no more in touch with the political realities of the world than their adversaries. For them, as well as for the reactionaries motivated by "essential fear," places like Palestine, Iran, Afghanistan, Lebanon, and Africa and the crises they face hardly exist. And for those who aspire to be leaders of those possessed of "derivative fear," rather than bring up these places and the political realities and problems they face, these aspiring leaders prefer merely to play on the fear of those who embrace "essential fear." In this sense, those who are consumed by "derivative fear" and those who lead them—the "opposition" as Badiou also describes them—are more removed from reality than even their conservative adversaries. Under any circumstances, neither group is in touch with "the real" according to Badiou. And, he concludes, "every chain of fear leads to nothingness, and voting is the operation of this."[36]

But, as Badiou also argues in the final pages of "Before the Election," the "chain of fear" he is describing doesn't lead only to nothingness. Rather, it serves to validate the state itself, and "once the state is occupied by fear, it can freely create fear." Moreover, this fear must assume the form of terror, a "democratic terror," because "fear never has any other future than terror."[37]

From these somewhat abstract—and oracular—pronouncements Badiou moves to the realities of the present, and then to his initial assertions concerning the meaning and relevance of Vichy and Pétainism to the current political situation. Fear and terrorism, Badiou writes, mean war, and a perpetual state of war at that. Indeed, war "is the global perspective of democracy."[38] Western democracies today are constantly at war with poorer countries, "rogue states" as well as "enemies" within: the poor, the disenfranchised, the *banlieusards.*

The toxic combination, or "alliance" of fear and war has a particular history in France, Badiou claims, and that alliance is called "pétainism." Philippe Pétain, he asserts, played on the fear of the destruction suffered between 1914 and 1918 in order to convince the French in 1940 that he would protect them in defeat, and he was largely successful in this endeavor. In fact it was Pétain "who said that we should fear war more than defeat,"[39] and the dishonorable outcome of embracing defeat and subservience was that the French suffered considerably less than those who actually fought Hitler, like the Russians and British.

Returning to the present, today's "analogous Pétainism" to quote Badiou consists in "maintaining that the French simply have to accept the law of the world—the Yankee model, servility toward the powerful, the domination of the rich, hard work for the poor, the surveillance of everyone, suspicion of foreigners living here, contempt for people who do not live like we do, and all will be fine."[40] Sarkozy, of course, embodies and promotes this state of mind, but, surprisingly, the threat of a "neo-Pétainism on a mass scale" is also embodied in the candidacy of Ségolène Royal. Both candidates ultimately champion neo-Pétainism rather than fascism, although in Badiou's presentation fascism almost seems superior to Pétainism: the latter represents "the subjective abominations of fascism (fear, informing, contempt for others) without its vital spirit."[41]

Badiou concludes his pre-election remarks by taking another shot at democracy, this time relying on the historical example of Vichy, and making a final claim concerning "Pétainism" in France today. On the first score, Badiou notes that by all accounts Pétain enjoyed the support of at least half of his fellow countrymen, a "democratic" majority by any measure. But given what this majority acquiesced to, why should that majority claim to speak for France, and enjoy the privilege of representing "the French?" The true French, those who deserve to speak for and represent France, Badiou argues, were the small minority that resisted Vichy and the Germans. And he adds, the nation will only continue to exist as a result of the "acts of those who have not accepted the abasements that the logic of the survival of privileges, or just 'realistic' conformity with the laws of the world, universally require."[42]

Badiou's final claim concerning Pétainism today in "Before the Election" also includes, not surprising, with another swipe at French democracy as it is currently practiced. Given that "voting is the fictitious figure of choice, imposed on an essential disorientation," that is, a false choice that both depends on and encourages the confusion of the voters, it is all the easier for the state to foster and sell the supposed protection of the "illusion of Pétainism." As Badiou explains, this illusion promises the voting public that they will remain "sheltered from global earthquakes, but at a terrible price: Jews handed over to be massacred, Africans handed over to the police, children chased out of schools."[43]

Part II of *The Meaning of Sarkozy*, based on Badiou's seminar at the *Ecole Normale Supérieure* of 16 May 2007 following Sarkozy's election, is frankly apocalyptic in tone. Alluding to the "distress" he acknowledges in his audience, Badiou affirms that the election of Sarkozy announces nothing less than "the coming to pass of a disgusting thing." Badiou then proceeds to sketch out the background, implications, and future consequences of the disastrous transformation he sees occurring. Among other events he points to the demise of the USSR and those responsible for it, the fading of a sclerotic Gaullism, the betrayal of the French Left, and the catastrophic approach of the single party state in France.

According to Badiou, a crucial and obvious factor in the demise of the Left in France and elsewhere was the collapse of the Soviet Union which, despite the fact of being a "worm-eaten state" at the end, was still the "ostensible guardian" of the "ideological bearings of Marxism." In laying blame for this collapse Badiou's wrath is directed not at Lenin and Stalin, leaders of the quintessential revolutionary elite formed by the Event of the October 1917, one presumes, but at more recent leaders. These include Brezhnev, "the man of stagnation" and especially Mikhail Gorbachev. Gorbachev, the man of "out and out reform," is responsible for plunging the world of the Left "into such a wretched state that no one knows when it will recover."[44] In Stalin's time, by contrast, things looked brighter, because "the political organizations of the workers and popular classes behaved infinitely better, and capitalism was that much less arrogant."[45] Badiou does not explain how such "good behavior" was established and maintained, nor does he provide examples of it.

In the French context, Badiou's judgments are equally peremptory, and more universally harsh: there are no exceptions to a blanket condemnation of the political class and the leaders of all parties. Chirac is the "Brezhnev of Gaullism": the latter only survived in a "pale and moribund form under [Chirac's] leadership." Gaullism no longer embodies the signal and single virtue of its namesake: courage, the strength to "never to be afraid." Thanks to Sarkozy's victory, it is now effectively dead.

But Badiou's anger at Chirac is nothing compared to his animosity toward Sarkozy, and especially those on the left who supported him. Resorting to language that outraged for its historical resonances—to be discussed shortly—Badiou repeatedly likens those on the left who flocked to Sarkozy's camp to "rats." Sarkozy himself is dubbed the "Rat Man." The rat, Badiou writes, is "the person who, internal to the temporality of opinion, cannot stand to wait. The next time around, as ordered by the state, is very far away. 'I'll be old,' says the rat. He doesn't want to stew in impotence, but even less in impossibility. The impossible offers very little sustenance to him."[46] And Badiou adds, Sarkozy "is deeply acquainted with the subjectivity of rats," due to his own political experience, and he is a "virtuoso" at attracting them. By finding "a state use for rat psychology,"[47] Sarkozy himself is richly deserving of the title of Rat Man.

What are the meaning and implications of the Left's betrayal, the "flocking of rats to the Rat Man?" In the end, Badiou writes, the "logic" of all this is the "logic of the single party": France is destined to become a one party state. And not just any one party state: Badiou reminds his audience of an assertion made by Slavoj Zizek to the effect that Stalinism and parliamentary democracy are not opposites, as commonly assumed. Rather, Stalinism, the quintessential one party state, is the *future* of parliamentary democracy, and French democracy is fast moving in that direction. Except that the consequences in the latter case will be even more dire: "the technological means of controlling the population are already such that Stalin, with his endless handwritten files, his mass executions, his spies with hats, his gigantic lice-ridden camps and bestial tortures, appears like an amateur from another age."[48]

Badiou concludes his comments in Part Two with a reflection on the meaning of May 1968, and Sarkozy's excessive preoccupation with and fear of that watershed moment. According to Badiou, in his speeches and other pronouncements about May 1968 Sarkozy argued that the event marked the perilous moment when the French people "stopped making a clear distinction between Good and Evil." This is why its continuing influence of French culture and society must be eradicated. But Badiou retorts, what May 1968 was actually about was precisely the opposite; it was about the *identification and recognition* of Good and Evil in France and the world: "Evil, for the rebel activists of the red decade between 1966 and 1976 meant the men of wealth and power who resembled the Rat Man. Basically, *he* is Evil. And Good was the politicized worker, the peoples in revolt, the revolutionary activists."[49] The real reason Sarkozy loathes May 1968 and is haunted by its shadow is that it represents, indeed embodies, a very dangerous idea, an idea that challenges the very foundations of the democratic and capitalist system. This is the idea of Communism. The Boogie Man of the bourgeoisie from time immemorial, it is the idea of Communism and the shadow that it casts through events like May 1968 that Sarkozy really wishes to be done with once and for all.

While the majority of the remaining sections of *The Meaning of Sarkozy* all further develop the general themes and ideas elaborated in the first two parts, Section 6, "France's Transcendental: Pétainism" focuses closely on the comparison of the present situation in France to the Dark Years, and explicates more thoroughly what Badiou means by "transcendental Pétainism."

First, despite earlier indications to the contrary, Badiou states that he is *not* saying that "circumstances today resemble the defeat of 1940, or that Sarkozy resembles Pétain."[50] Rather, "the mass subjectivity that brought Sarkozy to power, and sustains his actions, finds its unconscious national-historical roots in Pétainism." This subjectivity, he adds, is "something I call a 'transcendental': something that, without appearing on the surface—so that our situation does not 'resemble' the historical sequence of Pétain's reign—configures it from afar, gives law and order, to a collective mechanism."[51]

Having in effect abstracted "Pétainism" as he construes it from history, Badiou then re-introduces it into history by observing that "Pétainism goes back well beyond Pétain himself, indeed, as far as the Restoration of 1815. Then, as during the Dark Years, a reactionary government was established 'in the foreigners' baggage train, with the vigorous backing of émigrés, overthrown classes, traitors and opportunists of all kinds, and the consent of a worn-out population."[52] Also like *L'Etat Français,* the Restoration promised to restore public order and morals after the bloody anarchy of revolution. It spoke incessantly of the nation but was "installed by foreigners." And Badiou concludes, the current situation is a "wretched repetition of these severe historical depressions France has inflicted on itself."[53]

Summing up, Badiou delineates five characteristics of "transcendental Pétainism" as it manifests itself in French history. First, in a "Pétainist situation" capitulation and servility "present themselves as invention, revolution, and regeneration." Second a sense of crisis, and more specifically of moral crisis, predominates. Third the solution to the crisis, or its "correction," comes from abroad. Fourth—and most importantly according to Badiou—a concerted propaganda campaign affirms that "some time ago something damaging happened to crystallize and aggravate the moral crisis."[54] And finally, the fifth element is racism.

In illustrating these characteristics of "transcendental pétainism," Badiou draws almost exclusively on the election of Sarkozy and *Sarkozisme,* and this is where the comparison with historical Pétainism becomes most explicit. Where the first characteristic is concerned, *l'Etat Francais's* effort to turn military defeat and national humiliation into regeneration through Pétain's *Révolution nationale* are echoed in Sarkozy's call to break with the past and put the nation "back to work." But Sarkozy's calls for renewal only serve to mask what is really at stake, and that is complete subservience to global (read: American) capitalism and hegemony. Similarly, the moral crisis that Vichy propaganda touted that supposedly led to defeat finds its counterpart the Sarkozy's appeals to "moral correction, work, the household economy."[55] Badiou does not offer examples of these appeals, however. Third, "the paradigmatic function of foreign experience," the "correction" from abroad, in Pétain's day came from Mussolini's Italy, Franco's Spain, and especially Hitler's Germany. In the Sarkozy era, it comes from Bush's America, Blair's Great Britain, and even capitalist China. Fourth, the propagandistic exploitation of an earlier crisis to which the state and the nation must respond focused during the Vichy years on Léon Blum's Popular Front, whereas under Sarkozy the culprit is May 1968. Finally, the racism that characterized Vichy in the form of the persecution of Jews is echoed today in the subtler forms of animosity toward and ostracism of emigrants, the poor, and *sans papiers*. If, as Badiou claims, Sarkozy's France fulfills the five characteristics just elaborated, one can say "without hesitation that it falls under the Pétainist transcendental."[56] In this sense, as a "mass subjective form" Pétainism is very much alive in France today. To restrict Pétainism to "the leading personnel of collaboration between 1940 and 1944" would be, Badiou implies, a dangerous mistake in dealing with the present.

As the discussion of *The Meaning of Sarkozy* suggests, much of Badiou's diagnosis of French ills under Sarkozy and his account of the nation in the grips of a "Pétainist transcendental" draws on, reiterates, or recalibrates themes articulated in earlier writings on the Dark Years and their legacies, discussed above. As a result, it suffers from some of the same philosophical and historical shortcomings, while also raising additional concerns about the provocative ways in which Badiou chooses to address Jews, anti-Semitism, and the Holocaust.

In his comments on the Resistance in The *Meaning of Sarkozy* Badiou once again refers to an elite whose value is indicated here by the fact that even as a "minority" in electoral terms, it is the *real* French "elite" and should therefore speak for, and in the name of the "true France." But what that Resistance was in historical terms, how it came into being, and how that knowledge might be helpful *now* in the struggle against this new iteration of the "Pétainist transcendental," of an "analogous Pétainism" is not spelled out. Presumably a rebirth of Resistance in France requires "waiting for an Event" that may—or may not—come into being. Here, the Beckettian echo would in all likelihood be one that Badiou would not intend or approve.

If *The Meaning of Sarkozy* seems ultimately pessimistic on this score, it is equally pessimistic where the themes taken up in Badiou's essay on le Pen's first round victory in 2002 are concerned as well: democracy, the French Republic, and the character (or lack thereof) of the French people themselves. Once again, democracy is equated with dupery and conformism, and the republic is recognized for its failings, as opposed to it accomplishments. Although Badiou is more careful in his dissection and differentiation of Right and Left in political and historical terms in the more recent essay, both are in the end characterized by their "fear" and their cowardice. And if Sarkozy's supporters on the right fare better than his left-wing supporters in not being labeled "rats," they are in the end only marginally less abject than their left-wing counterparts. Both share the "subjective abominations" of fascism, without its "vital spirit."

The word "rat," of course, raises the more troubling and inflammatory topic of Badiou's comments on the origin and meaning of the word "Jew" and the Holocaust, discussed earlier, in that rats are indelibly associated in

French memory with the worst of Vichy's anti-Semitic propaganda. This resonance would certainly not be lost on Badiou himself. In a highly critical review in *Le monde des livres* of *The Meaning of Sarkozy* published shortly after it appeared in France, Pierre Assouline asserted that the last time images of "rats" and expressions like "Rat Man" were used in France to disparage political groups or ethnicities occurred during the Occupation in a 1942 anti-Semitic propaganda film denouncing the "Jewish peril." In using such terms, Assouline continued, Badiou had crossed the "Rubicon" into indecency. And to have made such pronouncements as a professor of one of France's elite institutions only made Badiou's comparisons all the more offensive.[57]

To be sure, there is no explicit connection between Badiou's use of the word "rat" to describe Sarkozy's leftist supporters in *The Meaning of Sarkozy* and his earlier, ambiguous reflections on the "predicate" Jew. Nevertheless, both words are cast in a harshly negative light in the political contexts in which Badiou applies them. Moreover, the use of an anti-Semitic slur that can hardly be detached from its Occupation roots gives it a special resonance and invites and encourages a particularly virulent form of hatred which itself is—at least hopefully—more reminiscent of the Dark Years than the present. The fact that some of these former leftists are themselves Jews—for example, André Glucksmann, whom Badiou denounces explicitly and who renounced his Maoist past to support Sarkozy and also George W. Bush's invasion of Iraq—is not lost on Badiou. This makes his use of the term "rat" all the more insensitive, not to say offensive.

To be precise, Badiou's interest in (and analysis of) the themes of betrayal, collaboration, and complicity implicit in his discussion of "rats" in *The Meaning of Sarkozy* have as a general rule not arisen in the context of evocations of Vichy and the Dark Years. Rather, they have been articulated in discussions of the political choices and evolution—the "renegacy," to use his term—of his former colleagues, former Maoists and other activists of the 1960s and 1970s who have since joined the political mainstream. In an interview in the *New Left Review* in Fall 2008, Badiou argues that some of these "renegades" were simply opportunists: when their radical politics did not provide a path to power, they simply chose to "play another card." That is, they chose a different politics. Other "renegades" were the victims of their own fanaticism, and ended up embracing precisely that which they had struggled against. As Badiou writes: "at a certain point, absolute commitment becomes indistinguishable from absolute slavery, and the figure of emancipation indistinguishable from barbarism." But regardless of how they arrived at their ultimate political destination, Badiou holds a special disdain for those who went all the way to "barbarism" by becoming "pro-American or cozying up to Sarkozy."[58]

The fact that Babiou's categories of "renegades" as delineated in the *New Left Review* interview can readily be applied to categories of collaborators with Nazism during World War II, and that the United States (along with its supposed minion, Sarkozy) is at least implicitly compared to Nazi Germany in its barbarism—a comparison made explicit *The Meaning of Sarkozy*—points to one of the most telling features of the latter essay and of Badiou's historical vision as a whole. This is the deliberate *slippage* between, or *conflation of* distinct historical epochs and, especially, crisis moments. As numerous examples of such epochs or moments alluded to in *The Meaning of Sarkozy* confirm, this tendency or predilection is by no means restricted to linking the Dark Years to the present in deliberately troubling ways. The current "fear" that haunts French society in the present recalls the "Great Fear" of the Revolutionary period. And the Pétainist moment of 1940s France is little—nothing?—more than a reiteration of the Restoration of 1815 in all of its most salient features. Of course these comparisons serve to validate Badiou's historical and ideological views, but they also lend themselves to historical distortions and contradictions that Badiou either doesn't notice or that don't seem to concern him. For example, in establishing the comparison between 1815 and 1940, Badiou remarks that the political regime in place came "in the baggage train of the foreigner." But in his denunciation of democracy and the rule of the majority Badiou reminds his reader that Pétain was "elected" and enjoyed the support of most of the French.

Stalinism and Stalinist Russia also come in for contradictory treatment. In comparing the Stalinist era to the sclerotic and decadent regimes of the likes of Brejnev and Gorbachev, Badiou states that the "political organizations and workers behaved" better under Stalin, and that the latter kept an "arrogant" capitalism in check. By contrast, it is the murderous, security-obsessed Stalinist regime of mass executions and the Goulag that Badiou invokes in discussing the one party state future in France that Sarkozy and his "rats" are preparing.

What is one to make of Badiou's historical comparisons and contradictions in *The Meaning of* Sarkozy? How do they relate to his vision and philosophy of history? And finally, do these articulations have an impact on Badiou's understanding of the meaning of Vichy, and how Vichy's memory is contoured and functions in the present?

On the first score, Badiou's historical contradictions point, superficially at least, to a lack of historical consistency and rigor that would tend to call his conclusions into doubt. But they also suggest that for Badiou historical moments are essentially isolated *loci*, or accretions of specific political and historical meanings that have no clear logical or necessary connection with each other—or with other moments. If this is the case, then his vision of history is not one of a dynamic continuum but something much more static and abstract. As Nick Hewlitt writes: "The division of political history [in Badiou's thought] into modes and sequences gives history a curiously immobile, stop-start air, apparently in keeping with the idea that there is no logic to the course of history but a series of events which come out of the blue and are inexplicable in terms of the circumstances in which they arose."[59] In the "sequel" to *The Meaning of Sarkozy* entitled *Sarkozy, pire que prevu*, ["Sarkozy: Worse Than Expected"] Badiou proposes just such a detached historical "sequence" in offering an allegorized account of post-Sarkozy France. The present, under the reign of the Socialists of François Hollande, is likened to a modernized "Platonic cave" in the form of a giant cinema in which the French people are imprisoned. Nailed to their seats and unable to look around them, they can only see manipulative shadows projected on the screen in front of them by politicians of the right and left whose job it is to dupe them eternally. Only an Event, in the form of a group of courageous radicals capable of leading them through a hitherto unforeseen exit to a clear "mountainside in spring" can save them and offer them, ultimately, a joyous and authentic existence. Because in Badiou's platonic cinema there is once again no real difference between right and left—both are "homogenous" to the system—in his lead-up comments to introduce his Platonic cinema Badiou proposes nothing in concrete political terms to account for Hollande's victory or to distinguish him from his opponent.

In this allegorized, frankly bleak and somewhat sterile and *ossified* vision of history, where does Vichy and its memory ultimately fit in? In the end, for Badiou, it marks an exception. First, if Pétainism, and by extension the Vichy regime itself form a "transcendental," which in effect shapes History and historical realities from afar, so to speak, why not choose earlier, more "original moments" like the 1815 Restoration (which, Badiou insists shares the same characteristics) to define or label the paradigm? Unless one assumes that Badiou chose Pétain and the memory of Vichy opportunistically, it seems clear that they have a special resonance for him as sources as well as symbols of moral and especially political evil. Vichy in fact embodies the quintessential moment of a national abjectness from which France has never really recovered. In the final analysis, the Events that the Resistance and May 1968 constituted for Badiou had no power to overcome or change the course of French history. This is presumably why even Gaullism, an integral part of the Resistance, declined and died under Chirac. It is also why Le Pen, "the old Pétainist" is not "heterogeneous" to the political system, but "homogeneous" to it. And this is also why Le Pen is not the "Other" to the French of today, but rather an expression of their darkest, most secret, and perhaps most authentic selves.

If, as the discussion here suggests, *The Meaning of Sarkozy* is ultimately a deeply flawed work of historical analysis, what accounts for its success, or more precisely, its *succès de scandale?* In Badiou's "episodic" and sclerotic or ossified history, in which historical sequences are readily conflated and even collapsed into each other, the lesson, it would appear, is that the French people have not really exited from the Vichy nightmare. In fact, in their abjectness, they are the *same people*, at least for Badiou. If the lesson of the scandal over Francois Mitterrand's past a little more than a decade earlier was that the Vichy past lived on in the person of the president, the lesson that Badiou seeks to teach in *The Meaning of Sarkozy* is that *all in France* are contaminated by that past. And, moreover, there is no way out. In a lecture entitled "The Three Negations" given around the time of Sarkozy's victory, Badiou dismissed the notion that an "Event" could emerge in the current French political climate. Only a false event, or "simulacrum" was possible. This, presumably, occurred with the election of François Hollande.[60] Hence Badiou's professed pessimism.

Finally, in what ways does Badiou's account of the meaning of Vichy, despite its particularities, coincide with the general paradigm laid out in the Introduction here? And, as a work of *political* analysis, what does *The Meaning of Sarkozy* reveal, or obscure, of Sarkozy's own take on the past and especially the memory of the Dark Years?

First, for Badiou as for Robert Frank, Vichy, "Pétainism" and the defeat of 1940 mark the watershed moment when French "decline" began in earnest. But as opposed to Frank, who merely diagnoses an *aspect* of the French mindset, for Badiou *le déclinisme* is *the* quintessential French reality of today. Additionally, for Badiou through its linkages with political evil past (1815) and present (Sarkozy), Vichy and Pétainism are transformed into the very embodiment of political and moral evil—hence Pétainism's transformation into a "transcendental" in Badiou's philosophy. Implicit in this move, also, is a retroactive judgment of that past in light of the political realities of the present. Finally, for Badiou, the assessment of the moral, as well as historical and even philosophical meaning of Vichy and Pétainism is inseparable from, and filtered through, his experience of May 1968 and his understanding of, and commitment to, 1960s and 1970s radicalism in France. At best, that "filter" or prism offers only a schematic understanding of the Dark Years, their impact and complexities—and their meaning for the present.

To conclude: what of Badiou's assessment of Sarkozy himself? What does Badiou "get right" about Sarkozy's electoral victory and its historic and political implications? What does he get wrong? Badiou is certainly correct in emphasizing Sarkozy's distaste for 1968. In Sarkozy's view—as he stated in numerous campaign speeches—France had lost its "moral compass," so to speak, as a result of that experience. Badiou is also correct that Sarkozy was successful in wooing voters from the far right, in articulating and implementing harsh anti-immigrant positions and measures, and in also undertaking initiatives in support of essentially mythical notions of *Français de souche*, or "true" French, not far removed from the mythical fantasies of Renaud Camus, for example, discussed in the previous chapter. Finally, President Sarkozy was successful in recruiting Badiou's so-called "rats" (former leftists) to his team. These included not only André Glucksmann, but also Bernard Kouchner of *Médecins sans frontières* who joined Sarkozy's cabinet.

But in reifying France's political present under the sign of the "Pétainist transcendental" and in refusing to acknowledge any real differences between the political parties and their leaders, including the National Front and Le Pen, Badiou deliberately obscures obvious and important differences. These include crucial policy differences in the present and, more central to our purposes here, profound differences in attitude toward the past and the Dark Years in particular. Le Pen's recent and not-so-recent pro-Pétainist and anti-Semitic provocations are well documented, and have been discussed earlier here. François Hollande's speech to commemorate the Vel d'Hiv roundups shortly after his inauguration as president has also been mentioned in the Introduction. It is important to stress that in Badiou's blanket condemnations of a decadent French Republic and its "homogeneous" democracy, these sharp not to say radical distinctions where history and historical vision are concerned are ignored.

To return to Sarkozy himself: Badiou's ideologically over-determined reading of the president and his historic significance leads to other, substantial interpretive blind spots and distortions. Most obviously, Sarkozy *overtly rejected* the Occupation and the Vichy past as an historical touchstone as part of his rejection of a politics and culture of "repentance" with which he felt France had been saddled. At the same time, Sarkozy embraced the legacy of the Resistance, not only in the Guy Môquet Affair, but also in his "pilgrimages" to the plateau of Glières. These events are not discussed in *The Meaning of Sarkozy* and thus the legacy of Gaullism itself appears subsumed in Badiou's relentless attempt to establish an "analogous Pétainism" in Sarkozy's 2007 victory and presidency.

Finally—and ironically—in reading the "meaning of Sarkozy" as he did in his 2008 book, and in linking Sarkozy and present day France to the "Pétainist transcendental," Badiou overlooks striking similarities between his vision of history and Sarkozy's own. If Badiou's vision of history is grounded not in an historical continuum but in a series of disconnected "sequences" and Events, Sarkozy's own narrative of France's past is also grounded in a vision of disparate phenomena, where the arrival on the scene of "great men" function essentially as Badioulian Events. And Sarkozy's narrative is articulated in such a way as to offer no substantive historical logic or cohesiveness. In a highly critical assessment of Sarkozy's historical vision and narrative, and the commemorative undertakings which define it, the historian Nicholas

Offenstadt underscores this incoherence by noting that that vision and narrative constitute "a huge hodgepodge, where everything bumps into everything else, just like in a night club with its spinning neon lights: great names (Jean Jaurès, Joan of Arc), great events (the Crusades, the Second World War) everything is mixed together without hierarchy, without context, without any concern for explanation."[61] Ultimately without intelligibility and substance, Sarkozy's vision of the past immobilizes, ossifies it as well. For Offenstadt, Sarkozy's vision of the past is nothing more than "Bling-Bling History."

Alain Badiou's admirers would of course reject any comparison of Badiou's philosophy of the Event and his dissection of France's ills and the "meaning" of Sarkozy in *The Meaning of Sarkozy* with the superficiality of the former president's "Bling Bling History." Still, in their reification of the past, and the Vichy past in particular, and their deliberate historical de-contextualization of that past for their own political purposes, the two men prove to be strange bedfellows indeed.

NOTES

1. "Eric Conan, Badiou, le star de la philo est-il un salaud?," *Marianne*, 27 February, 2010.
2. Ibid.
3. In a recent interview with the journalist Edwy Plenel, Badiou has stood by this argument. See Philippe Raynaud, *L'Extrême gauche plurielle* (Paris: Perrin, 2010), 256.
4. Philippe Raynaud, *L'extrême gauche plurielle* (Paris: Perrin, 2010), 174.
5. In the recent *Métaphysique du bonheur réel* (Paris: PUF, 2015), Badiou has also discusses the uprisings in Tahir Square in Cairo during the "Arab Spring" as an Event, 49–50.
6. Alain Badiou, "The Three Negations," *Cardoza Law Review* 29:5 (2008): 1878.
7. Ibid., 1881.
8. Ibid., 1882.
9. Barbara Will, "The Resistance Syndrome: Alain Badiou on Samuel Beckett," *South Central Review* 31:1 (Spring 2014): 124.
10. Ibid., 126.
11. Quoted in Hewlett, 345.
12. George Orwell, "Homage to Catalonia," in *Orwell in Spain* (London: Penguin, 2001), 33., emphasis added.
13. Simon Critchley, "Why Badiou is a Rousseauist and why We should be too." *Cardoza Law Review* 29:5 (2008): 1933.
14. Ibid.
15. For a discussion of the Badiou-Schmitt connection, see Colin Wright, "Event or Exception: Disentangling Badiou from Schmitt, or, Towards a Politics of the Void," *Theory and Event* 11:2 (2008).

16. Steve Corcoran, "Introduction to Badiou, *Polemics.,* xi.
17. *Polemics*, 161.
18. Ibid., 164.
19. Eric Marty, *Une querelle avec Alain Badiou, philosophe* (Paris Gallimard, 2007), 58.
20. Ibid., 67.
21. Ibid., 92.
22. For Badiou's frankly disappointing and ad hominem response to Eric Marty, see "The Word 'Jew' and the Syncophant," in *Polemics*, 230–47.
23. Ibid., 215.
24. Ibid., 76.
25. Ibid., 80.
26. Ibid., 83.
27. Ibid., 84.
28. Ibid., 86
29. Ibid., 93.
30. Ibid., 97.
31. Alain Badiou, *The Meaning of Sarkozy* (London: Verso, 2008), 8.
32. Ibid., 8.
33. Ibid., 8. In the Introduction to the English language edition, Badiou also refers to Ségolène Royale as a "painted goat," 6.
34. Ibid., 9.
35. Ibid.
36. Ibid., 12.
37. Ibid., 13.
38. Ibid., 14.
39. Ibid., 15.
40. Ibid., 16.
41. Ibid.
42. Ibid., 18.
43. Ibid., 19–20.
44. Ibid., 26.
45. Idid.
46. Ibid., 35.
47. Ibid., 36.
48. Ibid., 29.
49. Ibid., 37. As Badiou describes the event of May 1968 and the moral and ethical dichotomy it establishes here, it seems very much at odds with universal pretentions of a real, true Event, as opposed to its simulacrum. Gary Gutting writes that "a genuine event calls for fidelity from everyone and generates a truth process leading to universal truths." By contrast a "terroristic simulacrum, like Nazism, addresses itself to a particular group of individuals." (See Gary Gutting, *Thinking the Impossible: French Philosophy since 1960* [Oxford: Oxford UP, 2011], 81) As Badiou discusses May 1968 here, it sounds more like a simulacrum than an Event.
50. Ibid., 77.
51. Ibid.

52. Ibid., 78.
53. Ibid.
54. Ibid., 83.
55. Ibid., 80.
56. Ibid., 85.

57. In the Introduction to *The Meaning of Sarkozy* Badiou responds to Assouline, whom he describes as "a man of admittedly limited intelligence" (4) by stating that he is referring to Freud's "Rat Man," not to the disparaging images of Jews in Vichy propaganda during the Occupation.

58. Alain Badiou, interview with Eric Hazan, "Roads to Renegacy," *New Left Review 53* (September–October 2008).

59. Nick Hewlett, "Alain Badiou and the *idée communiste*," *Contemporary French Civilization* 37:1 (2012): 51.

60. Alain Badiou, "The Three Negations," *Cardozo Law Review* 29:5 (2008), 1883.

61. Nicholas Offenstadt, *L'Histoire Bling-Bling: le retour du roman national* (Paris: Stock, 2009), 23–24.

Chapter 4

Remaking the *Mode Rétro*
Perversion and the "Pulping" of History in Jonathan Litell's The Kindly Ones

When Jonathan Littell's novel *The Kindly Ones* appeared in France in fall 2006, it created a sensation.[1] Published by the nation's most prestigious publishing house, Gallimard, the novel was immediately praised as a literary masterpiece by many and condemned by others as nothing short of an obscenity, an apology for Nazism, and a work that should never have been published. Even though the novelist himself, a previously unknown young American writer and former NGO worker, anticipated only meager sales for his novel—he had written it, he stated in an interview, for "the happy few"[2]—the novel's sales were record breaking, reaching more than 700,000 copies in its first year. Praised by eminent intellectual and literary figures including Jorge Semprun, Julia Kristeva, and Pierre Assouline among others, *The Kindly Ones* also won the prestigious Goncourt Prize that year as well as the *Grand Prix du Roman de l'Académie Française*.

The fictional memoirs of SS Lieutenant Colonel Doctor Maximilian Aue, now living peacefully and anonymously in present-day France where he is the retired director of a lace factory, *The Kindly Ones* recounts Aue's wartime experiences over some nine hundred pages. A kind of Nazi Zelig or Forrest Gump, Aue has been almost everywhere in the war in the east, the so-called "Bloodlands," contested by Hitler and Stalin. He has followed the *Einsatzgruppen* into the Ukraine and has participated in the grizzly slaughter of Jews along the way, including at Babi Yar. Aue has also fought and been severely wounded at Stalingrad. After evacuation to safety in Berlin, he is assigned to deal with slave labor needs at the death camps, and visits Auschwitz

---

Portions of this chapter were originally published as Richard J. Golsan, "Perversion and Pulp: Reading Edgar Rice Burroughs and Figuring America in *Les Bienveillantes*," *Yale French Studies*, 121 (2012): 204–26.

and other camps as part of his duties. He vacations in Occupied Paris, where he meets collaborationist journalists and writers like Lucien Rebatet and Robert Brasillach, both of whom worked for the notorious pro-Nazi newspaper *Je suis partout*. Present at the fall of Berlin in Spring 1945, Aue ultimately murders his best friend Thomas, steals his *STO* papers,[3] and flees the German capital in the face of the oncoming Soviet army. During the course of his wartime adventures, Aue encounters almost everyone of significance in the Nazi hierarchy. He becomes acquainted with Heinrich Himmler, Albert Speer, Adolph Eichmann, and Rudolph Hoess, the commandant at Aushwitz. At novel's end, he meets Hitler himself, whose nose he twists in a comically gratuitous act.

Remarkable for its harrowing and horrifyingly graphic descriptions of the destruction wrought by Hitler's war against the Soviet Union, *The Kindly Ones* is also striking for its frank and detailed portrait of its protagonist's sexuality, his sadomasochistic impulses, and his murderousness. A homosexual who has also had incestuous relations with his sister, Una, (and with whom he has two twin sons, Tristan and Orlando) Aue's sexual partners include fellow Nazi officers, and a Russian prostitute, Mihaï. Evident intermittently throughout the novel, Aue's sadomasochistic impulses are most spectacularly indulged in a section near the end of the novel entitled *Aire*. Alone in his sister's deserted house, Aue abuses himself repeatedly, sodomizing himself with a tree branch, among other distasteful acts. He brutally murders his mother and stepfather, strangling the former and butchering the latter with axe blows. He also murders the aforementioned Thomas and Mihaï. Aue crushes Mihaï's neck with a mop handle. For these killings, as well as others, Aue expresses no remorse.

Given the historical scope and ambition of *The Kindly Ones* as well the novel's relentless focus on the psychosexual and other excesses of its protagonist,[4] it is not surprising that the novel's admirers as well as its detractors stressed these dimensions of the work in offering their assessments of it in the weeks and months following its publication. Its historical scope (and length) inspired some admirers to compare Littell's novel to such masterpieces as Tolstoy's *War and Peace* and Vasily Grossman's *Life and Fate*.[5] Other admirers praised the work for its alleged *historical* contributions, along with its literary accomplishments. In a special feature of *Le débat* devoted to the *The Kindly Ones* appearing in Spring 2007, Pierre Nora lauded the work as an "extraordinary phenomenon" both in literary *and* historical terms.[6] According to Nora, Littell had achieved nothing less than the "reintegration of the Shoah into the entire history of the war."[7] The French in particular, he added, were prone to "dehistoricizing" the former, and so *The Kindly Ones* constituted a necessary historical "correction" which, apparently, historians had not previously provided.[8]

Littell's detractors viewed the novel's historical dimensions, and especially its graphic depictions of the Nazis' slaughter of Jews, in starkly different terms. In *Holocauste ordinaire,* Pierre Emmanuel Dauzat decried the horror of these descriptions, attributing the extraordinary critical and popular success of Littell's novel in France to its status as "a feast of corpses" masquerading as literature. Kept thus at an "artistic" remove the crimes depicted titillated French audiences who remained nevertheless anxious to forget their country's very real and willing participation in the Nazi deportations, and the Final Solution itself.[9] In *Les Complaisantes: Jonathan Littell et l'écrture du mal,* the historian Edouard Husson and philosopher Michel Terestchenko went further. Rejecting the idea that history, and the history of World War II and the Holocaust in particular, can or should be recounted through the eyes of a *bourreau,* or perpetrator, Husson and Terestchenko accused Littell of historical revisionism of the worst sort. And, focusing on the novel's *outré* sexuality not only in its representations of Aue's own sexual adventures but, for example, in its depictions of men's bodies' ejaculating as they are being hung, Husson and Terschenko accused the novelist of "using sex to make [the reader] love Nazi violence."[10] Referring to works of the 1970s associated with the *mode rétro* such as Liliana Cavani's film *The Night Porter* (other critics referred as well to Visconti's film *The Damned* and Michel Tournier's novel *The Ogre*), Husson and Terestchenko emphasized that this linkage was nothing new. And although they ultimately dismissed *The Kindly Ones* as nothing more than a *canular,* or adolescent prank, the authors of *Les Complaisantes* stressed that the success of the novel was nevertheless symptomatic of a of a society which had lost its aesthetic and moral (not to mention its historical) bearings.[11]

From the standpoint of the present study, the possibility that Jonathan Littell's *The Kindly Ones* represents a kind of "repetition" or "remake" of a 1970s *mode rétro* work raises a number of interesting questions. First, why would Littell adopt an apparently outdated aesthetic model and historical vision to create a "memory of a memory" as it were, in writing his novel? What textual evidence in *The Kindly Ones,* aside from the general characteristics noted by Husson and Terstchenko above, confirms this inspiration? If Littell's novel relies essentially on a supposedly outmoded aesthetics and historical vision, what accounts for the novel's enormous popular success, as well as its critical *succès de scandale* in contemporary France? Finally, what does that success tell us about the memory of the Dark Years now? To answer these questions, it is first necessary to take a closer look at the *mode rétro* and what its critics have to say about aesthetic practices and historical vision of its most representative works.

THE *MODE RÉTRO*

Used to label a period in the early-to-mid 1970s in France (and elsewhere in Europe) as well as representative cinematic and literary works of that period, the *mode rétro* is characterized, first, by a nostalgia and fascination for the recent past, and Nazism and fascism in particular. In many if not most of its cultural manifestations, it is also characterized by an eroticization of these ideologies, most often through representations of sexual deviance.

Why Nazism—and fascism more broadly—and sexuality? And why the most extreme expressions of the latter in the form of sadomasochism and other deviant practices? In her recent book *Screen Nazis: Cinema, History, and Democracy* Sabine Hake (following earlier critics like Laura Frost)[12] argues that the "coupling of fascism and sexuality" became a means in the 1970s of "acknowledging both the enduring attraction of fascism as a system of total control and the necessity of post fascist societies to contain the threat, namely by identifying it with deviant sexuality."[13] This phenomenon is clearly evident in films like Luchino Visconti's 1969 film *The Damned* which features Nazi homosexuality, cross-dressing, and even incest. In Liliana Cavani's *The Night Porter*, a concentration camp survivor, played by Charlotte Rampling, is drawn back into a sadomasochistic romance with her former SS tormentor, played by Dirk Bogarde. They meet accidentally in a hotel in postwar Vienna, where Bogarde's character is now working clandestinely as the night porter. Other films in the genre include two 1975 films, Lina Wertmüller's *Seven Beauties* and Passolini's *Salò or the 120 Days of Sodom,* but they also include a string of "Nazi porn" or "Nazi sexploitation" films such as *Nazi Hell Camp* (1977), and *Caligula Reincarnated as Hitler* (1976). According to Hake, what distinguishes these lower budget and lower production value Nazi porn films from the more aesthetically accomplished films of the *mode retro* is that in the former, "porn and horror are merged, and the primary focus is on violence." Also "revulsion is the most important bodily affect."[14]

Hake is not alone in identifying fascism's continuing appeal as a crucial—the crucial—component of the advent of the *mode rétro* as well as its aesthetic manifestations. In her classic 1974 essay "Fascinating Fascism," on the works and political rehabilitation of the Nazi filmmaker Leni Reifenstahl, Susan Sontag writes that although National Socialism is generally associated with "brutishness and terror," it, and fascism more broadly, also stands for ideals that "are persistent today under other banners; the ideal of life as art, the cult of beauty, the fetishism of courage, the dissolution of alienation in ecstatic feelings of community: the repudiation of the intellect; the family of man (under the parenthood of leaders). These ideals are vivid and moving to many people. . ."[15]

For Saul Friedländer, the persistent attraction of Nazism is more sinister still. He argues, first, that historically, Nazism's appeal "lay less in any explicit ideology than in the power of emotion, images, and fantasms."[16] But the "new discourse" embodied in French *mode rétro* works like Michel Tournier's *The Ogre* reveals the underside of this appeal in exposing a "deep structure based on the coexistence of the adoration of power with a dream of final explosion—the annulment of all power."[17] This "dream of final explosion" is ultimately a longing for death, but not "real death in its everyday horror and tragic banality, but a ritualized, stylized and aestheticized death which ultimately appears as a poisonous apotheosis."[18] This is precisely where Nazism connects with sexual deviance and sadomasochism, in particular, at least in the imaginary of the 1970s. According to Sontag:

> Sadomasochism has always been the furthest reach of sexual experience: when sex becomes most purely sexual, that is, severed from personhood, from relationships, from love. It should not be surprising that it became attached to Nazi symbolism in recent years. Never before was the relation of masters and slaves so consciously aestheticized. Sade had to make up his theatre of punishment and delight from scratch, improvising the décor and costumes and blasphemous rites. Now there is a master scenario available for everyone. The color is black, the seduction is beauty, the justification is honesty, the aim is ecstasy, the fantasy is death.[19]

If the analyses of Sontag, Friedländer, and Hake more recently offer insights into the psychosexual dynamics of the *mode rétro*, what of its politics and historical vision? And what are its political and historical origins, especially in France? In his 1981 essay "History: A Retro Scenario," Jean Baudrillard offers answers to both questions in commenting on recent films in the genre. First, diagnosing the malaise of the historical moment that produced *mode rétro* movies, Baudrillard writes that history had "invaded" the cinema in the *rétro* period in the early seventies and beyond because the "historical stake" had been chased from contemporary life by what he describes as "this immense neutralization which is dubbed peaceful co-existence on a global level, and pacified monotony on the quotidian level."[20] Baudrillard adds: "Anything serves to escape this void, this leukemia of history and politics, this hemorrhage of values" and "it is in proportion to this distress that all content can be invoked pell-mell, that all previous history is resurrected in bulk—a controlling idea no longer selects, only nostalgia endlessly accumulates: war, fascism, the pageantry of the belle époque, or the revolutionary struggles, everything is equivalent and mixed indiscriminately in the same morose and funereal exaltation, in the same retro fascination."[21]

In his own comments on the *mode rétro* given in an interview appearing in *Cahiers du Cinéma* in Summer 1974, Michel Foucault detects a similar fundamental historical "indifferentiation" or nihilism in *mode rétro* works. But for Foucault, this historical indifferentiation or nihilism carries a politically reactionary message. Discussing Louis Malle's film *Lacombe Lucien* about a peasant boy in southwestern France in 1944 who joins the German police essentially by accident after being turned down by the Resistance,

Foucault states that the film's message is: "there are no heroes." But hidden in this phrase is a different—and truer—meaning of the film: "There are no heroes because there is no struggle." That is, the very idea of popular struggle, of revolution, so dear to the French left, is an illusion, simply a lie. Casting its vision backward in time, the film also articulates the message that the Resistance itself was a sham. Foucault writes: "Take something like the Resistance, even this glorious past you've talked about so much, just look at it for a moment . . . Nothing. Its empty, a hollow façade."[22]

What historical and political circumstance besides those identified by Baudrillard could also account for the advent of the *mode rétro?* Hake, for her part, insists on the importance of the revolutionary year of 1968 and the changing ideological, political, and sexual terrain it opened up.[23] In France, the revolutionary events of May 1968 were followed in short order by the downfall of Charles de Gaulle, and with him the prestige, sanctities, and myths associated with the Resistance. It is not surprising then, that the *mode rétro* roughly coincided with, and followed on what for Henry Rousso constitutes the "Broken Mirror" phase of the Vichy syndrome. During the "Broken Mirror" phase, encouraged by the release of films like *The Sorrow and the Pity* and *Lacombe Lucien,* the troubling realities of complicity and collaboration during the Dark Years came rushing back to public consciousness. Additionally, by way of explaining what some considered the shocking sexuality of *mode rétro* works, Lynn Higgins notes that early in his presidency, Valéry Giscard d'Estaing had loosened censorship laws, and sexual liberation was expressing itself in numerous films released at that time. In fact, the highest grossing film in France in 1974 was Just Jaeckin's *Emmanuelle,* which later became the first X-rated film released in the United States.

Although the analyses of the *mode rétro* discussed so far refer to earlier times and earlier works, it is not difficult to recognize general attributes of the genre in the historical and political vision it purportedly espouses in *The Kindly Ones.* Certainly, the fundamental historical nihilism to which Max Aue gives voice to in the novel, and which will be examined in greater detail here, ultimately diminishes or erases political and ideological differences rather than underscoring them. And in its Forrest Gump-like "been there, done that" narrative along with the narrator's historical ruminations, especially at the outset of the novel, it recalls Baudrillard's notion of history being recalled "in bulk" and indiscriminately mixed together "in the same morose and funereal exaltation, in the same retro fascination."[24] Also, obviously Aue's over-the-top sexuality and ultimately murderous sadomasochism fit the mold of 1970s Nazis, whether in more high-brow *mode rétro* films or Nazi porn works. There are other comparisons as well. In *Les Bienveillantes décryptés* Marc Limonier notes that the female entourage of Aue's mentor Mandelbrod, consisting of three SS "amazons" Hilde, Helga, and Hedwig, are deliberately reminiscent of precisely the sadistic, sex-craving "heroines" of Nazi films porn including not only those mentioned earlier, but also those like *Helge, She-Wolf of Stilberg* and *Erica, or the Final Days of the SS*.[25] One might also add that Max and Una's twin sons Orlando and Tristan recall SS twins in *The Ogre* with whom the novel's protagonist is much taken.

But to fully appreciate the ways in which the aesthetics, thematics, and historical vision associated with the *mode rétro* are woven into the fabric of *The Kindly Ones*, it is necessary to consider a curious "intertext" in Littell's novel. This intertext is comprised of references to the works of the American science fiction and pulp writer, Edgar Rice Burroughs. A close look at the "Burroughs connection," so to speak, should help elucidate not only the degree to which the novel "replays" the *mode rétro* or offers a "post" variation on the theme (in keeping with Littell's musical motif in the novel) and to what ends, but also what *The Kindly Ones* and its reception have to say about the memory of the Dark Years in France now.

THE BURROUGHS CONNECTION

In three significant instances in T*he Kindly Ones,* Maximilien Aue alludes to the works of Edgar Rice Burroughs. The first reference is to Burroughs's most famous creation, Tarzan the "Lord of the Jungle." After handing over a Ukrainian Jewish girl to a Waffen-SS soldier to be executed in the section of the novel entitled *Allemandes I and II,* Aue walks into the nearby forest. As the salvos announcing the girl's death crackle behind him, Aue recalls an episode from his own childhood when he received a three-volume set of Tarzan novels from his father. These he "read and re-read [. . .] with passion."[26] Emulating Burroughs' hero, Aue explains that he would enter the forests around Keil where his family lived, strip naked and then, lying down on beds of pine needles, enjoy "the little pricks on my skin."[27] Although Aue acknowledges that these were not "explicitly erotic games" because he was too young for that, he does state that through these games "the entire forest [became] an erogenous zone, a vast skin as sensitive as my naked child's skin, bristling in the cold."[28]

Later, however, the games in question do take an explicitly erotic—and sadomasochistic—turn. Stripping naked in the forest, Aue would "hang myself with my belt from a tree branch, and let myself go with all my weight; my blood, thrown into a panic, made my face swell, my temples beat to the point of bursting, my breath came in wheezes."[29] Having pushed his body's tolerance to the limit, Aue would then stand up, and begin again. Contrasting the forest of his childhood and adolescence with that of the present, Aue reminisces that the woods used to be "full of keen pleasure and boundless freedom." But now, as Jews are being murdered behind him, the woods fill Aue "with fear."[30]

The second substantial reference to the works of Edgar Rice Burroughs occurs in the section of the novel entitled *Courante*, when Aue is enraged with his mother for taking up with the Frenchman Moreau. While living with his stepfather and mother in France, Aue describes his discovery of Burroughs' Martian novels, which he "devoured with the same passion as the Greek Classics."[31] Like the Tarzan novels, the Martian novels are linked to Aue's burgeoning sexuality and sadomasochism. But here, they inspire much more extreme autoerotic and deviant sexual impulses:

> I locked myself in the large upstairs bathroom, running the water so as not to attract attention, and created extravagant scenes from my imaginary world. Captured by an army of four green men from Barsoom [The name Burroughs gives to the planet Mars in his novels], I was stripped naked, bound and led before a superb copper-skinned Martian princess, haughty and impassive on her throne. There, using a belt for the leather bonds and with a broom or bottle stuck in my anus, I writhed on the cold tiles while a half-dozen of her massive, mute bodyguards took turns raping me in front of her.[32]

Aue continues:

> But the brooms and bottles could hurt: I looked for something more suitable. Moreau loved thick German sausages; at night, I took one from the fridge, rolled it between my hands to warm it up, lubricated it with olive oil: afterward, I washed it carefully, dried it, and put it back where I found it. The next day, I watched Moreau and my mother slicing it up and eating it with great pleasure, and I refused my portion with a smile, offering a lack of appetite as my excuse, delighted at going hungry so that they could eat.[33]

The final substantial reference to the works of Edgar Rice Burroughs and his Mars novels in particular occurs near the end of *The Kindly Ones* in the section *Menuet (en Rondeaux)*. Aue is recovering from a fever and the Nazi Reich is shaken to its foundations by military reversals and the 1944 failed attempt on Hitler's life. Aue spends his recovery reading, and rediscovers his collection of Burroughs' Martian adventures. He reads "these three books at one go," fascinated, once again by the novels' "confused eroticism" and the presence in them of "warriors and princesses wearing nothing but weapons and jewelry" and "a whole weird jumble of monsters and machines."[34] But despite the Martian novels' apparent lack of "seriousness," in rereading them Aue makes a stunning discovery: "certain passages in these science fiction novels, in fact, revealed this American prose writer as one of the unknown precursors of *völkish* thinking."[35] Aue drafts a memorandum to his superiors in which he cites "Burroughs as a model of reform for *the profound social reforms that the SS should envisage after the war.*"[36] He proposes the civilization of the race of red Martians as a general model for the SS. But for the SS elite, Aue proposes the race of green Martians, "those three-meter-tall monsters with four arms and fangs." What interests Aue most is the green Martians' reproductive practices: *"Their mating is a matter of community interest solely, and is directed without reference to natural selection. The council of chieftains of each community controls the matter as surely as the owner of a Kentucky racing stud directs the scientific breeding of his stock for the improvement of the whole."*[37] Recalling that "the passages from Burroughs reminded me obscurely of the prophetic utopia [Himmler] had revealed to us in Kiev, in 1941," Aue sends his memorandum to the SS leader, Heinrich Himmler. Ten days later, Aue receives a personal response from the *Reichsführer* praising Aue for his "useful research" and expressing the desire to discuss this "visionary author" with Aue in more detail. However, nothing ultimately comes of the memorandum, or of Himmler's interest in what it proposes. Learning of Aue's memo, his mentor and protector Mandelbrod admonishes Aue not to indulge in such "childish pranks" and think instead about "Germany's salvation."[38]

In terms of graphic depictions of sexual deviance and its close relation to violence and death so characteristic of *mode rétro* films and novels of the 1970s, it is hard not to recognize worthy successors or replicas of these depictions in the first two episodes just described. In fact, in the revulsion Aue's sexual transgressions are undoubtedly intended to inspire, these scenes clearly veer towards the aesthetics of "Nazi porn" as described by Sabine Hake and discussed earlier here. Additionally, the fact that Aue's sadomasochistic impulses are reinforced by his allegiance to Nazism, and that they lead ultimately to homicide and death are suggested not only by Aue's feeding of the "tainted" sausage to his mother and stepfather before eventually murdering them, but also by his evocations of his Tarzan-inspired eroticism after turning the Jewish girl over to die. As the first Burroughs episode confirms, the transformation of the forest itself from a place of erotic fantasy to a place of murder and death marks a "closing in" of the former such that, for Aue, it is no longer synonymous with freedom. Rather, the forest becomes a kind of prison from which death is the only way out. This claustrophobic dimension of the forest, evident as well in the final episodes of the novel, is also reminiscent of earlier *mode rétro* works and their Nazi porn derivations. *The Night Porter* ends with the Charlotte Rampling and Dirk Bogart characters trapped in the night porter's apartment surrounded by his former fellow Nazis who are intent on killing them. The Nazi Porn films most often occur in prison camps or castles, where the worst abuses of all kinds can be carried out with impunity by the Nazis against their innocent victims. Even for film critics writing at the time, a feeling of claustrophobia could constitute the movie's most powerful effect. Describing his sensations while viewing *The*

Damned in the theatre, Roger Ebert wrote, "The effect is claustrophobic, and we want out. We want sun; we want light; we want to see."[39]

Despite these parallels between *The Kindly Ones* and *mode réetro* works in their fascination with sexual deviance and Nazi violence, Littell himself rejects the connection as "clichéd." He claims as well to have detested works like Visconti's *The Damned,* although he admits to having been "very much aware" (*très conscient*) of these films at the time. In his interview with Pierre Nora published in 2007, Littell argues that what distinguishes his work from those of Visconti and other *mode rétro* artists is the "inscription" of the "documented real" in *The Kindly Ones*.[40] It is precisely this commitment to historical accuracy and detail, he continues, which *mode rétro* works like *The Damned* lack.

If, as Littell claims, his novel distinguishes itself from *mode rétro* works through its commitment to historical accuracy, to the "documented real," do the Burroughs episodes in *Kindly Ones* support this claim? Or conversely, do they provide evidence of the kind of historical revisionism which many critics identified in *mode rétro* works and which often served (reactionary) political ends? Of the three episodes in which Burrough's fiction is invoked, the final episode, in which Aue recommends the green Martians' reproductive methods as models for the SS and characterizes Burroughs himself as a precursor of *volkische* thinking, is the most freighted historically and politically. In terms of historical accuracy, *was* Edgar Rice Burroughs a reactionary whose supposedly racist politics championed a Nazi-like commitment to eugenic practices on a national scale? Are his works essentially propaganda along these lines? Additionally, why the focus on Burroughs, an iconic American novelist but nevertheless a pulp-fiction author, to the exclusion of other, more artistically accomplished and at least equally iconic American writers? In a novel that bristles with "high-brow" literary and cultural references—Flaubert, Aeshylus, the poetry of François Villon, the music of Bach—the inclusion of Burroughs and his work is an anomaly.

In order to answer these questions and ultimately address the broader historical and political implications of the inclusion of the "Burroughsian intertext" in *The Kindly Ones*, a brief review of the life and career of Burroughs himself is helpful. Edgar Rice Burroughs began his career writing escapist popular fiction with the aforementioned *A Princess of Mars,* published in book form in 1912.[41] He went on to publish dozens and dozens of works of fantasy and science fiction, including the novels of the Mars or "Barsoom" series. Most famous as the creator of Tarzan, Burroughs is also widely remembered for creating other popular fictional heroes like John Carter of the Martian series, Carson Napier of Venus, the Julian Clan of *The Moon Maid* series and, lastly, Tangor of Paloda, a planet lost in spatial reaches literally *Beyond the Farthest Star,* the title of a posthumously published novel appearing in 1964.

That Burroughs was hugely successful as a popular writer is attested to by the large fortune he accumulated, the extraordinary global sales of his novels, and their translation into multiple languages. In 1939 the *Saturday Evening Post* declared Burroughs the "world's greatest writer" on the basis of these accomplishments.[42] By that year, Burroughs had earned more than ten million dollars for his work, sold twenty-five million copies of the Tarzan series alone, and seen his fiction translated into fifty-six languages.

Burroughs was himself a fascinating figure, and also, during his lifetime and afterwards, occasionally a politically controversial one as well. Born into a very comfortable middle class background in Chicago in 1875, Burroughs was the son of a minor industrialist and Civil War veteran. Despite his privileged origins, however, Burroughs' road to success was hardly uncomplicated. An indifferent student, Burroughs also proved equally feckless in his early efforts to find a vocation or launch a career. Eventually, with the help of his father, he sought and received a commission in the army. He served in the Arizona territory, where he was sporadically involved in chasing Indians. But health problems combined with the tedium of military life led Burroughs to resign his commission.

The list of Burroughs' subsequent occupations before he began his successful writing career at age thirty-five is quite long, and marked by failure. He worked as a railroad detective and briefly as a manager for Sears. While working as a pencil sharpener wholesaler and making inadequate money to support his wife and children, he began writing fiction. His first two works, *A Princess of Mars* and *Tarzan of the Apes* (1914) were both immediately highly successful, and his career as a writer was launched.

As his fame and fortune increased, Burroughs moved to California, where the estate he bought, developed, and sold eventually became the town of Tarzana. In California, he continued to efficiently exploit his successful creations. He also indulged his taste for horses and expensive cars. He took flying lessons, and became involved in the movie industry, writing and proposing screen-plays for Tarzan movies as well as picking their casts. Eventually, following the collapse of his first marriage and facing financial difficulties, Burroughs moved from California to Hawaii with his second wife. There he worked as a correspondent and witnessed the Japanese bombing of Pearl Harbor first-hand. His drinking increased dangerously, and his second wife left him. At the end of the war, Burroughs returned to California where he died on March 19, 1950, at the age of seventy-four.

If Burroughs' life and career appear at least superficially to be near-perfect examples of the fulfillment of the American Dream (and in some ways, its sad demise), his politics, like those of many "self-made men," were conventional and notably conservative. Burroughs was a staunch Republican. He detested "Democrats, the New Deal, and liberalism."[43] He was also extremely patriotic, even jingoistic. Strongly influenced by his background and upbringing, he was anti-labor and fiercely anti-Communist in his views. His anti-Communism became pronounced following World War I during the post-Bolshevik Revolution Red Scare. In an essay entitled "Red Blood and Red Flag," Philip R. Burger notes that a novella Burroughs wrote at the time that eventually became part of *The Moon Maid* saga dealing with the invasion of earth by moon men or "Kalkars" began as a story of a Communist takeover of the United States entitled "Under the Red Flag." As stand-ins for "Commies" the Kalkars, Burger stresses, are not just evil, they are "a potent symbol of the fears that pressed on white America at the time."[44] These fears included a perceived threat not only to the nation's class structure, but to its racial divisions as well. On the latter score, Richard Slotkin argues that Burroughs was influenced by Teddy Roosevelt, who believed in the "superiority of the White American racial stock, which had been highly selected from the best of the Nordic peoples."[45] Slotkin also claims that after 1916 (after the publication of *A Princess of Mars*) Burroughs was "directly influenced" by the works of racialist historians Madison Grant and Theodore Lothrop Stoddard, leaders of the eugenics movement whose activities and attitudes helped sustain segregation. However, in the Porges biography of Burroughs to which Slotkin refers in his latter claims, there is no mention of either Grant or Lothrop, nor of their work, although Burroughs' interest in eugenics in the 1920s is documented.

Burroughs' anti-Communism was also in evidence in the post–World War II years when, as Porges points out, his daily schedule included listening to the radio broadcasts of the conservative and reactionary commentator, Fulton Lewis. Like Burroughs an opponent of FDR and the New Deal before World War II, Lewis was also a strong supporter of Charles Lindbergh and his America First Committee that opposed American intervention in the "European War."[46] After the war Lewis was an outspoken admirer of Senator Joseph McCarthy, and continued to support him after the latter's disgrace.

On the basis of Burroughs' characterization of Kalkars as possessing "prominent, hooked nose[s]" of being unclean and thus fitting the stereotype of the "Dirty Jew," and of their leader Or-tis as possessing "'a thin, cruel upper lip and a full and sensuous lower, "highlighting the Jew's supposedly cunning and lustful nature," Burger acknowledges that it is not implausible to speculate on Burroughs own anti-Semitic tendencies. He adds that the charge has been formally leveled by critics, especially for Burroughs' portrayal of the Jew Adolph Bluber in *Tarzan and the Golden Lion*. But for Burger Burroughs' apparent prejudice toward Jews stems less from a globalized hatred of *all* Jews than it does to his hatred of Bolschevism, whose "carriers" were perceived to be the large numbers of Slavs and East European immigrants arriving in the Middle West after World War I. Moreover, in *The Moon Maid* itself one of the martyred heroes in the American struggle against the

Kalkars is the Jewish tanner Moses Samuels. Finally, in Burroughs' defense Burger points out that stereotypes like those used in *The Moon Maid* novels are the stock and trade of popular fiction because they "evoke an immediate response in the reader, thereby eliminating the need for elaborate (and in adventure fiction, usually dull) characterizations."[47]

If Burroughs' fiction occasionally portrays villains in a troublingly and stereotypically anti-Semitic guise, his work and correspondence also confirm anti-German sentiments on the writer's part. According to Erling B. Holtsmark Burroughs' was "vociferously anti-German."[48] Initially, Burger argues, this was in response to World War I–era anti-German propaganda featuring brutal, barbaric (and lascivious) caricatures of the "Hun." In *The Land that Time Forgot,* the arch-villain Baron von Schoenvorts is in fact the treacherous and patrician U-boat captain who, if not openly lecherous, covets the young American girl Lys La Rue. In the immediate postwar years as well, Burroughs did not back away from his animosity towards the Germans. During early negotiations over the translation of his works into German, Burroughs wrote to his agent in September 1921: "If they [German publishers] knew half of what I thought of the Germans they would not want any of my books."[49]

During the mid-1920s, Burroughs became involved in a controversy that obliged him to take a public and more qualified view of Germany and the Germans, for both financial and personal reasons. By 1925, the German publisher Charles Dieck had profitably and successfully published German translations of several Tarzan novels. Tarzan had in fact become a staple of German popular culture, much to the chagrin of high-brow literary critics, rival publishers, and German nationalists who resented the popularity of literary creation of a foreign author. Early in 1925, Stefan Sorel published *Tarzan the German-Devourer,* a work that underscored strong anti-German sentiment in the untranslated novel *Tarzan the Untamed,* which included an episode in which a German officer is eaten by a lion and several other German characters are described as "Huns." A firestorm of controversy followed, in which Burroughs was widely attacked in the German press as "the basest German devourer existing in the Anglo-Saxon countries."[50] Felix Salten, the creator of *Bambi*, attacked Burroughs in print and worried that his fellow Germans had been infected by a "Tarzan epidemic" and that the books themselves had inspired a "literary grippe." Another commentator stated that the name of Tarzan had begun "to stink in Germany." As Porges notes, the entire press campaign against Burroughs and his creation was organized around "an appeal to German nationalism."

Efforts by Burroughs to stem the tide of German animosity by writing an open letter to the German people protesting his general affection for them and attributing anti-German sentiments and episodes to World War I to wartime propaganda (*Tarzan the Untamed* and *The Land that Time Forgot* were both written during the conflict) did no good. Book sales of the Tarzan novels dropped precipitously in Germany, and the publication of other Burroughs novels, including *A Princess of Mars*, which had already been translated, were halted. In the end Burroughs lamented in his correspondence the financial losses suffered by Dieck, and speculated that the entire affair was the result of the jealousy of other publishers and writers of Tarzan's success.

If the "Tarzan Affair," so to speak, provides a context for anti-German sentiments expressed in Burroughs' novels written during World War I, it also forced Burroughs to think through more carefully his attitudes towards Germans and other foreigners, and to renounce the inclusion of "propaganda" in the future (a resolve he did always not keep).[51] More importantly for our purposes here, it also sheds new light on the meaning and accuracy of the references to Burroughs and his work in *The Kindly Ones*. First, neither *A Princess of Mars* nor the next two books in the series would have been available in German when Aue supposedly received the works as a gift from his father. Second, given the broad perception in Germany that Tarzan and Burroughs himself were German haters or "devourers" and that their condemnation was necessary in the name of German nationalism, it seems highly unlikely that Aue's nationalist, *Freicorps* father would have offered works by Burroughs to his son. Finally, in this light, Aue's passion for these works and their author would hardly seem to be in keeping with his commitment to Nazism or his loyalty to his absent, nationalist father. In fact, reading Burroughs could be construed as an act of rebellion, even subversion.

Returning to Burroughs and Germany: with the Third Reich in power, Burroughs' anti-German sentiment became manifest once again, this time subsumed in a broader distaste for totalitarian regimes in general. Hitler and the Nazis constituted in fact one of his "pet abominations."[52] In the 1937 novel *Carson of Venus*, the writer presents a caricature of Nazi society and of Hitler himself in the country of the "Zanis" who must repeatedly show absolute allegiance to their ruler Mephis by prefacing "every greeting and introduction with the phrase 'Maltu Mephis!'"–"Hail Mephis." All Zanis are also required to regularly attend a play in one hundred and one episodes celebrating episodes from their ruler's life. Like Hitler's Brown Shirts, Mephis's Zani Guard are brutes who detest intelligence and rule by intimidation and violence. Later in the posthumous and little-known *Beyond the Farthest Star*, Burroughs offers another portrait of a Nazi-like society—and of totalitarian regimes more generally—in the warlike and terror-dominated society of Kapara, where power is maintained through fear, treachery and the encouragement of the citizens' denunciations of each other.

If works like *The Moon Maid, Carson of Venus* and *Beyond the Farthest Star* offer interesting, if potentially conflicting, insights into Burroughs's political—and racial—views over time, it is of course not to these works that

Maximilian Aue refers in his claim that the American writer is a legitimate if "unknown" precursor of *volkisch* thinking. Rather, it is to the Mars or Barsoom novels which Burroughs wrote between 1912 and 1948, a period of time spanning virtually his entire writing career as well as of course, two world wars, the rise of Fascism and Communism, and the beginnings of the Cold War.

There are eleven novels in the Burroughs' Mars series. The first novel, *A Princess of Mars*, introduces the hero of the entire series and the protagonist of several of the novels, John Carter. As his name suggests, Carter is not a Martian but an Earthman, a former captain in the Confederate army and later adventurer and prospector in the American southwest. As presented by his "nephew" Edgar Rice Burroughs in the *Foreword* to *A Princess of Mars*, Carter is exemplary and indeed perfect in every way. He is, as Burroughs describes him,

> A splendid specimen of manhood, standing a good two inches over six feet, broad of shoulder and narrow of hip, with the carriage of the trained fighting man. His features were regular and clear cut, his hair black and closely cropped, while his eyes were steel gray, reflecting a strong and loyal character, filled with fire and initiative. His manners were perfect, and his courtliness was that of a typical southern gentleman of the highest type.[53]

Transported at the outset of the novel from earth to Barsoom after apparently dying in a cave in the Arizona Territory while fleeing marauding Apaches, Carter awakens on Mars, a dying planet filled with deserts and abandoned cities surrounding dead sea bottoms, and where the thin air is artificially maintained by atmosphere plants. Despite its general desolation, however, Barsoom is very much inhabited, and richly so. Carter first encounters the fearsome six-limbed green men, a warrior and nomadic race. But the green Martians are only one of several Martian races. Carter meets, falls in love with, and ultimately marries Princess Dejah Thoris of the Heliumite Empire, and a member of Mars's predominant red race. While pursuing Dejah Thoris across the planet and rescuing her from numerous, lascivious Martian villains over the course of the first three novels in the series, Carter also encounters the race of "very handsome and highly intelligent black men," who reside in the South Polar Region.[54] In the frigid North Polar Region are the yellow men of Mars. The red Martians, Burroughs explains, are the most similar to "ourselves," that is "Anglo-Saxon" whites, except for two important characteristics. They are oviparous, and their natural life span is one thousand years, although because of "their warlike activities and the prevalence of assassinations among them" few live to enjoy their full life expectancy.

It is important to note that with the possible exception of the white race or "Therns" who are the murderous and degenerate keepers of the false religion of Isis, none of the Martian races are innately evil or inferior. Burroughs does acknowledge that in the hands of the red Martians rests "the progress and civilization—yes, the very life of Mars."[55] The green race, on the other hand, is the most warlike, and the "hereditary enemy" of all the other races of Mars. Burroughs says of them: "They are a cruel and taciturn race, entirely devoid of love, sympathy or pity."[56] In *A Princess of Mars* Carter is captured by the green Martians shortly after his arrival on the planet, and lives among them. He confirms at least part of Aue's claim in *The Kindly Ones* that children are communal property, and child raising a community activity. Maturing in their eggs for five years and kept in a communal incubator, the children are captured upon hatching as they flee the incubator, and the woman who captures each child becomes its foster mother. The children, Carter adds, "are entirely unknown to their own mothers who, in turn, would have difficulty in pointing out the father with any degree of accuracy."[57] Before the eggs are placed in the incubators, they are carefully selected for quality in an effort to assure that the green Martian who emerges is the strongest and fittest for survival in a hostile world. Carter adds: "Should they prove deformed or defective in any way, they are promptly shot."[58]

If the green Martians' crude but thorough efforts at racial engineering and the perfection of a warrior race in *A Princess of Mars* bear some resemblance to Nazi eugenic practices the themes of biological engineering recurs under a very different light in a later Barsoom novel, *Synthetic Men of Mars*. Published in 1938—after the rise of Nazism—*Synthetic Men of Mars* focuses on a brilliant scientist Ras Thavas who conceives of the creation of "the perfect man, and a new race of supermen [who] will inhabit Barsoom—beautiful, intelligent, deathless." To implement his dream Thavas creates a "vat of life" of primordial human tissue, out of which he hopes will emerge perfect human beings, as if by a kind of "spontaneous generation." But what emerges instead are horribly flawed and defective, but indestructible sub-humans or "Hormads," who are quickly drafted by into the army of the city of Morbus by political leaders whose ambition is ultimately to conquer all of Barsoom. However, before this occurs, the "vat of life" begins to overflow. It eventually engulfs the city of Morbus, and threatens to engulf the entire planet. It is ultimately destroyed by John Carter at novel's end.

That *Synthetic Men of Mars* is a cautionary tale warning against the dangers of racial and genetic engineering and its potential political exploitation seems clear. Its message in fact, belies Aue's claims concerning Burroughs' *völkische* thinking and eugenicist views. That being said, it is possible to argue the case that some aspects of Burroughs "romantic fantasies," to use Mike Ashley's label,[59] can be ascribed to what Aue calls "*völkisch* thinking," broadly defined. The Martian novels, like virtually all of Burroughs other works, champion martial values, virility, and natural political and social hierarchies dominated by aristocratic elites. And Burroughs' description of John Carter in *A Princess of Mars,* coupled with the accounts of his adventures and exploits in later works in the series, single Carter out as the perfect embodiment of these values. As such, he can arguably be seen as a prefiguring of sorts of future Nazi or "Aryan elites," without the blond hair and blue eyes, of course. Similarly, the green Martians extremely martial society, their crude eugenic practices and social Darwinism do make Aue's claims for them seem legitimate in his memorandum to Himmler. Additionally—although these details relate to Burroughs' views as apparently manifested in works *other* than the Martian series—the writer's hatred of Communism, as well as his occasional use of anti-Semitic stereotypes in his novels can be broadly lumped in with *volkisch* and Nazi ideology as well.

But if these aspects of Burroughs work and his Martian novels in particular could be interpreted as supporting Aue's claims for them in political terms, the discussions thus far also provide more substantial evidence to the contrary. From Burroughs' distaste for Germans and Germany (and German aristocratic militarism in particular, if the villains in his novels are representative examples) to his animosity toward Nazi and other totalitarian regimes obliquely expressed in works like *Carson of Venus* and *Beyond the Farthest Star,* to grave concerns over eugenics and the biological engineering of a perfect race as explored in *Synthetic Men of Mars,* all of this evidence contradicts Aue's expressed views. Moreover, where the eugenic practices of the green Martians are concerned as they are described in *A Princess of Mars* and *The Kindly Ones,* Burroughs' editorializing on them through his alter ego John Carter in the first Martian novel leaves little doubt that they are negatively construed. For the green Martians, according to Carter, "parental and filial love is as unknown to them as it is common to us." Moreover, the "horrible system" of reproductive and child-rearing practices that "has been carried out for ages is the direct cause of the loss of all finer feelings and higher humanitarian instincts among these poor creatures."[60] While such a loss of "finer feelings and higher humanitarian instincts" may be desirable to the SS elite, it is certainly not to Burroughs' hero. In any case, while John Carter is no "revolutionary," as Burroughs critics' point out, and while his political efforts in the novels occasionally makes him a defender of the status quo, he is also portrayed as endlessly fighting against brutal, tyrannical, and illegitimate regimes, as well as cruelty and injustice. John Seelye describes Carter as "a militaristic advocate of planetary peace, a missionary of racial coexistence."[61] In short, he is hardly an exemplary Nazi Aryan.

As a final comment on Burroughs' views of Nazism, Hitler, and the racial politics of the Reich, in 1938 Burroughs proposed a synopsis of a film, ironically entitled "Heil Hitler!" to several major Hollywood studios. According to the fictional plot of the film, one of the doubles Hitler was known to use in real life successfully impersonates Hitler after the Fuhrer is assassinated. But rather than continue Hitler's policies, this "humanitarian Hitler" reverses course entirely. He purges Nazi army officers as well as "Goebbels and other Jew baiters." The synopsis continues:

> Master of Germany, he [Hitler] removes all bans against Jews: restores free speech and free press; restores Austria to her former position as an independent state; returns the Sudeten to Czechoslovakia; enters into a pact with France and Great Britain that insures the peace of Europe and the World.[62]

Max Aue, of course, would hardly be aware of Burroughs' 1938 film synopsis, nor for that matter would Jonathan Littell likely know of its existence. Nevertheless, the synopsis of *Heil Hitler!* casts into sharper relief the extent to which the presentation of Burroughs' political thought as exemplified in the Martian novels is deliberately distorted and in fact ultimately perverted in *The Kindly Ones*. The same holds true, moreover, for the erotic and sexual dynamics at play in Burroughs' fictional worlds. Despite Aue's claim to the contrary—and the graphic anal rape scene imagined by Aue in the first reference to the Martian novel above—there is no "confused eroticism" in Burroughs' fiction. Rather, the works in question rely on and promote a very conventional heterosexuality, a heteronormativity, typical of both the genre and the times in which they were written. Erotic responses to the scant attire of the Martians are, moreover, channeled directly into and by romantic love (except in the case of lascivious villains), and the relationships that result are exclusively and pointedly monogamous.

Why the perversion of Burroughs's thought and work both in their deliberate and persistent misinterpretation and indeed their political and moral inversions? Given the profile of Burroughs and his work sketched out here, it is not implausible to argue that it is the very "American-ness" of both—of Burroughs, as self-made man and fulfillment of the American dream, of the Martian novels as oblique parables of the American frontier mentality, as adventures of "the Virginian in Outer Space" to use Richard Slotkin's felicitous characterization of John Carter, that Aue seeks to undermine. Or, more accurately, in sending his memorandum to Himmler concerning Burroughs, Aue in effect seeks not only to link Burroughs and what he represents to Nazi ideology, but in so doing, to *implicate* both in Nazism's crimes.

If this is the case, then what the novel itself is actually saying about American culture and history, and the politics that characterize and derive from both needs to be brought into sharper focus. In the opening section of *The Kindly Ones* entitled *Toccata*, Aue makes the scandalous claim that all people are his "human brothers" that all individuals, given the right circumstances, are capable of the kinds and numbers of crimes he has committed.

Similarly, both implicitly and explicitly in his discussions of the number of those killed in World War II and other conflicts, Aue pointedly emphasizes the destructive capacity and murderous efficiency of other nations besides Nazi Germany. In the original French edition of the novel Aue notes that for every Frenchman killed in Algeria, ten Algerians were killed. Even by Nazi standards, he states, this was an "honorable effort."[63] In the American edition of the novel, Aue speaks of the fourteen-to-one ratio of Vietnamese killed compared to Americans in the Viet War and declares it "a fine effort even compared to our own." In both countries (and in both editions of the novel) Aue adds, these statistics are readily forgotten. While provocations like these are perhaps to be expected from the unrepentant Nazi Aue claims to be at the outset of *The Kindly Ones*, what the references to Edgar Rice Burroughs and his work accomplish is in effect to flesh out an implied equivalency between the American cultural and political context that led to Viet Nam, and the Nazi context that led to Nazism. If the crimes are ultimately the same, then the cultural and political contexts that spawned them are equally tainted.

It could be argued that the dubious historical equivalencies Aue's references to the Martian novels underscore are intended to show, through the narrator, Nazism's power to pervert and in fact *desecrate* not only the cultural and political context out of which it grew, but other cultural contexts as well. In simply presenting Burroughs and his work as potentially representative of American culture, one is after all by definition "pulping" the latter. Or, in a much narrower context, it could be suggested that through Aue's misrepresentations of Burroughs and his work what is targeted—what Nazism undermined and perverted—are traditional Western notions of heroism as well. (It is striking in this regard that in his ruminations on Burroughs and Barsoom, Aue never refers to John Carter, not only the central figure of the Mars series, but according to his critics, Burroughs' initial literary alter ego as well). But while both possibilities may provide insights into the mental workings of Littell's fictional *bourreau* as well as *his* understanding of Nazism, the claims themselves are so broad and lacking in historical specificity and perspective as to be highly dubious, if not ultimately meaningless. They imply, in effect, that all of Western culture led directly or indirectly to Nazism, and therefore that all of that tradition is subject retrospectively to Nazism's distorting and incriminating lens. If this is the case, then the adventures and ruminations of Littell's highly cultured and intellectual hero, along with the massive historical detail he provides in *The Kindly Ones* lead the reader not to a more concise historical understanding of Nazism itself, but precisely away from it.

To conclude: to the degree that the references to Burroughs and his fictional works provide a political-cultural and also psychosexual backdrop or reference point in *The Kindly Ones*, that backdrop or reference point challenges and ultimately undermines Littell's claims for the "documented real," for a documentary realism in his novel that distinguishes it from *mode rétro* works. In fact, subtending the enormous edifice of facts and figures and the graphic descriptions of violence is an historical and globalizing myth of sorts claiming dubious equivalencies between crimes and nations. By the same token, distorting and co-opting the conventional sexuality of Burroughs's novels to make them conform to Aue's Nazified sexual deviance links the American ethos these works invoke to the same longing for dehumanizing sexual excess that ultimately leads, as Susan Sontag suggests, to death. In the end, *The Kindly Ones* replays or reenacts the *mode rétro* in its subject matter, its thematics, and ultimately its aesthetics.

And if *The Kindly Ones* is in fact a repetition or "reenactment" of sorts of the *mode rétro* of the 1970s, long consigned by most critics to the "dustbin of history," what is the meaning of the novel's *succès de scandale* in modern day France? To be sure, Littell's novel follows the model of legal and political phenomena described in the preceding chapters according to which the past, and the Dark Years in particular, are recalled into the present, and judged, or misjudged, anachronistically. In conforming to the *zeitgeist* of France's "presentist" moment as described by Rousso in the Introduction here, the novel was bound to attract attention. But Littell's novel goes a step beyond this as well. In evoking and invoking the *mode rétro* in its thematics and aesthetics, it is not simply the World War II past that is called into question, but also the shapes and forms that its *memory* has assumed. And the fact that that memory still proves controversial, that sensibilities associated with the *mode rétro* are not extinct, so to speak, suggests that the "work of memory" undertaken with the trials, commemorations, presidential speeches, etc. of the 1990s intended to put the World War II past and subsequent traumas associated with it to rest, has not completely accomplished its aim. The nation is not in fact fully reconciled to the history of the Dark Years, nor to the avatars of its memory.

And what of the Burroughsian intertext? If, as Sabine Hake argues, the intent of the linkage of sexual deviancy with Nazism was intended to recognize the latter's attraction while shunting it outside the democratic system by attaching it to unsavory perversions, then in perverting Burroughs conventional, "wholesome" sexuality the novel is implicating *democracy*, or at least America democracy, in the perversions of Nazism. In the wave of anti-Americanism in France following George W. Bush's war in Iraq, this could certainly have contributed to the novel's appeal, at least in some quarters. But in suggesting, obliquely, that Nazism's perversions had overflowed their boundaries to contaminate *all* democracies (French democracy during the Algerian conflict, for example), and the ideal of democracy itself was another matter. In likening *The Kindly Ones* to a kind of contagion critics were not far off the mark. And in a France still haunted by the specter of Vichy and fascisms past as well as sporadic fears of the latter's return in one guise or another in the present, for Littell's critics at least, this was not a pleasant prospect.

NOTES

1. Richard J. Golsan, "Perversion and Pulp: Reading Edgar Rice Burroughs and Figuring America in *Les Bienveillantes*," *Yale French Studies*, 121 (2012): 204–26.
2. Jonathan Littell and Richard Millet, "Conversation à Beyrouth," *Le débat*, 144 (mars-avril, 2007), 19.
3. The *Service de Travail Obligatoire* consisted of French citizens conscripted to work primarily in German factories near the end of the war. Thus *STO* uniforms would allow their bearers entry into France at the end of the war.
4. In addition to Aue's sexual activities and homicidal actions, his bodily functions are described in abundant detail.
5. See Jonathan Littell, Richard Millet, "Conversations à Beyrouth," *Le débat*, 144 (March–April 2007), 12.
6. Pierre Nora, Jonathan Littell, "Conversation sur l'histoire et le roman," *Le débat* 144 (March–April, 2007), 25.
7. Ibid.
8. Henry Rousso takes issue with Nora's claim that in his novel Jonathan Littell had offered new and valuable insights into the World War II in *The Kindly Ones* that historians had ignored or overlooked. Rousso points out that the latter's erudition where the historical sources are concerned, while impressive, is dated. Littell, Rousso writes, appears to be unfamiliar with important historical works on the war and on Nazism appearing over the last decade. In the end, Rousso concludes, Littell is a skilled and informed "interpreter," but nothing more. See Henry Rousso, "A-t-on encore besoin d'historiens? Exception française et rapport contemporain au passé," in Marc Dambre and Richard J Golsan, eds., *L'Exception française et la France contemporaine. Histoire, imaginaire, littérature.* (Paris: Presses Sorbonne Nouvelle, 2010, pp. 17–18.
9. Pierre-Emmanuel Dauzat, *Holocauste ordinaire*. Histoires d'usurpation, Extermination, littérature, théologie. (Paris: Bayard, 2007), 12.
10. Edouard Husson and Michel Tereschenko, *Les Complaisantes: Jonathan Littell et l'écriture du mal.* (Paris: François-Xavier de Guibert, 2007), 48.
11. Ibid., 16.
12. See Laura Frost, *Sex Drives: Fantasies of Fascism in Literary Modernism* (Ithica: Cornell University Press, 2002), 7.
13. Sabine Hake, *Screen Nazis: Cinema, History, and Democracy* (Madison: U. of Wisconsin Press, 2012), 131.
14. Ibid., 150.
15. Susan Sontag, *Under the Sign of Saturn* (New York: Farrar, Strauss, Giroux, 1980) 96.
16. Saul Friedländer, *Reflections of Nazism: An Essay on Kitsch and Death* (New York: Harper and Row, 1984), 14.

17. Ibid., 19.
18. Ibid., 43.
19. Sontag, 105.
20. Jean Baudrillard, *Simulacra and Simulation* (Ann Arbor: U of Michigan Press, 1994), 43.
21. Ibid., 44.
22. Foucault's interview in C*ahiers du Cinéma* has been translated into English and republished in *Foucault Live; Selected Interviews* 1961–1983, Sylvère Lottringer, ed., (New York: Semiotext(e), 1989). The passage quoted here is from, p. 130.
23. Hake, 131.
24. Baudrillard, op. cit.
25. Marc Limonier, *Les bienveillantes décryptés* (Paris: Le Pré aux clercs, 2007), 40.
26. Jonathan Littell, *The Kindly Ones*, trans. Charlotte Mandell (New York: Harper Collins, 2009), 109. All references are to this translation.
27. Ibid., 109.
28. Ibid.
29. Ibid., 109–10.
30. Ibid.
31. Ibid., 372.
32. Ibid., 372.
33. Ibid.
34. Ibid., 822.
35. Ibid.
36. Ibid., 823.
37. Ibid.
38. Ibid., 832.
39. See http://www.rogerebert.com/reviews/the-damned-1970.
40. Pierre Nora, Jonathan Littell, 40.
41. The work was originally published in serial form as *Under the Moons of Mars* in *The All-Story Magazine*.
42. See article from the *Galveston Daily News* of 3 August 1939, reproduced in James Van Hise, *Edgar Rice Burroughs' Fantastic Worlds* (privately published by James Van Hise, Yucca Valley, Ca., 1970), 178.
43. Edwin Porges, *Edgar Rice Burroughs: The Man who Created Tarzan*, Volume II (New York, Ballantine Books, 1976), 1056. Although the Porges biography is published in two volumes, pagination in both volumes is sequential. Further references to this work in the text will provide volume number followed by page number.
44. Phillip R. Burger, "Red Blood vs. the Red Flag," in Edgar Rice Burroughs, *The Moon Maid, Complete and Restored* (Lincoln: University of Nebraska Press, 2002), 345.
45. Richard Slotkin, *Gunfighter Nation: The Myth of the Frontier in Twentieth Century America* (Norman; University of Oklahoma Press, 1998), 199.
46. There is no indication that Burroughs supported Lindbergh and the America First Committee, or a politics of non-intervention, although he had admired Lindbergh as the personification of an adventurer and man of action in the 1920s (701). In fact, in

one of his last works, *Beyond the Farthest Star*, those who oppose war are characterized as "slackers" (Porges, 1022). The novel was written during World War II.

47. Another biographer of Burroughs makes the same point. See Richard Lupoff, *Edgar Rice Burroughs: Master of Adventure* (New York: Canaveral Press, 1965), 162. If Burroughs' attitude toward and representation of Jews seems paradoxical or contradictory, the same can apparently be said of his attitude toward African Americans. In his unpublished autobiography, Burroughs praises the African American officers under whom he served in Arizona as "wonderful soldiers and as hard as nails." He adds, "without exception they were excellent men who took no advantage of their authority over us and on the whole were better to work under than our white sergeants." In the novel *Beyond Thirty*, Burroughs offers similar praise for the officers of a fictional Abyssinian army. But, where the rank and file are concerned, he reverts to racist stereotypes: the common soldiers have "thick lips and broad, flatter noses." While one could make the same argument about the negative characterization of blacks as Burger makes about the negative characterization of Jews, that is, that they conform to pulp fiction stereotypes, what seems more likely is that Burroughs was naturally inclined to a hierarchical and generally elitist vision of African Americans, as he was of whites. See Philip R. Burger, "The War to End All Wars," in Edgar Rice Burroughs, *Beyond Thirty* (Lincoln: University of Nebraska Press, 2001), 108–9.

48. Erling B. Holtsmark, *Edgar Rice Burroughs* (Boston: Twayne, 1986), 9.

49. Porges, I, 599.

50. Porges, I, 607

51. Porges, I, 610–15.

52. Porges, II, 923.

53. Edgar Rice Burroughs, *A Princess of Mars* in *John Carter of Mars* (New York: Fall River Press, 2009), 19.

54. In the Foreword to *A Fighting Man of Mars,* originally published in 1930, Burroughs offers a detailed description of the various races of Barsoom. References here are to the Ballantine Books paperback edition of 1964.

55. Burroughs, *A Princess of Mars*, xiv.

56. Ibid., xi.

57. Ibid., 53.

58. Ibid.

59. Mike Ashley, "Introduction: Science and Romance," to Edgar Rice Burroughs, *John Carter of Mars*, 9.

60. Burroughs, *A Princess of Mars*, 53.

61. John Seelye, "Introduction" to *A Princess of Mars* (New York: Penguin Publishers 2007), xvii.

62. Porges II, 917.

63. *The Kindly Ones*, 23.

Chapter 5

Revising History, Betraying Memory

Yannick Haenel's *Jan Karski* and the Jan Karski *Affair*

In late January 2010, Claude Lanzmann published a scathing review of the most recent winner of both the *Prix interallié* and the *prix du FNAC,* Yannick Haenel's novel *Jan Karski,* in the pages of the weekly magazine *Marianne.* Prior to the appearance of Lanzmann's hostile review, *Jan Karski* had generally been greeted favorably by critics and had enjoyed notable commercial success as well. Haenel's novel, a partially fictionalized account of the wartime experiences of the real life Polish Resistance hero after which it is named (Karski is also figured prominently in Lanzmann's *Shoah),* seemed destined to avoid the kind of controversy that exploded in France following the publication of Jonathan Littell's *Les Bienveillantes* some three years earlier. But in the wake of Lanzmann's hostile review, that situation changed abruptly.

In his review, Lanzmann denounced Haenel for writing a "false novel" that deliberately "falsified history." *Jan Karski* was, Lanzmann insisted, "an obscene book, dishonest, a disgrace."[1] The novel not only defamed the memory of the Polish Resistance hero, but that of other historical figures as well, including most notably Franklin D. Roosevelt. Where the latter was concerned, Haenel offered a portrait of Roosevelt that in Lanzmann's view constituted a "misery of the imagination" filled with "insulting platitudes."[2] The real Karski and Roosevelt met in Washington in an historic meeting on 28 July 1943. During their meeting Karski reported on the plight of occupied Poland. Toward the end of his visit with FDR, Karski also described the Nazis' destruction of European Jews, which he had witnessed firsthand in the Warsaw Ghetto as well as in the death camps. In Haenel's novel, rather than listen attentively to the Polish resistance hero as he is widely reported to have

---

Portions of this chapter were previously published in Richard J. Golsan, "L'Affaire Karski: Fiction, History, and Memory Unreconciled" *L'Esprit Créateur,* 50:4 (Winter 2010), pp. 81–96.

done by historical sources (including the real Karski himself),[3] Roosevelt is portrayed as profoundly indifferent to Karski's report. He is, moreover, self-satisfied and more interested in his secretary's legs than in what Karski has to say. For Lanzmann, this characterization of FDR's attitude and behavior were nothing short of defamatory. As Lanzmann stressed, there wasn't even a secretary present in the room during the historic meeting between the two men.

Lanzmann was equally critical of the portrait Haenel painted of Karski himself, which he characterized as "hateful and vulgar."[4] Rather than paint Karski as the heroic but also complex figure that he was, Haenel made him entirely one-dimensional, "sadly linear."[5] In Haenel's novel he is an overly zealous and even monomaniacal "whining and vehement prosecutor"[6] focused exclusively on accusing the entire world—and the Allies in particular—of willful complicity in the destruction of Europe's Jews. On a psychological level, Lanzmann insisted, the real life Karski was neither that simple nor that straightforward.

In addition to misconstruing and simplifying Karski in human terms, Haenel according to Lanzmann grossly distorted Karski's historical mission. During his meeting with Roosevelt, Karski was primarily concerned not with Nazi crimes against Jews but with the fate of Poland during and especially after the war, when the Polish nation would be confronted with ever-increasing Soviet threats to its sovereignty and territories. This was, in fact, the reason for his mission to Washington, as arranged by the Polish government-in-exile in London.

Taking egregious liberties with the characters and attitudes of real historical figures in *Jan Karski* was not the only abuse of history of which Haenel was guilty, according to Lanzmann. In the novel, Karski meets with the American Supreme Court Justice Felix Frankfurter before his meeting with Roosevelt. In reality, Lanzmann claims, based on his interviews with Karski for *Shoah*, he met with Frankfurter *after* his visit with FDR and at FDR's recommendation. The change is crucial, Lanzmann pointed out, because in the novel this leaves the impression that Roosevelt was totally indifferent to the plight of the Jews, and therefore let the whole matter drop. According to Lanzmann, Roosevelt sent Karski to see Frankfurter precisely because he *was* affected by Karski's report and the fate of Europe's Jews.

As for the novelist himself, Lanzmann charged Haenel with plagiarism for devoting the first part of his novel to a description, of sorts, of Lanzmann's interview with Karski in *Shoah,* and for lifting entire passages from the film's dialogue without receiving the filmmaker's permission.

In the weeks that followed the publication of Lanzmann's review, others attacked Haenel's novel along many of these same lines. Critics like Annette Wieviorka and the Polish president of the "Friends of Jan Karski" criticized Haenel for historical carelessness as well as egregious inaccuracies.

Wieviorka also charged Haenel with a dangerous historical revisionism by artificially imposing a more contemporary (and obviously calumnious anti-American) perspective onto the very different and complicated realities of World War II.[7]

Haenel responded to these criticisms in the weeks that followed in interviews in the press and in the media. He defended the historical credibility of his novel by arguing that the controversial third part of *Jan Karski*—a *fiction intuitive* or *"intuitive fiction,"* as the writer described it—was plausibly prepared by the first two "factual" parts. Part One of the novel describes the real-life Karski's interview by Lanzmann in *Shoah*. Part Two presents a synopsis of Jan Karski's memoir *History of a Secret State,* published in the United States in 1944, where it was a best seller. In offering an "intuitive fiction" of Karski's experiences and reactions in the United States in Part Three of the novel Haenel claimed that he was in effect "revealing" that part of Karski's wartime experience that did not figure in Lanzmann's film or in Karski's own wartime memoir. He added that, given the fact that Karski had "remained silent for thirty-five years after 1945" this silence left historians "helpless" in their efforts to understand him, his reactions and his motives. The best they could offer was a "fragmentary" (*parcellaire*) knowledge which would be "speculative" at best.[8] Therefore it was up to the novelist to "give new life to Karski."[9]

Haenel also did not back down from the historical claims and positions for which Lanzmann and others had attacked him. In interviews he reiterated the position that his novel constituted an interrogation of what he described as "this strange passivity of the Allies, confronted with the destruction of Europe's Jews,"[10] as well as the "anti-Semitism" of "certain persons" in the State Department in Washington, DC. His portrait of a lascivious Roosevelt ogling his secretary's legs, Haenel continued, was justified by the fact that Roosevelt was a known philanderer.[11] As for Lanzmann himself, Haenel proved to be as harsh as his recent critic. He denounced Lanzmann's tardy critique of his novel, and accused the director of *Les Temps Modernes* of being a publicity seeker in attacking *Jan Karski* as *Shoah* was about to be broadcast on the television channel *Arte*. Haenel responded to Lanzmann's charge that *Jan Karski* was a "false novel" by asserting that, for Lanzmann, the novel itself is "the discourse of the false" and therefore he Lanzmann could not understand a work like *Jan Karski*, let alone literature as a whole. Haenel went on to accuse Lanzmann of taking a proprietary attitude toward Jan Karski, as if the latter and his wartime experiences were Lanzmann's personal property. Going a step further, Haenel also charged Lanzmann with "betraying" Karski in not doing in *Shoah* what he had supposedly promised the Polish resistance hero he would do in the first place, that is, evoke the Allies' culpability in failing to rescue the Jews alongside the film's insistence on Polish complicity in the Holocaust. The subject of Allied culpability must certainly have come up in Lanzmann's "long hours of conversation" with Karski but the filmmaker, Haenel submitted, chose deliberately to leave that portion of the footage on the cutting room floor in preparing the final version of *Shoah*. Jealous of and infuriated by the success of *Jan Karski* Lanzmann, Haenel concluded in 25 January 2010 editorial in *Le Monde,* even harbored homicidal thoughts against him.

Bitter exchanges between Lanzmann and Haenel like those just described continued through the late winter and into the early spring. These exchanges did credit to neither man, while also lowering the intellectual bar through increasingly ad hominem exchanges. For example, in a televised interview aired in February, Lanzmann once again condemned Haenel's novel, this time describing it as an "unbelievable anti-American tirade" by a novelist who "writes like a pig." But the *Affaire Jan Karski,* as the controversy had come to be known, took a more interesting and substantive turn when the excised portions of Lanzmann's interview with Karski in *Shoah* were aired on the channel *Arte* on 17 March 2010. Entitled *"Le Rapport Karski,"* the interview addressed directly Karski's meeting with FDR, his mission to Washington and his meeting with other American officials. Toward the end of the interview it also included Karski's reflections on the meaning of Hitler's destruction of European Jewry, some thirty years after the fact. Lanzmann also chose to publish the text of the interview in the January–March 2010 issue of *Les Temps Modernes,* alongside the text of his original review in *Marianne* and a brief prefatory note.[12]

Several things are striking about the exchanges between Lanzmann and Karski in *"Le Rapport Karski."* First, Karski's statements about Roosevelt are lavish in their praise of the American president. At no point in the interview does Karski give voice to a negative reaction to Roosevelt.[13] When Lanzmann raises the issue of FDR's response to his description of his visit to the Warsaw ghetto and the Nazi extermination camp, Karski does tell him that Roosevelt said nothing. But following his visit, Karski states, Roosevelt arranged for him to meet important and influential members of the American Jewish community including, most notably, the supreme court justice Felix Frankfurter. Karski's statement in this instance directly contradicts the chronology of events in Haenel's novel.[14]

In *"Le Rapport Karski"* the Polish Resistance hero also discusses his meeting with Frankfurter. This meeting is clearly more unsettling to Karski than his meeting with FDR because, after Karski describes to Frankfurter the fate of European Jews, Frankfurter responds: "I'm telling you that I don't believe you." But as Karski goes on to explain to Lanzmann, Frankfurter's statement, in his view, was made not to accuse him of lying, but to acknowledge that in 1943 the monstrosity of the crimes being perpetrated by the Nazis against the

Jews was simply incomprehensible. Karski quotes Frankfurter as explaining: "I am a judge of men. I know humanity I know what a man is. No! No!"[15] When Lanzmann questions Frankfurter's sincerity, Karski defends him, reminding Lanzmann again that "this was a problem without precedent, an unheard-of atrocity."[16]

The conversation that follows this exchange between Lanzmann and Karski underscores a second, striking feature of the film, and that is Karski's actual reflections on the historical and even epistemological dimensions and implications of the Holocaust. For Karski, the Holocaust was unquestionably unique and unprecedented in history, and therefore was, and to a certain degree remains, incomprehensible, beyond the understanding of "sane and rational human beings." Especially at the time he made his report, Karski continues, the people with whom he spoke had absolutely no basis for comparison of the events he witnessed and described, and this explains their incredulity. Then, speaking of his own reaction over time, Karski adds:

> I cannot deal with it. What I saw—the extermination of the Jews—is incomprehensible to me. I cannot deal with it. I can deal with the Polish problem perfectly well, I speak of it to my students, the Czechs, the Serbs, the Russians—I understand it all. I can speak of it, calmly, rationally. History is cruel to many countries and many individuals. But where the Jews are concerned, I flee, I try to eliminate that. Not only has an event like that never occurred before, but nothing like it has happened since.[17]

There is one final aspect of "*Le Rapport Karski*" that should be stressed, especially in light of the polemics of the "Affair." While, as already noted, to a significant extent the exchanges during the "Affair" focused on Karski's report on the fate of the Jews and Roosevelt's supposed indifference and indeed complicity with the Nazi crime through his inaction, in the televised interview Karski insists on reminding Lanzmann that reporting on the fate of the Jews in Europe was not his primary objective. Rather, the trip had been organized and painstakingly prepared by the Polish government-in-exile in order for Karski to report on the fate of Poland: "For me, the crucial problem was Poland, Soviet exigencies, the presence of Communists in the resistance movement, the fear experienced by the Polish nation. What was going to happen to Poland? That was what was most important for me."[18]

In light of "*Le Rapport Karski*," it is clear in *Jan Karski* that Yannick Haenel has taken considerable and—depending on one's perspective—egregious liberties both with the historical realities of the Polish Resistance hero's trip to Washington DC in Summer 1943 and with the historical and ideological outlook of the real life Karski at the time of the Lanzmann interview. These novelistic liberties become even more numerous when other historical considerations not emphasized in the media polemics that constituted the *Affaire Karski* are factored in. A closer look at Haenel's novel itself makes this clear.

One should recall that in the August 2009 interview in *Le Nouvel Observateur* Haenel stated that the "intuitive fiction" that constitutes Part Three is prepared for, so to speak, by the first two parts of the novel. These two "factual" or nonfictional parts, he claimed, present the real-life Karski as he presented himself in word in *Shoah* and in writing in *Story of a Secret State*. But what actually occurs in certain instances in the text of the first two parts is that Haenel has recourse to a kind of skewed "indirect free style" or better, ventriloquism, in order to attribute thoughts and attitudes to Karski that, for example, are expressed neither directly nor indirectly, either in *Story of a Secret State* or in *Shoah*. Just before Part Three begins, Karski draws in Part Two what amounts to a Manichaean contrast between a misunderstood and entirely heroic Poland and a culpable and corrupt Allied side: "When it comes down to it, no one understood the heroism of that nation which refused to collaborate with Germany; no one understood the notion of an 'underground state,' while everywhere else compromise prevailed." By contrast, in *Story of a Secret State*—the supposed source of Part Two—Karski does acknowledge that the "outside world could not comprehend the two most important principles of Polish resistance," the first being the very idea of a "secret state" and the second, that resistance had prevented a "Quisling" from coming to power in Poland, as had been the case elsewhere in occupied Europe.[19] But at no point does Karski accuse the Allies (or the world) of living in a state of complete "compromise" with Nazi Germany. Following his meetings with American leaders, he states "Again I heard the same questions from the most prominent men in the country: What can we do for you? What do you expect from us? How can we help?"[20] Shortly thereafter, Karski emphasizes a kind of global solidarity, *including* Poland, in writing: "I realized to what extent the entire world is unified. It seemed to me as though the network of which I was a part performed some function in a single, world-wide organism—an organism from which no member, not even the most powerful, could separate itself."[21]

In the first part of *Jan Karski*, in which Haenel describes the interview between Karski and Lanzmann in *Shoah* as well as the documentary itself, there are other glosses by the novelist that set the stage for the "intuitive fiction" of Part Three and the interpretation of history which it constructs. In the first instance, while Karski is describing his message from the Warsaw ghetto "to the world," Lanzman's camera scans the Statue of Liberty in the New York harbor. At this point, Haenel speculates:

Does Claude Lanzmann want to pay tribute to Jan Karski's *liberty* in this way? Or rather, by playing on the contrast between the voice and the image, to highlight the tragic difference between the battered Europe which Jan Karski is evoking and the striking symbol of "Liberty enlightening the world"? Or between the suffering of Europe's Jews, as expressed in Jan Karski's voice, and what America actually did to save them?[22]

Given Lanzmann's reaction to *Jan Karski* and his rejection of Haenel's interpretation of history and the role of the Allies and especially the United States during the war, this speculation as to the filmmaker's intent in *Shoah* seem doubtful, to say the least.

Shortly after this moment in the text, the novelist speculates on an image of the Washington DC in *Shoah,* and writes:

We see the White House, then travel around the capitol, which is filmed from a car. Here, too, the contrast between the terrible words being pronounced by Karski and the images of the monumental composure of American democracy evokes a distance, a misunderstanding, a dialogue of the deaf. Who heard this message? Who really listed to it? Is it possible that nothing was done? Jan Karski says nothing.[23]

In structuring the passage the way he does, Haenel once again attributes historical and political perspectives to Karski that may well not be his, but are the novelist's instead.

In turning to Part Three, Haenel's "intuitive fiction": while the historical perspectives—and distortions—presented are striking in themselves, what is equally evident is the utterly pessimistic, condemnatory (even damning) and cynically insolent tone Haenel attributes to Karski in the latter's narrative. In his review of *Jan Karski* in *Marianne*, Lanzmann had taken strong exception to Haenel's Karski's description of FDR as preoccupied with his [imaginary] secretary's legs. But he had also been highly critical of the fictional Karski's description of FDR as "*a man who is digesting*—he was in the process of digesting the extermination of Europe's Jews."[24] and as an individual whose profound indifference to their fate is underscored by his tendency to express himself through yawning. On the latter score, what Lanzmann does not mention is that, in Haenel's novel, at *precisely* the moment when Karski describes to Roosevelt the horrors of the Warsaw Ghetto and the fate of Europe's Jews under Nazism, FDR reaction is to suppress a yawn; "He said nothing; his mouth remained a little twisted, then he stifled a yawn."[25]

Roosevelt's callous and indeed obscene indifference to the fate of the Jews as portrayed in *Jan Karski* is, moreover, part and parcel of a profound condescension on the part of the American president that betrays an intolerance toward the Other that borders on racism: "Despite everything, I sensed a curiosity in him, that haughty curiosity that people have for foreigners they despise. After all, the ambassador and I were merely vulgar Poles. . ." Karski then adds: "And then we were Catholics, in other words, for Americans, rather like fanatics."[26]

If Americans supposedly share Roosevelt's bias toward Catholics, they also share his profound, and ultimately "criminal" indifference to the plight of the Jews, which is itself an expression of their own anti-Semitism. What is true of America and its leader is, moreover, true of America's British ally as well. The text of Part Three of *Jan Karski* is in fact crowded with passages that directly link "the Anglo-American consensus" to "a shared interest *against* the Jews."[27] More egregiously, Haenel's Karski charges that in exterminating Europe's Jews Hitler was in fact solving a "problem" for the Allies that they could not solve themselves. In this sense the two sides in the conflict are deeply complicit. Haenel's Karski states bluntly that any time an advisor to Roosevelt or Churchill "wondered what to do about the Jews, he was asking the same question as Hitler was asking and adopting the same thought process." And he concludes: "Fortunately for the British, and fortunately for the Americans, Hitler did not expel the Jews of Europe, he exterminated them."[28]

Given these attitudes on the part of the fictional Karski, no wonder that toward the end of his interview with Roosevelt, he is force to ask "myself the same question as I had in the Gestapo office, while being tortured by the SS: how can I get out of here?" He then adds: "I had confronted Nazi violence, I had suffered from Soviet violence, and now, completely unexpectedly, I was being introduced to the insidious violence of the Americans. A cosy violence, made up of couches, tureens and yawns."[29] In its insidiousness, and its ability to disguise itself behind the "beautiful word of democracy" as Karski states elsewhere, American violence appears ultimately more dangerous and destructive than the violence of the totalitarian regimes. Haenel's Karski claims he finally understood what really went on in Roosevelt's Oval Office "only when the atomic bomb destroyed Hiroshima and Nagasaki."[30]

Given these claims of a fundament equivalency (or worse) between Nazi and Soviet totalitarianisms and the Western democracies where a reliance on extreme violence is concerned, coupled with claims of a radical, if thinly disguised, anti-Semitism on the part of Allied leaders and their respective peoples, it is not surprising that in *Jan Karski* the Holocaust is essentially a *shared* enterprise. As Haenel's Karski puts it: "On one side, there was extermination, and on the other was abandonment."[31] And just as the Jews are abandoned so, too, is the Polish nation, except that the latter suffers the double onus of being caricatured and reduced to the status of a state and people given over entirely to its own anti-Semitism. Haenel's Karski states: "They [the Allies] continue to heap Poland with infamy, to reduce it to that anti-Semitism which it suits their countries to inflict on it, because it gives them the illusion of cleansing themselves, even though they all collaborated in way or another with the Nazis."[32] In his diatribe, Haenel's Karski makes no acknowledgement of Poland's very real history of anti-Semitism and anti-Semitic acts before and during the war as well as afterward.

Given the depth and reach of Haenel's Karski's pessimistic and indeed highly cynical outlook, his reaction to both the Allied victory and their efforts to deal with Nazi crimes at Nuremberg are predictably uniformly negative. As the fictional Karski states on numerous occasions in Part Three, Nuremberg is merely another effort to hide Allied complicity in the Holocaust by blaming the Nazis exclusively. The hypocrisy of this gesture is confirmed by the bombing of Hiroshima in the same year. The latter, Karski affirms, is "in other words the continuation of barbarity by the so-called 'free world.'"[33] The end of the war, the Allied victory, marks for Haenel's Karski not the victory of freedom over oppression, what remains in 1945 are not "winners," but only "accomplices and liars."[34] And what Karski claims to have experienced toward the end of Haenel's novel is nothing less than "the end of humanity itself."[35]

Given this reading of Yannick Haenel's *Jan Karski* it is fair to say that the criticisms of the historical (and psychological) accuracy of the work made by the likes of Lanzmann, Annette Wieviorka, and others are legitimate. Moreover, Haenel's Karski's conclusion at novel's end that there were no victors in 1945, but only "accomplices" and "liars" is morally troubling, in light of the sacrifices made by millions in order to defeat the Nazi menace. As Lanzmann asserted in his review in *Marianne,* the fictional Karski's cynical conclusion concerning the outcome of the war makes a mockery, for example, of those American and Allied troops who fought and died in Normandy, not to mention Soviet forces who were, after all, primarily responsible for the defeat of Nazism.

Leaving aside for the moment the troubling moral implications of the novel, there are other historical concerns that need to be addressed. First, as Yannick Haenel indicated in interviews, two of the principle sources he used in writing his novel were *Story of a Secret State* and also *Karski: How One Man Tried to Stop the Holocaust,* by E. Thomas Wood and Stanislaw M Jankowski. The second work is particularly interesting from an historical as well as a psychological standpoint for several reasons. First Woods and Jankowski raise the tantalizing possibility that in his meeting with Roosevelt, Karski did not even discuss with the American president his visit to the Warsaw ghetto or to the death camps. In fact, Wood and Jankowski state that in his report written at the time Karski did not speak of these visits, and later "denied having mentioned the experiences to the President."[36] While this now appears unlikely, it does suggest that Karski himself was not always a completely reliable and consistent witness. Moreover, Wood and Jankowski note that Karski was already practiced in the art of intrigue and deception by the time he arrived in Washington, and that he was secretly spying and sending critical reports on the Polish Ambassador in Washington to London while he was the Ambassador's guest in the American capitol. While this does not ultimately diminish his stature or compromise his wartime heroism, it does suggest that the real life Karski was the more complicated figure Lanzmann describes rather than the more one dimensional deeply pessimistic character Haenel portrays in his novel.[37]

Wood's and Jankowski' book also tends to support the positive impression Karski had of Roosevelt as he expresses it in "Le Rapport Karski" The biographers report Karski as describing Roosevelt in glowing terms: "He really projected majesty, power, greatness" Karski would recall. He had the aura of "a master of humanity."[38] *Karski: How One Man Tried to Stop the Holocaust* also strongly argues that, unlike Haenel's FDR, the real FDR *was* affected by Karski's report on the fate of Europe's Jews. Wood and Jankowski note that John Pehle, first head of the War Refugee Board appointed by Roosevelt, stated that Karski "made a difference. Roosevelt's willingness to set up the Refugee Board in an attempt to help those Jews who were still alive resulted from his moving encounter with Karski."[39] Shortly after his meeting with Karski, Roosevelt also personally intervened with Treasury Department officials to encourage the freeing-up of funds to "facilitate the possible evacuation of 70,000 Jews from Romania."[40]

As for FDR's supposed indifference to the fate of Poland, Woods and Jankowski stress that twelve million dollars in lend-lease money were approved for the Polish underground following Karski's meeting with the American president.[41] However, in fairness to claims made in Haenel's novel, Wood and Jankowski also argue that, to the extent that Karski's mission was to encourage the re-establishment of Polish sovereignty and restore the integrity of its prewar borders, that mission was rendered "futile" by Roosevelt's political aims before Karski "reached American shores."[42] Roosevelt's prime objectives as the end of the war neared were to get the Soviet Union to join the Allied struggle against Japan after Nazi Germany had been defeated, and to secure Soviet participation in the planned creation of the United Nations. Given these objectives, Roosevelt did not wish the fate of Poland to prove to be an insurmountable obstacle. And by the time of the Yalta Summit in February 1945 the realities on the ground gave Roosevelt and Winston Churchill no leverage in negotiating a future independent and democratic Poland with Joseph Stalin. As David Reynolds writes:

By February 1945 when the big three convened at Yalta, the Soviets were in control of much of Eastern Europe. They could not be evicted except by force, and it was politically impossible for Britain or America to turn on their ally in this way.[43]

Nevertheless, as S. M. Plokhy has written more recently, both leaders strove—ultimately unsuccessfully—to persuade Stalin to be more flexible on the future of Poland.[44] Their failure in this effort weighed on both men, although Roosevelt believed that the settlement that had been reached was "the best that I can do for Poland at this time."[45]

Finally, as for any unspoken complicity, or secret sympathy on the part of the Allies for Nazi Germany both in their attitude toward Jews and in their recourse to extreme political violence, this is ludicrous, both in terms of intentions and motives as well as outcomes. Where Roosevelt himself was concerned, the president entertained an abiding dislike of the German "character," and referred to Hitler as a "wild man." These opinions were moreover, based on fairly extensive personal experience. Travels in Germany, as well as a German school class as a youth had left Roosevelt hostile to German militarism and expansionism, and his reading of *Mein Kampf* had made him very much aware of Hitler's ambitions along these lines. In 1940 Roosevelt expressed "little patience with those who seek to draw a clear distinction between the German government and the German people."[46] Besides, to ask an obvious question, if collusion and sympathies of this sort existed at all, why would the Allies be involved in a struggle to the death with Nazi Germany in the first place?

In the same issue of *Les Temps Modernes* in which he published the transcript of excised portions of his interview with Karski in *Shoah*, Lanzmann speculates in a prefatory note on the motives of young writers like Yannick Haenel and others of his generation who take up the World War II past and revise it in their novels according to their own lights. These writers Lanzmann states, are "to be pitied," living as they do "in obscure times, without reference points or things to be hoped for, where the future is indecipherable, where there is nothing to inspire confidence, enthusiasm, or total commitment. The utopias are dead, it is the end of History."[47] But, refusing to resign themselves to this state of affairs, Lanzmann continues, these writers turn to the past. They

> throw themselves voraciously on the preceding century, so close and yet so far away. Feeling guilt for never having suffered—an intolerable emptiness in their lives—they reactivate and replay a past in which they have no part, transforming into thunderous 'new discoveries' what has been known and chewed over for quite some time.... But, as opposed to what Racine wrote in *Bazajet*: 'respect grows with distance in time' this very same distance authorizes these young writers, they believe, to take the most cavalier of approaches and offer up the worst distortions, in the name of a maudlin and retrospective moralism.[48]

Lanzmann's judgment here of Haenel and other writers of his generation may be overly harsh and too general as well, but it does raise important issues of artistic motivation and inspiration. It also focuses needed attention on the ethical, moral, and historical responsibilities of the novelist who chooses to write about the most traumatic moments of the recent past, moments that are still disturbing and controversial for many today. In addressing these issues in relation to the author of *Jan Karski*, it is helpful to look more closely at Haenel's conception of the function of literature, its relationship to history, and the prerogatives and obligations of the writer in dealing with historical subjects. For the purposes of the present study, it is also necessary to examine Haenel's vision of history as it is elaborated both in *Jan Karski* as well as in other works. As will be shown, that vision conforms in important ways to the paradigm of the memory of the Vichy and World War II past elaborated in earlier chapters here.

In a lengthy interview or "conversation" with Marc Dambre published in 2013, Haenel makes several strong claims for literature, its function and purpose, that begin to explain both the historical liberties taken in *Jan Karski* and also the deeply pessimistic vision of history that the novel articulates. Haenel affirms, first, that literature poses the question of that which is "unrepresentable." One such "'unrepresentable' phenomenon is evil."[49] Evil, as it is experienced by the protagonists of Haenel's novels, is something that "comes from very far away, from a memory without name: a memory that is without reason."[50] As an example of both evil and memory without reason, Haenel sites an episode that haunts him in Primo Levy's *If This Be a Man*. In that episode Levy, suffering from terrible thirst, breaks a window pane to get at the ice formed outside. A kapo intervenes and forbids him to take the ice. When asked why by Levy, the guard responds that "there is no 'why?'." If literature exists at all, Haenel states, it must situate itself in relation to this kind of reasonless evil, this "absolute barbarity" of the kind Levy's experience with the kapo represents.

Haenel's novelistic poetics as described in the conversation with Dambre point to an important connection in his work between evil, memory, and history, and specifically the memory and history of the Holocaust. In fact, the latter resonates strongly not only in the novelist's creative process, but also in the lives of his characters. Indeed, Haenel affirms elsewhere in the conversation that History [Haenel's capitalization] as exemplified in the Holocaust is a nightmare "that lies at the heart of literature."[51] The epigraph of Haenel's 2007 novel *Cercle* (of which *Jan Karski* was originally intended to form a part) is a quote from James Joyce: "History is a nightmare from which I try to wake up."

But what precisely is the connection between evil, memory, and history, evidently exemplified in its purest form in the Holocaust? In *Cercle* a character named Oleg, whom the narrator encounters, appropriately enough, in Berlin, sums up this connection:

> "There is only one single person of importance to Western history" said Oleg, "and that is Hitler. Through Hitler," he continued, "all the criminal penchants of Western Europe were condensed together." In Hitler's name the true object of European History crystalized, which is crime, integral crime—extermination. The name Hitler sums up all that is malevolent in the heart of History. Because History, whether one likes it or not, has as its horizon the death of the human species. The extermination of the Jews is the prelude to complete extermination.[52]

Oleg continues:

> The Russians and the Americans opened the camps, but the doors to the camps were never closed again. The camp extended its reach to the entire world. Besides, there is no more world. When the world becomes synonymous with the camp, all that remains is the non-world. There is no more global catastrophe because the world itself is the catastrophe. The process of the coincidence of the space of the world and the space of the camp is called History.[53]

If the core of European history—indeed of Western history and human history *tout court*—is geared toward crime and the ultimate annihilation of the species, then one perverse but very logical response to this reality is the embrace of guilt on a communal, even a national (or European) scale. This embrace of guilt is in fact invoked in Haenel's 2001 novel *Introduction à la mort française*. At the end of the novel, the French president gives a speech to celebrate the recently announced Day Zero, the day when all of France, all the French, acknowledge and assume their part in the nation's past crimes. In his speech, the president announces that "where culpability is concerned, in our country, we are all experts."[54] He continues that the feeling of making the past *badly* is not an "unworthy sentiment," but rather a "beautiful one." And he adds, all the crimes of the French past, including most notably "the dossiers of the trials since 1940" henceforth will be archived and available for public consumption in a new, national institution, the *Museum of Guilt*. The French, he adds, "need to feel badly" about the past, and a visit to the *Museum of Guilt* will enhance that feeling. There, the president states,

> You will know, my friends, the ambiguous links between evil and public consent. From the Francisque [the highest award given by the Vichy regime] to the sacks of contaminated blood[55] which splattered our national honor, the emblems of the worst will not be lacking. On video screens . . . will be projected the great

moments of French guilt: from the most touching speeches of Marshall Pétain to the most beautiful torture sessions. A small [heretofore] censored film dating from the 1960s will even show Algerians being pushed expeditiously into the Seine.[56]

Following the speech and a presidential procession up the Boulevard Saint-Michel, the president inaugurates the Pantheon itself, where the French Republic's national heroes are entombed, as the site of the new *Museum of Guilt*. In response to all this, the novel's narrator acknowledges that "A great popular élan is growing in the country since the announcement that we are all guilty, and that it is good to be guilty."[57] Walking the streets of Paris, he adds,

> I pass men who cling to the Second World War, to the war in Indochina, to the Algerian war, to all the secret crimes in francophone Africa, these men are sad and beautiful, distraught, hungry, they tell you everything while you sit with them on a bench, they know everything. They still believe in justice, they repeat the words "French justice," they believe in it in order to vituperate against it . . . old tragic howlers, they demand "reparation" . . . that's their word, "reparation."[58]

In summing up what *Cercle* and *Introduction à la mort française* have to say about Haenel's vision of history it is clear, first, that that vision—despite claims made elsewhere for the novelist as a kind of clairvoyant historian—is fundamentally an *ahistorical* one. History as presented in these works is, in effect, an account of a latent, essentially apocalyptic and genocidal evil that erupts into the world with the arrival of Hitler (but that does not originate with him) and that has remained and subsumed subsequent historical events ever since. And guilt, like memory itself, becomes a kind of undifferentiated and endless obsession with and meditation on all the crimes of the past. Although this obsessive guilt is treated ironically in *Introduction à la mort française*, it is nevertheless a logical response to the novelist's dark and essentially nihilistic vision as described in *Le sens du calme*, a kind of memoir that Haenel published in 2011 in reaction to the controversy over *Jan Karski*. In *Le sens du calme*, Haenel affirms that his "first memory" is of watching Alain Resnais' famous films about the Nazi death camps, *Night*, and that this memory was, appropriately enough about "human criminality."[59] And, he adds, "The horror of the images of *Night and Fog* grab me by the throat. Do they coincide with the world? On that day, on the town square at Lucques, I thought this: what are called 'men' comprise a tortured community where abandonment crushes all relations."[60]

What are the implications of these observations for the novel *Jan Karski* and its eponymous protagonist and hero? First, the vision of History as essentially a politically and ideologically undifferentiated continuum of crime and extermination is confirmed by the equation made between Nazi and Allied intentions and also their destructiveness. To Hitler his Holocaust with, of course the implicit complicity of the Allies; and to Roosevelt his Hiroshima and Nagasaki. As noted earlier, Haenel's Karski states that he only "understood" what went on in Roosevelt's office when the atomic bombs were detonated over Japan.

And what of the novelist's portrayal of Karski himself? In *Le sens du calme* Haenel states that he received admiring letters from fans of the novel wishing to know from whence came the voice of the Polish hero that the novelist had "resuscitated." Haenel responds that this is tantamount to knowing from whence comes *his own* voice, since, apparently, his voice and Karski's are one and the same. In his conversation with Marc Dambre however, Haenel casts his depiction of Karski in somewhat different terms. He acknowledges here as well that he wanted to resuscitate Karski, to make him "live again."[61] But he also states that the original title he had in mind for his novel was not merely the Polish resistance fighter's name, but rather *Saint Karski*,[62] and in recounting Karski's visit to the White House—which he refers to ironically as *le saint des saints*—he wished to show that it was "this man," Karski, "who was innocent, not Roosevelt."[63] Returning to his scandalous portrayal in the novel of the American president, Haenel adds, "Tell me where the true indecency lies: in the charges I bring against Roosevelt or in the Allies' indifference to the extermination of the Jews."[64]

As these passages confirm, even in his depictions of Karski—who in the end, it appears, is little more than Haenel's mouth piece, his alter ego—the novelist's inspiration is less historical than it is anachronistically judgmental and moralizing. Moreover, the judgments made, for example, the evident anti-Americanism implicit in Haenel's language, are those of the novelist, rather than those of his protagonist. They are certainly not those of the Karski of history, of that historical moment who, in addition to praising Roosevelt and despite Haenel's claims concerning his postwar "silence," went on lecture tours abroad making propaganda speeches for the US government. Karski also wrote secret reports for the CIA in the postwar years.[65] Finally, in first conceiving of Karski as *Saint Karski* as the embodiment of a "saintly" innocence as opposed to the guilt and corruption of others Haenel betrays hagiographic intentions that veer toward the religious, the "timeless" as opposed to the temporal and historical.

There is a striking irony in Haenel's inspiration for depiction of his hero as just described, in that the "real" Jan Karski was, by any measure, a deeply and profoundly *historical* individual. Plunged into the history of his times to the point of risking his life almost daily in the Polish Resistance, in his visit with Roosevelt and other Allied leaders it was precisely to *recount historical truth* that Karski had committed himself. In abjuring the responsibility to do the same in his portrayal of the historical figure he so admired, Haenel unfortunately betrays the memory of the latter in order to remain faithful to his own ahistorical poetics.

If as these remarks suggest, Yannick Haenel ultimately fits the mold of a new generation of novelists writing about World War II who according to Lanzmann judge the past retroactively and impose their own moralizing vision upon it in their fictions, his work and historical vision are also more broadly representative of the "presentist" French and European moment and its anachronistic mindset. As described by Henry Rousso in *La dernière catastrophe,* this mindset ceaselessly recalls the recent past in order to re-experience it and also to judge it anew. In speaking—revealingly—of the "charges" he brings against Roosevelt through his alter ego in *Jan Karski*, Haenel indulges in just such an anachronistic judgment in a past made present, while also linking his fiction to the "legalistic turn" of memory that saw its most spectacular manifestations in the trials for crimes against humanity of the 1990s and the Memorial laws of the new millennium, described in Chapter One. Finally, in articulating a vision of history in *Jan Karski* as well as other works discussed here which deliberately and explicitly conflates the crimes of the past, the novelist ultimately strips these crimes of their historical specificity and meaning. In his interview with Lanzmann in *Shoah*, this is precisely the kind of blurring and conflation that Karski rejects in his reaction to the Nazi extermination of European Jewry. The latter he states as noted earlier was unique, and unprecedented in history before or since. In this kind of conflation and distortion as well, Haenel's fiction is symptomatic and representative of the skewed memory of the Vichy and World War II past as it manifests itself in France today.

Is there a price to be paid not only for re-judging history in this manner, but also for deliberately revising it through a canny mixture of fact and fiction? In an essay published in the Summer 2011 issue of *Le débat*, the British historian Anthony Beevor denounces the "perils" of what he labels "faction." Works of "faction"—movies and television series as well novels—are works which in Beevor's view skillfully and dangerously mix fact and fiction to the detriment of the former. Why dangerously? Because as Beevor notes, in a world in which historical illiteracy is increasingly becoming the norm, ill-informed readers and spectators take the false version of the past as the truth, and this has potential politically and psychologically nefarious consequences in the present. As one example of "faction," Beevor cites the British television series *Cambridge Spies* which falsely promulgated a version of the World War II past according to which the British government knew of the impending German invasion of the Soviet Union in Summer 1941, but deliberately kept the information from Stalin. In point of fact, Beevor notes, the British repeatedly warned Stalin of Hitler's intentions and preparations, to no avail. Not only does this constitute an egregious revision of the past, it also gives the British spectators a falsely negative understanding of their government's role in history. And he warns, "A country that does not respect its history has very little chance of learning the lessons from that past, or of respecting the history of other countries."[66]

Beevor cites other examples of "faction" as well, Steven Spielberg's *Saving Private Ryan* being one of them. According to Beevor, despite its obvious merits in its depiction of warfare itself, *Saving Private Ryan* also represents and promulgates a picture of a fundamental American "innocence." This troubling national psychological trait, Beevor continues, encourages both a naïvité in foreign affairs and also a dangerous adventurism, resulting all too often on global calamities.

In discussing these works peddling what he describes as "counter knowledge" Beevor also speculates on works that have not yet been written or produced, but whose impact would prove most dangerous. Beevor imagines a "blockbuster film denying the Holocaust," skillfully marketed as a thriller on the model of *The Da Vinci Code.* And while the film would be welcomed in the Middle East, for example, it would be censored by law in several European countries. This, Beevor writes, would only increase its popularity and encourage a paranoid suspicion of a government or Zionist conspiracy, both of which would also promote the view that the Holocaust never happened.

So what do Beevor's observations about the "perils" of "faction" tell us about Yannick Haenel's *Jan Karski* and the potential problems it poses? First, it is clear that *Jan Karski is* a work Beevor would characterize as a work of "faction." Moreover, the novelist might well recognize this label as appropriate to *Jan Karski* not in order to acknowledge his work's shortcomings but as a means of underscoring the "arrogance" of historical discourse[67] as opposed to fiction. In this sense, in his overt denigration of historical discourse Haenel goes even further than the works of "faction" Beevor describes In the latter, the works themselves do all the talking, not their creators.

And what are the historical dangers *Jan Karski* poses, when considered as a work of "faction"? In addition to the frankly calumnious portrait of Franklin Roosevelt and a characterization of Allied motives and actions that, among other things, disregards (or perhaps disrespects) those who fought and died in the struggle against Nazism, it also leaves aside the historical fate and complexity of the Polish nation and people for whom the real Jan Karski wished to be the spokesperson and champion. Presented in Haenel's novel as just one more victim of Allied and American indifference and racism, Poland and the Polish represented and represent in fact a kind of microcosm or "perfect storm" of all the horrors of World War II. Hitler's stated purpose in attacking Poland was its "annihilation" and as Timothy Snyder has noted recently, the absolute barbarity experienced by the Poles was the result of an invasion "undertaken on the logic that Poland did not, had not, and could not exist as a sovereign state." And he continues, "[Polish] soldiers taken prisoners could be shot, since the Polish army could not have existed as such."[68] At the same time, however, Poland, and certain actions of the Polish people are representative of both the nation's own anti-Semitism and complicity in the Nazi Holocaust, evidence of which of course abounds in *Shoah* and the memories of which still leave scars on the Polish psyche.[69] Nothing of course obliges Haenel to incorporate these complexities in his novel. Except that, according to Wood and Jankowski, it was precisely because as a student Karski had remained silent in the face of *Polish* anti-Semitism that he had personally witnessed—"I simply didn't want to get involved," Karski later ruefully confessed—that he later worked so hard to inform the world of its murderous Nazi variant.[70]

Finally, what of France and the French context in which Haenel's novel created such controversy? In *Karski: How One Man Tried to Stop the Holocaust* Wood and Jankowsky write of the historical Jan Karski's animosity toward France and the French. The latter he considered to be "alot of sniveling collaborators." In answering a question from Roosevelt during their interview about the mood in France (where Karski had briefly hidden) Karski is reported to have responded: ". . .my general impression is that the broad classes of French society simply want life and peace."[71] In Haenel's novel, French collaborationism is contrasted with Polish resistance: "En Pologne, il n'existe pas de gouvernement de collaboration avec les Allemands, comme il en existera par exemple en France. Et contrairement à la France où la Résistance va mettre du temps à s'organiser, plus encore à agir, la Pologne bascule immédiatement dans la Résistance."[72] ["In Poland, there was no collaborationist government, as there was, for example, in France. And, also unlike France, where the Resistance took some time to organize itself, and even longer before acting, Poland started resisting immediately."] Whether as part of an effort to remain as faithful as possible in his portrayal to the real-life Karski or for another reason, the very negative reference to France and to the Resistance itself is also unquestionably in keeping with France's ongoing pre-occupation with French collaborationism and criminal complicity in the Holocaust, with the nation's obsessive *déclinisme* since 1940, as defined by Robert Frank. In this light, the official guilt, the "tyranny of penitence" so vividly described at the conclusion of Haenel's *Introduction à la mort française* is not just a fiction, but an appropriate historical outcome as well. If this is the case, then Haenel's "intuitvie fiction" in *Jan Karski* does less to illuminate the Europe's past than to affirm France's status quo.

NOTES

1. For the sake of convenience of access, all references to Lanzmann's essay in *Marianne*, "*Jan Karski* de Yannick Haenel: un faux roman," are from the reprinted version in *Les Temps Modernes No. 657* (January–March 2010), 1–10.
2. Ibid., 10.
3. Jan Karski, *Story of a Secret State* (Boston: Houghton Mifflin, 1944, 387–88.
4. "*Jan Karski* de Yannick Haenel: un faux roman," 5.
5. Ibid., 5.
6. Ibid., 4.
7. Wieviorka's review of *Jan Karski* appeared in *L'Histoire* 349, (2010, under the title of "Faux Temoignage." The quotes from the review here are taken from *Le monde,* 25 January 2010.
8. Yannicik Haenel, "Précisions sur *Jan Karski*, in Marc Dambre, Richard J. Golsan, and Christopher Lloyd, eds., *Mémoires occupées: Fictions françaises et seconde guerre mondiale* (Paris: Presses Sorbonne Nouvelle 2013), 237.
9. Yannick Haenel, "Le recours à la fiction n'est pas seulement un droit, il est nécessaire, "*Le monde*," 25/1/2010. Consulted 11/16/2015.
10. In an interview published in the *Le Nouvel Observateur* on 27 August 2009, for example, Haenel had addressed the "passivity" of the Allies, but added that this passivity "without doubt went all the way to complicity." He also spoke of "a secret pact among the allies to let it happen" where the extermination of the Jews was concerned, and this "for all sorts of reasons," although Haenel does not provide any.
11. Haenel, "Précisions," 241.
12. All quotes from the "Le Rapport Karski" interview are taken from the text in *Les Temps Modernes.* No. 657 (January–March, 2010).
13. Some of Karski's gestures could indicate that he believes Roosevelt is a bit full of himself, although for Lanzmann, these gestures would reveal Karski's "hammy" (*cabotin*) side which he acknowledges in his original *Marianne* essay.
14. A number of historical sources suggest that Karski was wrong in this instance, and that he did meet Frankfurter before his meeting with Roosevelt. For example, see E. Thomas Wood and Stanislaw Jankowski, *Karski: How One Man Tried to Stop the Holocaust* (New York: John Wiley and Sons, 1994) 186–96. In *Story of a Secret State*, Karski is not clear on this point.
15. "Le Rapport Karski," 19.
16. Ibid., 19.
17. Ibid., 20.
18. Ibid., 14.
19. Jan Karski, *Story of a Secret State* (Boston: Houghton Mifflin Company, 1944), 385.
20. Ibid., 386.
21. Ibid., 387.
22. Haenel, *Jan Karski*, 19.
23. Ibid., 22.
24. Ibid., 125.

25. Ibid.
26. Ibid., 126–27.
27. Ibid., 129.
28. Ibid., 131.
29. Ibid., 128.
30. Ibid., 128–29.
31. Ibid., 118.
32. Ibid., 120.
33. Ibid., 153.
34. Ibid., 115.
35. Ibid., 165.
36. E. Thomas Wood and Staislaw M. Janikowski, *Karski: How One Man Tried to Stop the Holocaust* (New York: John Wiley and Sons, 1994), 200.
37. To all appearances, Haenel's portrait of Karski is largely inspired by statements made by Karski in his review of *Shoah,* published in French in *Esprit* in 1986. In that review, Karski is blunt in his condemnation of Allied Western governments for abandoning Europe's Jews. He states "The governments of nations either lead the extermination of Jews or were indifferent to it." (114) But it is important to stress that Karski's review appeared initially in the Polish publication *Kultura* at precisely the moment when, in its relentless evocations of Polish complicity in, and in some instances approval of the Nazi extermination of the Jews *Shoah* was generating a storm of protest in Poland. Moreover, in the same review Karski argues that "humanity" did not abandon the Jews, and states that "hundreds of thousands" of Jews were saved by Europeans and "tens of thousands" saved by Poles. Although as we shall see Karski was in fact sensitive to Polish anti-Semitism, for obvious reasons in this instance he does not mention it.
38. Woods and Jankowski, 197.
39. Ibid., 201.
40. Richard Breitman and Allan J. Lichtman, *FDR and the Jews* (Cambridge: Belknap-Harvard UP, 2013), 227. Breitman and Lichtman show that the effort met with only limited success, due to administrative obstacles.
41. Woods and Jankowski, 206.
42. Ibid., 193.
43. David Reynolds, *Summits: Six Meetings that Shaped the Twentieth Century* (New York: Basic Books, 2007) 108.
44. See S. M. Plokhy, *Yalta, The Price of Peace* (New York: Viking, 2010) 241–51.
45. Quoted in Plokhy, 251.
46. Reynolds, 108.
47. Lanzmann, prefatory note to the republication of "*Jan Karski* de Yannick Haenel," *Les Temps Modernes*, 1.
48. Ibid.
49. The other "unrepresentable" phenomenon Haenel identifies in the interview is eroticism. With the exception of *Jan karski,* much of Haenel's fiction gravitates in fact around these two themes. The erotic dimension being absent from *Jan Karski* and to all appearances disconnected from the writer's treatment of history, it will not be discussed here.

50. "Entretien avec Yannicik Haenel: Précisions sur *Jan Karski*, 233.
51. "Entretien avec Yannick Haenel," 242.
52. Yannick Haenel, *Cercle* (Paris: Gallimard, 2007) 386.
53. *Cercle*, 387.
54. Yannick Haenel, *Introduction à la mort française* (Paris: Gallimard, 2001) 192.
55. A reference to the national scandal in 1985 over the distribution of HIV-contaminated blood and the government cover-up that followed.
56. *Introduction à la mort française*, 193.
57. Ibid., 184.
58. Ibid., 59.
59. Yannick Haenel, *Le sens du calme* (Paris: Mercure de France, 2011), 39.
60. Ibid.
61. *Le sens du calme*, 40.
62. "Entretien avec Yannick Haenel," 235.
63. Ibid., 241.
64. Ibid.
65. Wood and Jankowski, *Karski: How One Man Tried to Stop the Holocaust*, 249–50.
66. Anthony Beevor, "La fiction et les faits: Périls de la 'faction,'" *Le débat 165* (May–August 2011) 35.
67. "Entretien avec Yannick Haenel," 238.
68. Timothy Snyder, *Black Earth; the Holocaust as History and Warning* (New York: Tim Duggins Books, 2015) 105.
69. On this score, see Anna Bikont's recent book, *The Crime and the Silence: Confronting the Massacre of Jews in Wartime Jedwabne* (New York: Farrar, Strauss, and Giroux, 2015).
70. Wood and Jankowski, 39.
71. Wood and Jankowski, 198.
72. Haenel, *Jan Karski*, 58.

Conclusion

Will the memory of Vichy and the World War II past eventually fade and die out in France? Will the trauma it represents cease to serve as an historical and moral touchstone against which many contemporary social and political ills are measured and assessed—or mis-measured and poorly assessed, as the chapters here suggest? Will that memory continue to fire the literary imagination in a present that, according Anthony Beevor and Claude Lanzmann at least, seems drab and uninspiring by comparison?

Answers to these questions would of course be speculative and anecdotal at best. And in the wake of the 13 November 2015 terrorist attacks in Paris that killed 130 people and wounded dozens more, both questions and answers might seem misplaced, or even irrelevant. Most indicators are that France today is very much a society focused on the present and the urgent problems and threats the present poses. As a literary indicator of the current focus, certainly the most controversial novel published in 2015 is Michel Houellebecq's *Submission*, a chillingly matter-of-fact tale of an Islamic assumption of power in France. In Houellebecq perverse and provocative telling the resulting "Islamification" of France is not without certain "advantages." In removing women from the work force, it resolves overnight the problem of unemployment, as women's jobs now fall all to men. And for Houellebecq's louche and misanthropic narrator, François, it offers the additional advantage of forbidding women from wearing sexually provocative clothing, thus eliminating temptation.

But even given its apparent timeliness in focusing on *l'extrême contemporain,* Houellebecq's novel is not lacking in historical echoes, and this perhaps contributed in some measure to its *succès de scandale* following publication. In its title the novel recalls one of the most painful aspects of the history and memory of the Dark Years: a resigned "submission" to a "foreign" occupying power and the complicity of France's political elites in that capitulation. In Houellebecq's novel, the leftist Socialist Party supports the Islamic party to head off the threat posed by the now-dominant National Front (the novel takes place in 2022). And the narrator François—in his name at least a stand-in for the French "everyman"—succumbs with little resistance. Indeed he collaborates with the new order of things by apparently converting to Islam to keep his job as professor at the Sorbonne. Shades of the oath of loyalty to Pétain under Vichy.

If this reading of Houellebecq's novel seems fanciful, suggesting historical comparisons where the author, at least, may not have intended them, explicit connections between the troubled memory of the Dark Years and the current Islamic threat have been made in a number of other contexts recently. In an editorial appearing in the newspaper *Libération* two weeks after the 13 November terrorist attacks entitled "Lacombe 'Jidad' Lucien," Thomas Clerc likened the jihadists who carried out the attacks in Paris to the eponymous antihero of Louis Malle's classic 1974 film. Like Lucien Lacombe, who as noted earlier joins the French auxiliaries of the German police after being turned down by the Resistance, the November 2015 terrorists and the *Charlie Hebdo* killers of the previous January are essentially a disenfranchised, apolitical "rabble" recruited to a "nihilist" and "totalitarian" ideology because they are rejected and excluded by a French Republic given over entirely to capitalism and the all-consuming dream of "Profit." Like Lucien they are essentially victims. But unlike Lucien they are effectively "doubly" excluded in that their religion, Islam, is rejected, "unintegrateable" into French society and culture. In Malle's film, Lucien essentially has no religion (He is raised Catholic, but mocks that religion in one of the film's early scenes).

The number of dubious historical analogies—and questionable moral judgments—in "Lacombe 'Jihad' Lucien" are striking. Most obviously, the implicit analogy drawn between Vichy's French State and François Hollande's Fifth Republic is strained to say the least. And the claim that Malle's protagonist and the Paris terrorists are essentially *déclassé* victims of an indifferent and cruel society is a facile simplification of multi-faceted problem. Malle certainly never intended for Lucien Lacombe to be simply a victim. If he were, Lucien would lose all the complexity and ambiguity that made him fascinating to moviegoers at the time as well as a source of continued reflection and debate about the myths and realities of Dark Years. And, as opposed to the Paris Jihadists, Lucien at least tried to join "the right side" before succumbing to the seductions of brutality and power represented in his case by French Nazi minions. Finally, the suggestion that Islam is an excluded, a "bad" faith in contemporary France, just as Jews and Judaism were excluded and vilified in the 1930s and especially under Vichy, points to an equation that hardly stands up to the evidence. (It must also certainly have proven shocking to at least some of the editorial's readers.) Among other things, as Alain Finkielkraut has observed in a recent interview in the *Revue des deux mondes*, there were no Jewish terrorists in the France of the 1930s, as there are Islamic jihadists today.[1] Equally importantly according to Finkielkraut, the equation itself occults another troubling reality in France today, and that is a rising anti-Semitism.

In the same interview, Finkielkraut points to other ways in which the current Islamist and terrorist threats are interpreted through the prism of the World War II past. This is understandable, he states, because in equating radical Islam with fascism, with "papa's dirty beast" as Finkielkraut labels it, one makes it seem less threatening because that "dirty beast" is at least familiar. But if they make sense in this way, the comparisons between past and present still generate historical and political confusions that have unfortunate consequences today. Citing a recent controversy over Charles de Gaulle's statement at the conclusion of the Algerian War that France must welcome peoples of all races, but that for it to remain France it must remain predominantly white and European, Finkielkraut asserts that those who retroactively condemned de Gaulle as racist are in effect "making a gift of the 'man of 18 June' to the National Front"[2] It is one of the paradoxes of the present in France, and what Finkielkraut labels "the progressive *doxa*" that "anti-fascist memory is in the process of becoming anti-Gaullist."[3]

The heated debates in late 2015 and early 2016 over a constitutional amendment proposed by President Hollande to withdraw French citizenship from French-born, dual nationals convicted of terrorism also frequently drew comparisons with the World War II and Vichy pasts. For critics of the amendment, this kind of exclusion smacked of Vichy's statutes stripping Jews of their rights and citizenship during the Occupation. It also recalled fascistic dreams of "national purity" that characterized the politics of France's far right during the interwar years as well as earlier. But even those in favor of withdrawing French citizenship from binational terrorists recalled the Dark Years and their immediate aftermath in framing their support for the measure. For Finkielkraut what should also be done with these terrorists is that they be convicted and sentenced to *indignité nationale*, a Liberation-era punishment handed down to those found guilty of collaboration which prevented them from exercising their rights as citizens. In both instances, the analogies were historically problematic. In the first instance, the Fifth Republic's Islamic terrorists (or potential terrorists) were implicitly equated with Vichy's Jews in their exclusion by a racist state. In the second, *l'indignité nationale*, was a sentence handed down to many non-violent collaborators—writers, for instance—whereas violent collaborationists who fought on behalf of the Nazis, or for Vichy's *milice* for example, were imprisoned and/or executed. *L'indignité nationale* thus seems a strange punishment for potential or actual jihadists and, at least arguably, serves as another misapplication of the Vichy and World War II past to the present.

If the examples cited thus far invoke the Dark Years in relation to the realities and debates of the post-13 November moment in France, more globalizing comparisons have also been invoked to address the broader threat of Islam. The term "Islamo-fascism" has in fact been used in certain circles in France as it was in this country, especially in the post 9/11 years. But in a recent interview with the Algerian writer Boualem Sansal—widely known for his 2009 novel *The German Mujahid*, in which the dangers of Islamic fundamentalism in France are compared to those of Nazism—the connection between Islam and fascism is not one of comparison, but of *identity*. Sansal affirms in fact that "Islamism, Nazism, fascism, they are all the same thing."[4] And in his recent prize winning novel, *2084,* Sansal imagines a future Islamic-fascist state which, however, as the choice of title at least, borrows more from George Orwell's Communist-inspired dystopia than from the realities of historical Nazism and fascism.

To be sure, the World War II and Vichy pasts are not the only historical references brought to bear to explain radical Islam and Jihadist violence and the menace they pose to democratic France, or to propose ways of dealing with the threat.[5] Nor for that matter, is France the only European country in which comparisons of political practices by the Nazis and their minions are invoked to denounce current political decisions and policies by European governments. On the latter score, in January 2016 a measure by the Danish government requiring all refugees entering Denmark to hand over valuables and money as they enter Denmark to help support the Danish social security system that would support them drew cries of outrage and also comparisons to the Nazis' fleecing of Jews and others. But, if Finkielkraut is correct that the French in particular live "under the regime of historical analogy" the evidence gathered in the present study suggests that the Vichy and World War II past still assume pride of place, and that other traumas of the past as well as the present live under its shadow and are subject to its distorting lens.

But as the chapters here also confirm, the "distorting lens" in question is itself also the creation, the result of the misinterpretation or manipulation of the history and memory of the Dark Years by politicians, novelists, philosophers, and others, either for political ends in the present or, in some instances, as a means to relive the past vicariously in search for a more authentic existence. But while the literary examples of Jonathan Littell's *The Kindly Ones* and Yannick Haenel's *Jan Karski* discussed at length here offer bleak assessments of that past in part as a means to condemn the present, other writers whose work is not discussed at length in these pages draw more positive lessons for the present from the horrors of World War II. In his international bestseller *HHhH*, dealing with the assassination of Reinhard Heydrich in

Prague by Czechoslovakian partisans in May 1942 Laurent Binet draws lessons in courage, heroism, and self-sacrifice for the present from the partisans' actions. In Boualem Sansal's aforementioned *The German Mujahid*, one of the novel's protagonists, recognizing dangerous similarities between his deceased father's Nazism and the brutal authority of the local Imam in his own neighborhood in present-day Paris, resolves to struggle against and resist the latter's hegemony in the name of a better and freer future for his community.

Are these more optimistic visions of the World War II past helpful? Are they beneficial for the present? In a compelling essay entitled (appropriately enough) "The Revenge of History" Bruno Tertrais argues that they are not, for two reasons. First he argues that almost if not all historical analogies of this sort, whether positive or negative, serve to stoke nationalist sentiments, and often territorial ambitions. Moreover, each country indulges in comparisons of the present with a real (or imagined) national past that is different from that of neighboring countries, and therefore frictions between these countries and their respective pasts becomes inevitable. Where the Word War II past and positive narratives of it are concerned, Tertrais argues that "heroic" narratives of it are emerging precisely because those who experienced the full weight of its horrors and destruction of the war are dying out, and only its historically misleading "heroic" dimensions remain. And this, Tertrais adds, encourages the instrumentalization of the memory of the war to fuel new nationalisms and, potentially at least, new conflicts.[6]

As the present study confirms, there is little danger in France of a simplistic or "heroic" account of the World War II past taking hold, and leading to excessive nationalism or territorial expansionism. In fact, the evidence provided here suggests that on balance the reverse is the problem: can France move beyond largely negative images of its World War II past that continue to weigh on the present? And, as Bruno Tertrais argues, even if the nation succeeded in finally "reconciling" itself to the past, while necessary earlier 'reconciliation" with that past is hardly relevant today, seventy years after the Liberation. In fact Tertrais asserts, it is both ludicrous and dangerous now, in that reconciliation per se implies that all parties are equally at fault, equally guilty, which is certainly not the case where the Vichy past is concerned.[7]

What is to be done? What can break the cycle of recurring scenarios, recurring "memories" that have the potential at least to monopolize and distort debate in the present, and often seem to require rehashing old and stale arguments rather than stimulate fresh insights into current events and crises? In his interview in *Revue des deux mondes* Finkielkraut, in response to a question from his interviewer, addresses the old charge that he and other "New Reactionaries" and "racists" including Houellebecq, Michel Onfray and Régis Debray are once again opposing the "camp of the good" in the current circumstances and promoting the agenda of the far right on the national stage.[8] As the discussion in Chapter 2 here indicates, the question as well as the historical scenario it implies constitute a reprise of the 2002 debate following the publication of Daniel Lindenberg's *Le Rappel à l'ordre*. It should come as no surprise that Lindenberg's incendiary pamphlet has been re-issued by the *Editions du Seuil* and that in some quarters at least, it is being hailed anew as "clairvoyant" and "prophetic."[9]

Recognizing the need to come to terms with, and move beyond traumatic memories of the past, and Vichy and World War II pasts foremost among them, figures including Tzvetan Todorov, Pascal Bruckner, and others have proposed various types of solutions. In a brief essay entitled *Les abus de la mémoire* published originally in the mid-1990s Todorov argued for the primacy of what he called "exemplary memory" over "literal memory." Whereas the latter involves an incessant, obsessive and uncritical rumination on a trauma experienced and a demand for retribution or reparation in the present, the former implies something else. Exemplary memory implies acceptance of the trauma one has undergone, along with the obligation to understand it in critical terms and to turn one's knowledge and understanding into positive lessons for, as well as positive actions in the present. For Todorov, the latter eliminates not only an unhealthy dwelling on the past at the expense of the present, but also the tendency to see all traumatic memories in similar terms, which encourages their competition. Universal analogies of this sort, he writes, "make all cats in distress in the night gray."[10]

Todorov's solution to the problem of memory is it would seem more applicable on an individual or group level than on a national level. To address the problem of memory on a national level, Pascal Bruckner proposes a different solution. Alongside the need to recognize and come to terms with the crimes of the past, to fulfill a "duty to memory," France needs also to acknowledge what he labels a "duty to our past glories," to recognize what the nation and the French have accomplished as a people. In his call for a renewed national pride of sorts, as a counterbalance to the nation's recognition of its crimes, Bruckner's assertions echo in fact statements made earlier by Albert Camus at the height of the Algerian war, and recorded in the *Chroniques algériennes*: "It is good for a nation to be strong enough in its traditions and its honor to find the courage to denounce its errors. But that nation must not forget the reasons it has for self-esteem."[11]

Both of these approaches have their merits as well as their limitations (as both writers would likely acknowledge), and both entail an "activist" dimension, an approach which poses its own problems. So perhaps a more fundamental step is necessary, and one which is suggested by a statement made in Sudhir Hazareesingh's recent book, *How the French Think*. According to Hazareesingh, "there remains to this day a sacred and quasi-messianic dimension to French views of the nation." He continues: "Republicanism, France's dominant political tradition long operated as a civic religion, with its own cults, martyrs, missionaries, holy texts—and it is no coincidence that the hallowed Parisian cenotaph for national heroes, the Panthéon, is a deconsecrated church."[12] In its many representations in this book and elsewhere, the Vichy past and through it the Dark Years of World War II and Nazism have come to embody the absolute *antithesis* of the nation and republican France. If this is the case, and if one accepts Hazareesingh's claims for the sacredness of the nation and the Republic in French eyes, then the Vichy past, the Dark Years themselves, are not only an historical aberration but in moral and even religious terms, something *sacrilegious,* something *blasphemous.* Alongside Rousso's discussion of France's "presentist" obsession with the past, this perception would account for the continuing urgency and scandal of that past in moral terms.

So for France to move beyond a preoccupation with the repetitive and sclerotic memory of the Dark Years, a first step would appear to be to "disarm," to "desacralize" that past as a foil as well as a distorting mirror to the nation's self-image, to let it become truly "past." But that "desacralization" of the World War II past would also logically require something else, and that is a parallel effort to move away from the "sacred and quasi-messianic dimension to French views of the nation" that Hazareesingh describes. As this study confirms, in recent years and indeed up to the present, a crucial dimension of this sacralization of the nation and of the French Republic has involved the celebration in numerous contexts of the Resistance during World War II, along with its heroes. The inclusion in the Panthéon of Geneviève de Gaulle, Pierre Brossolette, and Germaine Tillion in 2015 is one example of this phenomenon. So were the 2014 celebrations of the D-Day landings described in the Introduction here. But as Finkielkraut's defense of Charles de Gaulle discussed above suggests, the central figure around which this repeated consecration of the Resistance centers is the "man of 18 June." While Finkielkraut is not wrong in defending de Gaulle against the anachronistic distortion of his politics in the present, that defense remains uncritical of the General's legacy in ways that *are* appropriate in historical terms. As noted in the Introduction here, *Libération's* account of the liberation of Paris in August also featured a similar heroization of de Gaulle in ways that at least partially erased the historical backdrop against which the Liberation of Paris occurred. All of these examples constitute only a few among many instances in which the Resistance and its heroes are deployed in the present to shore up a national self-image and make it somehow impregnable to the vicissitudes of the present and the troubling memories from the past.

Perhaps ironically then, it would seem that the way out of the apparent impasse of the memory of Vichy and World War II in France is to renounce the "cure" applied, to seek Pascal Bruckner's "national glories" not in instances of extreme heroism and courage but in more mundane and "everyday" gestures of solidarity and support that do not rely on grandiose and tragic historical contexts for their meaning. When Camus published *The Plague,* his allegory of resistance to Nazi terror in 1947, he was roundly criticized for using the metaphor of an epidemic to capture the horrors of Nazism. But one result of this choice was that the self-sacrifice and generosity his "heroes"—Dr. Rieux, Tarrou, Grand, and the rest—were all the more moving for their simplicity, their timelessness, and the fact that did *not* arise out of a struggle with radical *human* evil. The lesson Camus draws from the more modest and humble circumstances of these men's struggle is that "there is more to admire in men than to despise,"[13] something that dwelling on the Vichy past obscures. So, to paraphrase Jack Burden, the narrator of Robert Penn Warren's *All the Kings Men,* where the Vichy and World War II pasts are concerned it is better for the French to move "out of history" in order to move back "into history," and face "the awful responsibility of time."[14]

NOTES

1. Alain Finkielkraut, "Qu'avons-nous fait du 11 janvier?" *Revue des deux mondes* (December 2015–January 2016), 10.

2. Ibid., 14.

3. Ibid., p. 13. It is of interest to note that in the same interview in which Finkielkraut denounces sweeping historical linkages between the present European crisis and the World War II past, he describes Germany's generous immigration policy as a moment of "redemption" and contrasts Angela Merkel's openness to the other to the Nazis hatred of the other (16).

4. Boualem Sansal, "Dans cinquante ans le totalitarianisme islamique est possible," *Revue des deux mondes* (December 2015–January 2016), 112.

5. In the December 13–14, 2015 issue of *Le monde* Tzvetan Todorov invoked his childhood and adolescence in Communist Bulgaria to underscore the dangers of a totalitarian regime's dehumanization of its enemies. That dehumanization, he adds, eventually justified the latter's extermination. According to Todorov, in the wake of events like 9/11 and the Paris attacks political leaders in Western democracies—like Communist and totalitarian leaders before them—are adopting a Lenin's maxim "exterminate without pity the enemies of freedom." In this case, the enemies to be annihilated are not only terrorists who carry out attacks in America and Europe but those Islamists in spawning grounds like war-torn Syria and Iraq. For Todorov, violence against these enemies both close and far-flung only breeds more violence, and one would be better served to follow the example of Nelson Mandela, who brought down the apartheid system in part by refusing to dehumanize his adversaries.

6. Bruno Tertrais, "La revanche de l'histoire," *Revue des deux mondes* (December 2015–January 2016), 158–59.

7. Tertrais, 160.
8. Finkielkraut, 11.
9. See the review by Sonya Faure and Cécile Daumas of the republication of Lindenberg's pamphlet, "Nouveau Réacs: piqûre de 'Rappels'" in *Libération*, 20 January 2016.
10. Tzvetan Todorov, *Les abus de la mémoire* (Paris: Arléa, 1995), 46.
11. Albert Camus, *Chroniques algériennes* in *Oeuvres complètes IV, 1957–1959* (Paris: Gallimard, Editions de la Pléïade, 2008), 302.
12. Sudhir Hazareesingh, *How the French Think: An Affectionate Portrait of an Intellectual People* (New York: Basic Books, 2015.), xi–xii.
13. Albert Camus, *La peste* in *Oeuvres complètes*, vol. II (Paris: Gallimard, 2006), 248.
14. Robert Penn Warren, *All the Kings's Men* (New York: Harcourt, Brace, Jovanovich, 1946), 464.

Acknowledgements

This book has been several years in the making. It has benefitted enormously from the support, ideas, and criticisms offered by family and friends on both sides of the Atlantic. As always, my wife Nancy and our children James, Jody and Ashley are the reasons why. Their love—and their patience—have always kept me going. Friends and colleagues in College Station/Bryan have made my life here rich and rewarding. These include colleagues at Texas A&M Terry Anderson, Nathan Bracher, Stefanie Harris, Melanie Hawthorne, Brian Linn, Larry Reynolds, Bob Shandley, Apostolos Vasilakis, Arnie and Jan Krammer (who gave me the commemorative Pétain plate whose photograph adorns the cover) and the indispensable Ede Hilton-Lowe. They also include the wonderful staff and student apprentices at the Glasscock Center: my Associate Director, Sarah Misemer, and also Donna Malak, Hannah Waugh, Amanda Elsner, Kelsey Morgan, and Desiree Embree. Kelsey and Desiree prepared the final versions of this manuscript. Terry Anderson and Larry Reynolds, along with Brian Harley, have been tennis partners as well as friends for years, and Brian is the world's best stringer! I would also like to thank my sister-in-law Ultima Morgan, in whose beautiful Lake Winnisquam home two chapters of this book were written.

One of the most admirable traits of the French character in my opinion is that the French greatly value friendship and are wonderful and constant friends. I would like to thank the following friends for sharing their lives and ideas with me, making France a second home: Pascal Bruckner, Marc and Sylvie Dambre, Jean-Jacques Fleury, Guy Hareau and Christine Scenazi, Annette Lévy-Willard and Ludi Boeken, Pat and Hervé Picton, Henry Rousso, and Tzvetan Todorov.

Over the years, colleagues and friends at other institutions have shared their ideas and enthusiasms, and working with many of them on a variety of projects has made my professional life and career a genuine pleasure, and indeed a privilege. There are too many to mention them all here, but I am most grateful to Chris Flood, Leah Hewitt, Lynn Higgins, Mary Jean Green, Mary Byrd Kelly and Van Kelly, Don Reid, Susan Suleiman, and Phil Watts, who died tragically young three years ago.

I have had the great pleasure of being invited to present parts of this work at other universities in this country and abroad, and I would like to thank the following institutions and individuals for inviting me to visit their campuses: Lynn Higgins and Barbara Will at Dartmouth College; Susan Suleiman at Harvard University, Margaret Atack at the University of Leeds; Hugo Frey at the University of Chichester; Marc Silverman and Florence Vatan at the University of Wisconsin-Madison; Helen Solterer at Duke; the French Graduate Student Association and Lie Brozgal at UCLA; Debarati Sanyal at UC-Berkeley; Phil Watts at Columbia; Julia Elsky at MIT; Noit Banai at Tufts University; Lex McMillan at Albright College; Leah Hewitt at Amherst; Christian Delage at the Cardozo School of Law; and Marc Dambre and Bruno Blanckeman at *Université Paris III-Sorbonne Nouvelle*.

The writing of this book has also witnessed the passing of loved ones whose presence on this earth made it a better place not just for me, but for many, many others as well. These include dear friends Wayne Ahr, Mary Reid, and Phil Watts. Most importantly, my mother, Lucy Golsan, died just as this book was being completed. Among the many, many gifts she gave to me was a love of France and the French, and I am sorry she never got to read this book which, I hope, expresses these sentiments, if indirectly or imperfectly. She also taught me the value and meaning of friendship, which has enriched my life immeasurably. When she died she left many, many friends behind.

Finally, I would like to thank the journals *SubStance*, *Yale French Studies*, and *L'Esprit Créateur*. Portions of Chapter 2 originally appeared in *SubStance*; of Chapter 4, in *Yale French Studies*; and of Chapter 5 in *L'Esprit Créateur*.

Bibliography

Allègre, Claude. "Le crepuscule de l'intellectuel cru." *L'Express* (January 25, 2001).
Anderson, Perry. *The New Old World*. London and New York: Verso, 2009.
———. "Union Sacrée." *London Review of Books* 26, no. 18 (September 23, 2004): 10–16.
Apter, Emily. "Laws of the 70's: Badiou's Revolutionary Untimeliness." *Cardozo Law Review* 29, no. 5 (2007–2008): 1885–1904.
Arbor, Madam Justice Louise. *War Crimes and the Culture of Peace*. Toronto, Buffalo, and London: University of Toronto Press Incorporated, 2002.
Ash, Timothy Garton. "The Life of Death." *The New York Review of Books* 32, no. 20 (December 19, 1985). http://www.nybooks.com/articles/1985/12/19/the-life-of-death/.
Atack, Margaret and Christopher Lloyd, ed. *Framing Narratives of the Second World War and Occupation in France, 1939–2009*. Manchester: Manchester University Press, 2012.
Azouvi, François. *Le Mythe du Grand Silence: Auschwitz, les Français, la mémoire*. Paris: Fayard, 2012.
Badiou, Alain. *The Meaning of Sarkozy*. Translated by David Fernbach. London: Verso, 2008.
———. *Metapolitics*. Translated by Jason Barker. London: Verso, 2005.
———. *Polemics*. Translated by Steve Corcoran. London: Verso, 2006.
———. *Sarkozy: pire que prévu. Les autres: prévoir le pire*. Paris: Nouvelles Éd. Linges, 2012.
———. "Le rouge et le tricolore." *Le Monde*. Last Modified January 27, 2015. Accessed February 2, 2015. http://www.lemonde.fr/idees/article/2015/01/27/le-rouge-et-le-tricolore_4564083_3232.html.
———. "The Three Negations." *Cardozo Law Review* 29, no. 5 (April 2008): 1877–883.
Baruch, Marc Olivier. *Des Lois Indignes?* Paris: Tallander 2013.

Baudrillard, Jean. *Paroxysm: Inverview with Philippe Petit*. Translated by Chris Turner. London and New York: Verso, 1998.
Bédarida, Fançois. *Touvier, Vichy et le Crime Contre l'Humanité: le dossier de l'accusation*. Paris: Seuil, 1996.
Birnbaum, Jean. "Pierre Rosanvallon: 'Il faut refaire le baggage d'idées de la démocratie française.'" *Le Monde* (November 21, 2002).
———. "Trois questions à Pierre Nora." *Le Monde* (November 21, 2002).
Birnbaum, Jean, and Nicolas Weill. "Ce livre qui brouille les familles intellectuelles." *Le Monde* (November 21, 2002).
Blanchard, Pascal, and Isabelle Veyrat-Masson. *Les Guerres de Mémoires: La France et son historie*. Paris: La Découverte, 2008.
Boons-Grafé, Marie-Claire. "Un Autre portrait d'Alain Badiou." *Le Nouvel Observateur*. Last modified July 4, 2010. http://bibliobs.nouvelobs.com/essais/20100407.BIB5180/un-autre-portrait-d-039-alain-badiou.html.
Braganca, Manuel. "Faire parler les morts: sur Jan Karski et la controverse Lanzmann-Haenel." *Modern and Contemporary France* 23, no. 1, (2015): 35–46.
Bruckner, Pascal. *Un bon fils*. Paris: Benard Grasset, 2014.
———. *The Tyranny of Guilt: An Essay on Western Masochism*. Translated by Steven Rendall. Princeton and Oxford: Princeton University Press, 2010.
Camus, Renaud. *Du sens*. Paris: P.O.L., 2002.
Chandernagor, Françoise. "The Historian at the Mercy of the Law." *Liberté Pour l' Histoire CNRS Edition* (2008). http://www.lph-asso.fr/index.php?option=com_content&view=article&id=150&Itemid=&lang=en.
Chaumont, Jean-Michel. *La Concurrence des Victimes: génocide, identité, reconnaissance*. Paris: Découverte, 1997.
Clerc, Thomas. "Lacombe 'Jihad' Lucien." *Libération*. Last Modified November 27, 2015. Accessed December 4, 2015. http://www.liberation.fr/chroniques/2015/11/27/lacombe-jihad-lucien_1416690.
Conan, Éric. "Badiou, la star de la philo est-il un salaud?" *Marianne* no. 671, (February 27, 2010).
———. "La fin des intellectuels français." *L'Express* (November 30, 2001).
———. *Le Procès Papon: Un Journal d'audience*. Paris: Gillimard, 1998.
Conan, Éric, and Henry Rousso. *Vichy: an Ever-Present Past*. Translated by Nathan Bracher. Hanover and London: University Press of New England, 1998.
———. *Vichy, un passé qui ne passe pas*. Paris: Fayard, 2013.
Coquery-Vidrovitch, Catherine, Giles Manceron, and Gérard Noiriel. "Les Historiens n'ont pas le monopole de la mémoire." *Le Monde*. Las modified July 11, 2008. Accessed February 7, 2015. http://www.lemonde.fr/idees/article/2008/11/07/les-historiens-n-ont-pas-le-monopole-de-la-memoire-par-catherine-coquery-vidrovitch-gilles-manceron-et-gerard-noiriel_1116082_3232.html.
Courtois, Stéphane, Nicolas Werth, Jean-Louis Panné, Andrezej Paczkowki, Karel Bartošek, Jean-Louis Margolin. *The Black Book of Communism: Crimes, Terror, Repression*. Translated by Jonathan Murphy and Mark Kramer. Cambridge, MA and London: Harvard University Press, 1999.
Crémieux-Brilhac, Jean-Louis. "La Complexité du cas fançais." *Le Débat* no. 183 (2015): 168–92.

Dambre, Marc, Christopher D. Lloyd, and Richard J. Golsan, ed. *Mémoires Occupées: Fictions Françaises et Seconde Guerre Mondiale*. Paris: Presses Sorbonne Nouvelle, 2013.

Dean, Carolyn J. *The Fragility of Empathy After the Holocaust*. Ithaca and London: Cornell University Press, 2004.

Debray, Régis. "L'intellectuel a été piégé par le vedettariat." *L'Express* (November 30, 2000).

Denieul, Séverine. "Les habits neufs d' Alain Badiou." *Lieux Communs*. Accessed July 6, 2013. https://collectiflieuxcommuns.fr/482-les-habits-neufs-d-alain-badiou-1?lang=fr.

Finkielkraut, Alain. "Une interview du Grand Homme défiguré." *Le Figaro* (November 14, 2002).

———. *Remembering in Vain*. Translated by Roxanne Lapidus and Sima Godfrey. New York: Columbia University Press, 1992.

Finkielkraut, Alain, Marcel Gauchet, Pierre Manent, Philippe Maury, Pierre-André Taguieff, Shmuel Trigano, and Paul Yonnet. "Manifeste pour une pensée libre." *L'Express* (November 28, 2002).

Forcari, Christophe, and Laurent Joffrin. "Août 1944: la liberté Guidant Paris." *Libération*. 22 Août 2014. http://www.liberation.fr/societe/2014/08/22/aout-1944-la-liberte-guidant-paris_1085140.

Frank, Robert. "La France est passée de l'idée de déclin à celle de décadence." Interview by Béatrice Vallaeys. *Libération*. July 11, 2014.

———. *La hantise du déclin: La France de 1914 à 2014*. Paris: Belin, 2014.

Friedländer, Saul. *Reflections of Nazism: an Essay on Kitsch and Death*. Translated by Thomas Weyr. New York: Harper & Row, 1984.

Grollmus, Denise. "In the Polish Aftermath." *Tablet*. April 17, 2013. http://www.tabletmag.com/jewish-arts-and-culture/129082/in-the-polish-aftermath.

Golsan, Richard J., "L'Affaire Karski: Fiction, History, Memory Unreconciled." *L'Esprit Créateur* 50, no. 4 (2010): 81–96.

———. "The American Reception of Max Aue." *SubStance* 121, no. 39 (2010): 174–83.

———. ed. *Memory, the Holocaust, and French Justice*. Translated by Lucy Golsan and Richard J. Golsan. Hanover and London: University Press of New England, 1996.

———. "The Poetics and Perils of Faction: Contemporary French Fiction and the Memory of World War II." *Romanic Review* 105, no. 1–2. Edited by Vincent Debaene and Richard J. Golsan, 53–68. Lillington, NC: Edwards Brothers, Inc., 2014.

———. ed. *The Papon Affair: Memory and Justice on Trial*. Translated by Lucy B. Golsan and Richard J. Golsan. New York and London: Routledge, 2000.

———. "What Does 'Vichy' Mean Now?." In *Being Contemporary: French Literature, Culture, and Politics Today*. Edited by Lia Brozgal and Sara Kippur. 127–43. Liverpool: Liverpool University Press, 2016.

———. "Where the Past is Always in the Present Tense." *The Los Angeles Review of Books*. Last Modified February 10, 2015. Accessed March 14, 2015. https://lareviewofbooks.org/article/past-always-present-tense/.

Guérin, Jeanyves, and Alain Schaffner., ed. *La portée de l'Histoire: Études sur le roman français moderne et contemporain.* Villeneuve d'Ascq: Roman 20–50, 2011.
Guéry, Christian. "Faisons confiance au juge." In *Juger Sous Vichy.* Paris: Seuil, 1994.
Gutting, Gary. *Thinking the Impossible: French Philosophy Since 1960.* Oxford: Oxford University Press, 2011.
Haenel, Yannick. *Cercle: roman.* Pars: Gallimard, 2007.
———. *Introduction à la mort française: roman.* Paris: Gallimard, 2001.
———. *Jan Karski: roman.* Paris: Gallimard, 2009.
———. *The Messenger.* Berkeley, CA: Counterpoint, 2012.
———. "Le recours à la fiction n'est pas seulement un droit, il est necessaire." *Le Monde.* Last Modified January 25, 2010. Accessed November 16, 2015. http://www.lemonde.fr/idees/article/2010/01/25/le-recours-a-la-fiction-n-est-pas-seulement-un-droit-il-est-necessaire-par-yannick-haenel_1296378_3232.html.
———. *Le sens du calme.* Paris: Mercure du France, 2011.
Hake, Sabine. *Screen Nazis: Cinema, History, and Democracy.* Madison, WI: The University of Wisconsin Press, 2012.
Hautin-Guiraud, Denis. "'Nouveaux réactionnaires': un manifeste en réplique." *Le Monde* (November 21, 2002).
Hazareesingh, Sudhir. *How the French Think: An Affectionate Portrait of an Intellectual People.* New York: Basic Books, 2015.
Hewlett, Nick. "Engagement and Transcendence: The Militant Philosophy of Alain Badiou." *Modern & Contemporary France* 12, no. 3 (2004): 335–52.
Higgins, Lynn A. "Old Waves, New Waves: French Cinema in 1974." *Contemporary French and Francophone Studies* 14, no. 5 (2010): 469–76.
Hochmann, Thomas. "Le Problème des lois dites 'mémorielles' sera-t-il résolu par les résolutions? La référence à l'article 34–1 de la Constitution dans le discours contemporain sure les relations entre le Parlement et l'histoire." *Droit et cultures* 66 (2013): 57–69.
Hollande, François. "The 'Crime Committed in France, by France.'" *New York Review of Books.* Las Modified August 18, 2012. Accessed May 14, 2015. http://www.nybooks.com/daily/2012/08/18/france-hollande-crime-vel-d-hiv/.
Houellebecq, Michel. *Soumission.* Paris: Flammarion, 2015.
Husson, Édouard, and Michel Terestchenko. *Les Complaisantes: Jonathan Littell et l'écriture du mal.* Paris: François-Xavier de Guibert, 2007.
Hutton, Margaret-Anne. "Jonathan Littell's *Les Bienveillantes*: Ethics, Aesthetics and the Subject of Judgement." *Modern & Contemporary France* 18, no. 1 (2010): 1–15.
Huyssen, Andreas. *Present Pasts: Urban Palimpsests and the Politics of Memory.* Stanford: Stanford University Press, 2003.
Igounet, Valérie. *Le Front National de 1972 à nos jours Le parti, les hommes, les idées.* Paris: Éditions du Seuil, 2014.
Jankélévitch, Vladimir. *Forgiveness.* Translated by Andrew Kelley. Chicago and London: University of Chicago Press, 2005.

Jenkins, Joseph. "Violence in Badiou's Recent Work." *Cardozo Law Review* 29, no. 5 (2007–2008): 2121–31.

Johnston, Adrian. "The Right Left: Alain Badiou and the Disruption of Political Identities." *Yale French Studies* 116/117 (2009): 55–78.

Judt, Tony. *Reappraisals*. London: Penguin Press, 2008.

Julliard, Jaques. *L'Année des Dupes*. Paris: Éditions du Seuil, 1996.

———. *L'année des fantômes: Journal 1997*. Paris: Bernard Grasset, 1998.

Karski, Jan. *Story of a Secret State*. Boston: Houghton Mifflin Company, 1944.

Kershaw, Ian. "'Working Towards the Führer.' Reflections on the Nature of the Hitler Dicatorship." *Contemporary European History* 2, no. 2 (July 1993): 103–18.

Klarsfeld, Serge. *Mémoires*. Paris: Fayard Flammarion, 2015.

Klarsfeld, Serge, Didier Daenickx, Danis Tanovic, and Alain Jakubowicz., First Signatories. "Ne mélangeons pas tout." (Manifesto) *L'OBS* (December 20, 2005).

Kristeva, Julia. "De l'abjection à la banalité du mal." Accessed May 5, 2014. http://www.kristeva.fr/abjection.html.

Laborie, Pierre. *Le Chagrin et le vénin: La France sous l'Occupation, mémoire et idées reçues*. Montrouge: Bayard Éditions, 2011.

Lacoste, Charlotte. *Séductions du bourreau*. Paris: Presses Universitaires de France, 2010.

Lagasnerie, Geoffroy de. "De quoi Badiou est-il le symptôme?." *Libération*. Last modified Janurary 10, 2008. Accessed July 19, 2015. http://www.liberation.fr/tribune/2008/01/10/de-quoi-badiou-est-il-le-symptome_62312.

Laignel-Lavastine, Alexandra. "Marcel Gauchet, au chevet de la démocratie." *Le Monde* (November 21, 2002).

———. *La pensée égarée: Islamisme, populisme, antisémitisme: essai sure les penchants suicidaries de l'Europe*. Paris: Bernard Grasset, 2015.

Lançon, Philippe. "La traque des nouveaux réacs." *Libération*. (November 19, 2002).

Lanzmann, Claude. "Historique de 'L'affaire Badiou-Winter.'" *Les Temps Modernes* 3 no. 637, 638, 639 (2006): 728–68.

———. "L'Humanitaire et le Tragique de l'Histoire." *Les Temps Modernes* 2, no. 627 (2004): 1–9.

———. "*Jan Karski* de Yannick Haenel: Un Faux Roman." *Les Temps Modernes* 657, (January–March 2010): 1–10.

———. "Universalité des victims, singularité des événements historiques." *Les Temps Modernes* 1–2, no. 635–36 (2006): 1–3.

"La République et ses héros [Pierre Brossolette, Geneviëe de Gaulle Anthonioz, Germaine Tillion, and Jean Zay]: La panthéonisation, un ritual daté?." *Esprit* 5, no. 414 (2015).

Lévy-Willard, Annette. "Paxton enfonce le clou." *Libération*. Last Modified October 13, 2015. Accessed October 14, 2015. http://annette.blogs.liberation.fr/2015/10/13/paxton-enfonce-le-clou/.

Lévy, Bernard-Henri. *Archives d'un Procès: Klaus Barbie*. Paris: Le Livre de Poche, 1986.

Liauzu, Claude, and Gilles Manceron. *La Colonisation, la loi et l'histoire*. Paris: Syllepse, 2006.

Lilla, Mark. "France: The Ground Shifts." *NYR* (blog). January 14, 2015 (5:50 p.m.). http://www.nybooks.com/daily/2015/01/14/france-after-terror-ground-shifts/.

Lindenberg, Daniel. *Le procès des Lumières*. Paris: Èditions du Seuil, 2009.

———. *Le rappel à l'ordre: Enquête sur les nouveaux reactionaries*. Paris: Éditions du Seuil et La République des idées, 2002.

———. "Rester à gauche après le totalitarisme." *Le Monde* (November 21, 2002).

Littell, Jonathan, and Pierre Nora. "Conversation sur l'histoire et le roman." *Le débat* 144, (May–April 2007): 25–44.

Littell, Jonathan, and Richard Millet. "Conversation à Beyrouth." *Le débat* 144, (May–April 2007): 4–24.

"Ce livre qui brouille les familles intellectuelles." [on Daniel Lindenberg, *Le Rappel à l'ordre*.] *Le Monde* (November 21, 2002).

Lorcin, Patricia, M. E., and Daniel Brewer. *France and its Spaces of War: Experience, Memory, Image*. New York: Palgrave Macmillan, 2009.

Maier, Charles S. "A Surfeit of Memory? Reflections on History, Melancholy and Denial." *History and Memory* 5, no. 2 (Fall-Winter, 1993): 136–52.

Maillard, Jean de. "À quoi sert le procès Papon?" *Le débat* 4, no. 101 (1998): 32–42.

Manent, Pierre. *Situation de la France*. Paris: Desclée de Brouwer, 2015.

Marrus, Michael R., and Robert O. Paxton. *Vichy et les Juifs*. France: Calmann-Lévy, 1981. (Revised Edition, 2015).

Marty, Éric. *Un querelle avec Alain Badiou, philosophe*. Paris: Gillmard, 2007.

Mathy, Jean-Philippe. *Melancholy Politics: Loss, Mourning, and Memory in Late Modern France*. University Park, PA: The Pennsylvania State University Press, 2011.

Maximin, Daniel, Stéphane Pocrain, and Christiane Taubira. "Quelle mémoire de l'esclavage?" *Esprit* 332. (February 2007): 62–70.

Minc, Alain. *L' Homme Aux Deux Visages: Jean Moulin, René Bousquet: itinéraires croisés*. Paris: Grasset, 2013.

Nora, Pierre. "Liberté pour l'histoire!" *Le Monde*. Last modified October 11, 2008. http://www.lph-asso.fr/index/php?option=com_content&view=article&id=4%3Apierre-nora-l-liberte-pour-lhistoire-r&catid=4%3Atribunes&Itedmid=4&lang=fr.

Nora, Pierre, and Françoise Chandernagor. *Liberté pour l'histoire*. Paris: CNRS Éditions, 2008.

Offenstadt, Nicolas. *L'Histoire Bling-Bling: Le retour du roman national*. Paris: Stock, 2009.

Onfray, Michel, Elisabeth Lévy, Eric Zemmour and Alain Finkielkraut. "Néoréacs: piqûre de 'Rappel.'" *Libération*. Last modified Janurary 20, 2016. http://www.liberation.fr/debats/2016/01/20/neoreacs-piqure-de-rappel_1427832.

Orwell, George. *Orwell in Spain*. London: Penguin, 2001.

Pauchet, Catherine. "Soyons réactionnaires." *Libération* (November 9, 2002).

Paxton, Robert. "How Vichy Made it Worse." *The New York Review of Books* 61, no. 7 (April 24, 2014). http://www.nybooks.com/articles/2014/04/24/how-vichy-made-it-worse/.

Péan, Pierre. *L'Extrémiste: François Genoud, de Hitler à Carlos*. Paris: Fayard, 1996.

Rateau, Paul. "La Vérité, Le Mensonge et la Loi." *Les Temps Modernes* 4, no. 645–46, (2007): 26–58.

Rémond, René. "Quand l'État se mêle de l'Histoire." Paris: Stock, 2006.
Rioux, Jean-Pierre. "Les avatars du 'devoir de mémoire.'" *Le débat* 3, no. 170 (2012): 186–92.
Robin, Corey. "Dragon-Slayers." *London Review of Books* 29 no. 1, (January 4, 2007): 18–20.
Rothberg, Michael. *Multidirectional Memory*. Stanford: Stanford University Press, 2009.
Rogozinski, Jacob. "Le philosophe et le djihadiste." *Le Monde*. Last Modified February 26, 2015. Accessed November 23, 2015. http://www.lemonde.fr/idees/article/2015/02/20/le-philosophe-et-le-djihadiste_4580674_3232.html.
Rosanvallon, Pierre. "Il faut refaire le baggage d'idées de la démocratie française." *Le Monde* (November 21, 2002).
Rousso, Henry. *Face au Passé. Essais sur la mémoire contemporaine*. Paris: Belin, 2016.
———. "La France a-t-elle eu la mémoire qui flanche?" *Marianne* 3 (November 2012): 92–95.
———. *Le Régime de Vichy*. Paris: Presses Universitaires de France, 2007.
———. *The Latest Catastrophe: History, the Present, the Contemporary*. Translated by Jane Marie Todd. Chicago and London: The University of Chicago Press, 2016.
———. *The Vichy Syndrome: History and Memory in France since 1944*. Translated by Arthur Goldhammer. Cambridge and London: Harvard University Press, 1991.
Runia, Eelco. *Moved by the Past: Discontinuity and Historical Mutation*. New York: Columbia University Press, 2014.
Salvan, Chloé. "Pour aujourd'hui: Badiou?" *Etudes*. Last modified October 25, 2010. Accessed July 3, 2013. https://www.revue-etudes.com/article/pour-aujourd-hui-badiou-13353.
Samuels, Maurice. "Alain Badiou and Antisemitism." In *Being Contemporary: French Literature, Culture, and Politics Today*. Edited by Lia Brozgal and Sara Kippur. 107–23. Liverpool: Liverpool University Press, 2016.
Sandberg, Eric. "'This Incomprehensible Thing'" Jonathan Littell's *The Kindly Ones* and the Aesthetics of Excess." *Cambridge Quarterly* 43, no. 3 (2014): 231–55.
Scruton, Roger. "A nothing would do as well." *The Times Literary Supplement* 5709 (August 31, 2012). http://www.the-tls.co.uk/articles/private/a-nothing-would-do-as-well/.
Semelin, Jacques. *Persécutions et Entraides dans la France Occupée: Comment 75% des Juifs en France ont Échappé à la mort*. Paris: Seuil and Le Arènes, 2013.
Silverman, Max. *Palimpsestic Memory: The Holocaust and Colonialism in French and Francophone Fiction and Film*. New York and Oxford: Berghahn Books, 2013.
Snyder, Timothy. *Black Earth: The Holocaust as History and Warning*. New York: Time Duggan Books, 2015.
———. *Bloodlands: Europe Between Hitler and Stalin*. New York: Basic Books, 2010.
Suleiman, Susan Rubin. *Crises of Memory and the Second World War*. Cambridge and London: Harvard University Press, 2006.

Taguieff, Pierre-André. "Le Nouvel opium des intellectuels." *Le Figaro* (November 27, 2002).

Tarnero, Jacques. "Badiou: misère de la lumpen-philosophie." *Causeur* (2 February 2015). http://www.causeur.fr/alain-badiou-etienne-balibar-terrorisme-31311.html.

Tertrais, Bruno. "La revanche de l'histoire." *Revue des Deux Mondes* (December 2015–January 2016): 150–60.

Theweleit, Klaus. "On the German Reaction to Jonathan Littell's *Les Vienveillantes*." *New German Critique* 106, no. 36 (Winter 2009): 21–34.

Todorov, Tzetan. *Les Abus de la mémoire*. Paris: Arléa, 2004.

———. *Hope and Memory: Reflection on the Twentieth Century*. London: Atlantic Books, 2003.

———. "Letter from Paris." *Salmagundi* no. 88/89 (Fall 1990-Winter 1991): 33–37.

———. *Memory as Remedy for Evil*. Translated by Gila Walker. London, New York, and Calcutta: Seagull Books, 2010.

———. *La Signature Humaine*. Paris: Seuil, 2009.

Toranian, Valérie. "Alain Finkielkraut. 'Qu'avons-nous fait du 11 janvier?'" *Revue des Deux Mondes,* (December 2015–January 2016): 8–22.

———. "Les raciness du mal." *Revue des Deux Mondes* (December 2015–January 2016), 5–6.

Turowicz, Jerzy. "'Shoah' and Poland." *The New York Review of Books* 33, no. 8 (May 8, 1986). http://www.nybooks.com/articles/1986/05/08/shoah-and-poland/.

Varaut, Jean-Marc. *Plaidoirie de Jean-Marc Varaut devant la cour d'assises de la Gironde: au procès de Maurice Papon, fonctionnaire sous l'occupation*. Paris: Plon, 1998.

Vergès, Fançoise. *L'homme prédateur: ce que nous enseigne l'esclavage sur notre temps*. Paris: Albin Michel, 2011.

Vidal-Naquet, Pierre. *Assassins of Memory: Essays on the Denial of the Holocaust*. Translated by Jeffrey Mehlman. New York: Columbia University Press, 1992.

———. *Le Trait empoisonné: Réflexions sur l'affair Jean Moulin*. Paris: La Découverte, 1993.

Watts, Phillip, and Richard J. Golsan. "Interview with Henry Rousso." *Romanic Review* 105, no. 1–2. Edited by Vincent Debaene and Richard J. Golsan, 91–96. Lillington, NC: Edwards Brothers, Inc., 2014.

———. "Interview with Laurent Binet." *Romanic Review* 105, no. 1–2. Edited by Vincent Debaene and Richard J. Golsan, 87–90. Lillington, NC: Edwards Brothers, Inc., 2014.

Wieviorka, Annette. *The Era of the Witness*. Translated by Jared Stark. Ithaca and London: Cornell University Press, 2006.

Wieviorka, Olivier. *Divided Memory*. Translated by George Holoch. Stanford: Stanford University Press, 2012.

Will, Barbara. "The Resistance Syndrome: Alain Badiou on Samuel Beckett." *South Central Review* 31, no. 1 (Spring 2014): 114–29.

Weill, Nicolas. "Daniel Lindenberg: rester à gauche après le totalitarisme." *Le Monde* (November 21, 2002).

———. "Intellectuels français et 'coup de barre' à droite." *Le Monde* (November 21, 2002).

Wolin, Richard. *The Wind from the East*. Princeton and Oxford: Princeton Universty Press, 2010.

Zaoui, Michel, Noëlle Herrenschmidt, and Antoine Garapon. *Mémoires de Justice: Les procès Barbie, Touvier, Papon*. Paris: Seuil, 2009.

Zemmour, Éric. *Le suicide français*. Paris: Éditions Albin Michel, 2014.

Zuckerman, Laurence. "FDR's Jewish Problem." *The Nation*. Last Modified July 17, 2013. Accessed November 9, 2015. http://www.thenation.com/aritcle/fdrs-jewish-problem/?print=1.

Index

Note: Page numbers followed with "n" refer to footnotes.

Accoyer Commission, and Memorial Laws, 15–16
Act of Accusation, 18n25
"acts of Resistance," 4
Affaire Jan Karski, 92
African slave trade, 13
Algerian War, 14, 15, 113, 116
Allemandes I and II, 71
All the Kings Men (Warren), 118
anachronism, 2, 8, 13, 14
analogous Pétainism, 52, 56, 61
Anglo-Saxon whites, 79
anti-Communism, 76–78
anti-German sentiments, 77–78
anti-Semitism, 11, 37, 39, 47, 91, 96–97, 106, 113;
   destruction of, 91;
   French, 11;
   Le Pen, 61;
   Pétainist, 7;
   Polish, 106;
   refined, 33;
   violent, 37
anti-totalitarian ideology, 38
A Princess of Mars (Burroughs), 78–81
Arendt, Hannah, 2
Armenian genocide, 13–14

Armenian law, 19n42
Aue, Maximilian, 65–66, 71–73, 78, 81–83

Badinter, Robert, 22
Badiou, Alain, 43–62;
   fascination, 46–47;
   homogeneity principle, 49;
   Martian novels, 72, 80–83;
   revolutionary politics, 47
barbarism, 57–58
Barbie trial, 1–4;
   crimes against humanity, 7, 14;
   crimes against Resistance, 5–6
Bardèche, Maurice, 31, 33, 34
Baudrillard, Jean, 69, 70
Beevor, Anthony, 105–6
Beyond the Farthest Star (Burroughs), 78
Beyond Thirty (Burroughs), 87n47
"Bling-Bling History," 61–62
"Brezhnev of Gaullism," 53
"Broken Mirror" phase, 70
Brunerie, Maxime, 21
Burger, Philip R., 76
Burroughs, Edgar Rice, 71–72, 74–78;
   anti-Communism, 76–78;

anti-German sentiments, 77–78;
Beyond the Farthest Star, 78;
Beyond Thirty, 87n47;
characterization of Kalkars, 76;
Courante, 71–72;
life and career, 75;
Nazism, 81–83;
A Princess of Mars, 78–81;
sexuality of his novel, 84

Camus, Renaud, 29–34;
"Frenchness," 30–32, 34;
ideas on racism, 31;
intellectual abstractions, 31;
politically disturbing writings, 32–33;
pseudo-"reasonable" approach, 32;
racism and, 31;
"Shoah," 30, 31
Carson of Venus (Burroughs), 78
Cercle (Haenel), 101, 103
Chandernagor, Françoise, 15
"Chaos," 31–32
Charlie Hebdo attack, 17, 112
Chevènement, Jean-Pierre, 23–25
Chirac, Jacques, 21–23, 26–28, 50, 53, 59;
"Brezhnev of Gaullism," 53;
victory of, 27
Churchill, Winston, 96, 99
Circonstances, 3: Portées du nom juif (Badiou), 47
Clerc, Thomas, 37
Conan, Eric, 43–44
"confused eroticism," 72, 82
Courante (Burroughs), 71–72
crimes against humanity:
French trials, 3–4, 7–10, 14–16;
Memorial Laws, 14–16
crimes against Resistance, 5–6

"the Dark Years," 34, 38, 39, 55–58, 84;
memory of, 44, 60, 111
"The Dawn of Time," 30–32
de Gaulle, Charles, 4

derivative fear, 51
desacralization of World War II, 117
"dirty beast," 113
Durafour, Michel, 26

Eichmann before Jerusalem (Stagneth), 17
Eichmann in Jerusalem (Arendt), 2, 17n4
Eichmann trial, 2, 17n4
"The Enlightenment on Trial" (Lindenberg), 38–39
essential fear, 51

faction, 105–6
fascism, 26, 28, 29, 114;
and sexuality, 68;
threat of a renewal, 37.
See also Nazism
Fifth Republic's Islamic terrorists, 113
Finkielkraut, Alain, 5–6, 32, 34, 37–38, 113, 114, 118n3
first round victory of Le Pen, 22–23, 27–28, 35–36, 38–40, 48–50, 40n4
Foucault, Michel, 69–70
Frachon, Alain, 17
fractured legal vector of memory.
See French trials for crimes;
Memorial Laws
Français de souche, 22
French affair, 4
French anti-Semitism, 11
French collaborationism, 107
Frenchness, 30–32, 34
French Resistance, during World War II, 45–46
French Revolution, 30–32
French trials for crimes, 1–3;
Barbie. *See* Barbie trial;
against memorial laws, 3;
and Memorial Laws, 13–14;
Nazi Final Solution, 8, 10, 11;
1980s and 1990s, 2;
Papon. *See* Papon trial;

Touvier trial. *See* Touvier trial
Friedländer, Saul, 68, 69

Gayssot Law, 12–15, 17
genocide, 15;
  of Armenians, 12–14, of 13;
  Turkish, 12
German crime, 7
German Mujahid (Sansal), 114, 115
Gorbachev, Michael, 53, 58
"Great Fear" of French, 50–51, 58
"Great Upheaval," 31–32
Gulag Archipelago (Solzhenitsyn), 38

Haider, Jorg, 35
Hake, Sabine, 68
harki population, 14
Heil Hitler, 81–82
"History: A Retro Scenario" (Baudrillard), 69
History of a Secret State, 91
Hitler, 81–82, 99–100, 103, 106
Hollande, François, 59–61, 113
Houellebecq, Michel, 111, 112
How the French Think (Hazareesingh), 116–17
human criminality, 103
Hyper Kacher attack, 17

If This be a Man (Levy), 101
indifferentiation/nihilism in, *mode rétro*, 69–70
"intellectual abstractions," 31
intelligent fascism, 36
Introduction à la mort française (Haenel), 102, 103, 107
intuitive fiction, *Jan Karski* (Haenel), 91, 94, 95, 107
irrational process, 50
Islam, criticism of, 25
Islamic jihadists in France, 112–13
Islamic threat, 112–13
"Islamification" of France, 111
Islamism, 114
"Islamo-fascism," 114

Jan Karski (Haenel), 89–106, 114;
  criticisms on, 89–91;
  faction, 106;
  as false novel, 91;
  intuitive fiction of, 91, 94, 95, 107;
  liberty, 95
Jankowski, Stanislaw M., 98–99
"Jewish peril," 57
Jihadist violence, 114
Jospin, Lionel, 22, 23

Karski: How One Man Tried to Stop the Holocaust (Wood and Jankowski), 98, 106
The Kindly Ones (Littell), 65–84, 85n8;
  Aue's wartime experiences, 65–66;
  critics, 67;
  Nazi violence and, 67, 74;
  as remake of *mode rétro*, 67;
  sexual deviance and, 68, 69, 73–74, 84

"Lacombe 'Jidad' Lucien," 112
"la France seule," 22
Laguiller, Arlette, 27
Lanzmann, Claude, 6, 89–100, 105, 113;
  Karski and, 92–93
Left's failure, 24, 38
Lepenization of the minds, 36
Le Pen, Jean-Marie:
  anti-Semitism, 61;
  first round victory of, 22–23, 27–28, 35–36, 38–40, 48–50, 40n4;
  moment, *and Le Rappel à l'ordre* (Lindenberg), 34–40;
  politicians opposition to, 26;
  protest for the candidacy of, 25–26;
  psychosis, 50
Le Procès des Lumières (Lindenberg), 38–39
Le Rappel à l'ordre (Lindenberg), 34–39, 116;
  critics of, 35, 37;
  "New Reactionaries," 35–39
"Le Rapport Karski," 92, 98
Les abus de la mémoire (Todorov), 116

Le sens du calme (Haenel), 103
Levy, Primo, 101
l'extreme contemporain (Houellebecq), 111
Lindenberg, Daniel, 34–39;
  acts of anti-Semitism in France and, 37, 39;
  critics of his book, 35, 37
l'indignité nationale, 113–14
louche (Houellebecq), 111

Malle, Louis, 112
"A Manifesto for the Freedom of Thought," 38
Martian novels, of Barsoom, 72, 80–83
Martian races, 79–80.
  See also Anglo-Saxon whites
The Meaning of Sarkozy (Badiou), 43–62;
  After the Election par, 50;
  analogous Pétainism, 52, 56, 61;
  "Bling-Bling History," 61–62;
  derivative fear, 51;
  Before the Election part, 49, 51, 52;
  essential fear, 51;
  France's Trancendental Pétainism, 54–55;
  "Great Fear" of French, 50–51, 58;
  neo-Pétainism, 52;
  pessimistic, 56;
  Pétainism, 52, 55–56, 60;
  transcendental pétainism, 43–62
Meckachera Law, 12, 13, 15
Mégret, Bruno, 22
Mein Kampf (Hitler), 99–100
Memorial Laws, 3;
  concerns, 15;
  critics of, 13, 14;
  Gayssot Law, 12–15, 17;
  Meckachera Law, 12–13, 15;
  Turkish genocide of Armenians in 1915, 12
mode rétro, 67;
  comments of Baudrillard on, 69;
  comments of Foucault on, 69–70;
  indifferentiation/nihilism in, 69–70
  and *The Kindly Ones* (Littell), 70, 71, 74, 84;
  Nazi violence, 73, 74;
  psycho-sexual dynamics of, 69–70;
  sexual deviance, 73;
  sexuality in, 68–69
The Moon Maid (Burroughs), 76–78
Museum of Guilt, 102

Nazi, 5–6;
  crimes, 2, 90, 97;
  crimes against Jews, 90, 93;
  revolution, 48;
  sexploitation, 68;
  terror in 1947, 118;
  violence, 67
Nazi Final Solution, 8, 10, 11, 15
Nazi porn, 71–73;
  films, 68, 70
Nazism, 81–83, 114, 117;
  Burroughs' views of, 81;
  and fascism, 68;
  in *mode rétro,* 68–69;
  and sadomasochism, 69;
  and sexual deviance, 69;
  during World War II, 45, 47, 58, 117
Nazi Zelig, 65
negationism, 13, 14, 37, 39
neo-Pétainism, 52
neo-Stalinist politics, 38
"New Reactionaries," 35–39
Nora, Pierre, 36

Papon trial, 1–4, 8–12, 15, 16, 19n27;
  crimes against humanity, 9, 10;
  crimes against Algerians, 9;
  imprisonment, 9;
  "inner circle" of, 17n2.
  See also Barbie trial; Touvier trial
parliamentary fetishism, 50
Parti du peuple algérien (PPA), 9
Pauchet, Catherine, 36
pensée unique, 22
Pétainism, 52, 54–56, 60

Pétainist anti-Semitism, 7
Pétainist moment, 58
Pétainist transcendental, 56, 61
Peulvast-Bergeal, Annette, 22
The Plague (Camus), 118
Plenel, Edwy, 32–33
Polish anti-Semitism, 106
politics of ideological hegemony, Nazis, 7, 8
Pompidou, Georges, 3, 4
post-Bolshevik Revolution Red Scare, 76
PPA. *See Parti du peuple algérien*

racism, 31, 37;
   Camus ideas on, 31
radical Islam violence, 114
"Rat Man," 53–54
Rebérioux, Madeleine, 15
"Red Blood and Red Flag" (Burger), 76
refined anti-Semitism, 33
Rémond, René, 15
return of fascism, 39
"The Revenge of History" Bruno Tertrais, 115
Revue des deux mondes (Finkielkraut), 115
Reynolds, David, 99
Roosevelt, Franklin D., 89–91, 96–100, 104–4, 106
"Round Two" of the *Affaire Camus*, 33, 34
Rousso, Henry, 16, 85n8

sadomasochism, 68–72
Saint Karski, 103–4
Sansal, Boualem, 114
Sarkozy, Nicholas, 44
Saving Private Ryan (Spielberg), 105
Screen Nazis: Cinema, History, and Democracy (Hake), 68
séisme Le Pen, 25, 29
"Shoah," 30–32
Shoah (Lanzmann), 13, 90–92, 94, 100, 105

simulacrum, 60, 63n49
Snyder, Timothy, 106
Socialist petty bourgeois, 51
Sorel , Stefan, 77
Spielberg, Steven, 105
Stalinism, 36, 43, 54, 58
Story of a Secret State (Karski), 94, 98
Submission (Houellebecq), 111
Synthetic Men of Mars (Barsoom), 80–81

Taguieff, Pierre-André, 37
"Tarzan Affair," 78
Tarzan the German-Devourer (Sorel)
Taubira Law, 12–16
terrorist attacks in Paris, 111, 112
Thavas, Ras, 100
"Therns," 79
"The Three Negations," 60
Todorov, Tzvetan, 6, 14, 118n5
Touvier trial, 1–4, 6–8, 11, 16;
   1989 arrest, 13;
   presidential pardon, 3
transcendental pétainism, 43–62;
   characteristics of, 55
"true fascist peril," 36
"true Frenchness," 35
Turkish genocide of Armenians in 1915, 12–14

Wood, Thomas, 98–99
World War I, 76, 77, 84
World War II, 11, 31, 38, 39, 67, 83–84, 100, 104–5, 113–18;
   Burroughs' anti-Communism, 76;
   Dark Years of, 117;
   desacralization of, 117;
   French Resistance during, 45, 117;
   Nazism during, 45, 47, 58

Yannick, Haenel, 89–106

"Zanis," 78

About the Author

Richard J. Golsan is University Distinguished Professor and Distinguished Professor of French at Texas A&M University. His research interests include the history and memory of World War II in France and Europe and the political involvements of French and European writers and intellectuals with antidemocratic and extremist politics in the twentieth and twenty-first centuries. His most recent book is *French Writers and the Politics of Complicity* (Johns Hopkins, 2006). Golsan served as a visiting professor at the University of Paris III-Sorbonne Nouvelle in 2001. He has been recognized by the Italian government in being named to the *Ordina Della Stella Della Solidarieta Italiana* and by the French government by being awarded the *Palmes Academiques*. He has served as editor of the *South Central Review* (SCMLA) since 1994, and is also director of the Melbern G. Glasscock Center for Humanities Research at Texas A&M and the *Centre Pluridisciplinaire*, funded by the French government.

CPSIA information can be obtained
at www.ICGtesting.com
Printed in the USA
BVOW08*1937161216
R7719900001B/R77199PG470016BVX2B/2/P

9 781498 550321